Dear Educator,

Thank you for your interest in American Book Company's state-specific test preparation resources. We commend you for your interest in pursuing your students' success. Feel free to contact us with any questions about our books, software, or the ordering process.

Our Products Feature	Your Students Will Improve
Multiple-choice and open-ended diagnostic tests	Confidence and mastery of subjects
Step-by-step instruction	Concept development
Frequent practice exercises	Critical thinking
Chapter reviews	Test-taking skills
Multiple-choice practice tests	Problem-solving skills

American Book Company's writers and curriculum specialists have over 100 years of combined teaching experience, working with students from kindergarten through middle, high school, and adult education.

Our company specializes in effective test preparation books and software for high stakes graduation and grade promotion exams across the country.

How to Use This Book

Each book:

*contains a chart of standards which correlates all test questions and chapters to the state exam's standards and benchmarks as published by the state department of education. This chart is found in the front of all preview copies and in the front of all answer keys.

*begins with a full-length pretest (diagnostic test). This test not only adheres to your specific state standards, but also mirrors your state exam in weights and measures to help you assess each individual student's strengths and weaknesses.

*offers an evaluation chart. Depending on which questions the students miss, this chart points to which chapters individual students or the entire class need to review to be prepared for the exam.

*provides comprehensive review of all tested standards within the chapters. Each chapter includes engaging instruction, practice exercises, and chapter reviews to assess students' progress.

*finishes with two full-length practice tests for students to get comfortable with the exam and to assess their progress and mastery of the tested standards and benchmarks.

While we cannot guarantee success, our products are designed to provide students with the concept and skill development they need for the graduation test or grade promotion exam in their own state. We look forward to hearing from you soon.

Sincerely,

The American Book Company Team

Basics Made Easy

Writing Standards and Benchmarks Chart
McREL Level III

The materials in this book are based on the 4th edition of *Content Knowledge*, an online collection of standards and benchmarks created by McREL (Mid-continent Research for Education and Learning). The standards and benchmarks are based on extensive research into state standards across the nation and explain what a student should know and be able to do at a certain level in a given subject. To see the database of McREL standards and their references to state and professional standards, visit **www.mcrel.org/standards-benchmarks**. The following chart correlates the Level III writing standards and benchmarks with chapters in this book and with all questions in the diagnostic test and two practice tests.

Benchmark Chapter(s)	Diagnostic Writing Test	Practice Writing Test 1	Practice Writing Test 2
McREL Standard 1: Uses the general skills and strategies of the writing process			
1. Prewriting: Uses a variety of prewriting strategies (e.g., makes outlines, uses published pieces as writing models, constructs critical standards, brainstorms, builds background knowledge)			
Ch 3	All prompts	All prompts	All prompts
2. Drafting and Revising: Uses a variety of strategies to draft and revise written work (e.g., analyzes and clarifies meaning, makes structural and syntactical changes, uses an organizational scheme, uses sensory words and figurative language, rethinks and rewrites for different audiences and purposes, checks for a consistent point of view and for transitions between paragraphs, uses direct feedback to revise compositions)			
Ch 4, 5	All prompts	All prompts	All prompts

Benchmark Chapter(s)	**Diagnostic Writing Test**	**Practice Writing Test 1**	**Practice Writing Test 2**
3. Editing and Publishing: Uses a variety of strategies to edit and publish written work (e.g., eliminates slang; edits for grammar, punctuation, capitalization, and spelling at a developmentally appropriate level; proofreads using reference materials, word processor, and other resources; edits for clarity, word choice, and language usage; uses a word processor or other technology to publish written work)			
Ch 5, 6	All prompts	All prompts	All prompts
4. Evaluates own and others' writing (e.g., applies criteria generated by self and others, uses self-assessment to set and achieve goals as a writer, participates in peer response groups)			
Ch 14	All prompts	All prompts	All prompts
5. Uses content, style, and structure (e.g., formal or informal language, genre, organization) appropriate for specific audiences (e.g., public, private) and purposes (e.g., to entertain, to influence, to inform)			
Ch 2, 3, 7–11	All prompts	All prompts	All prompts
6. Writes expository compositions (e.g., states a thesis or purpose; presents information that reflects knowledge about the topic of the report; organizes and presents information in a logical manner, including an introduction and conclusion; uses own words to develop ideas; uses common expository structures and features, such as compare-contrast or problem-solution)			
Ch 3, 8	prompt 2	prompt 2	prompt 2
7. Writes narrative accounts, such as short stories (e.g., engages the reader by establishing a context and otherwise developing reader interest; establishes a situation, plot, persona, point of view, setting, conflict, and resolution; develops complex characters; creates an organizational structure that balances and unifies all narrative aspects of the story; uses a range of strategies and literary devices such as dialogue, tension, suspense, figurative language, and specific narrative action such as movement, gestures, and expressions; reveals a specific theme)			
Ch 10	prompt 1	prompt 1	prompt 1
8. Writes compositions about autobiographical incidents (e.g., explores the significance and personal importance of the incident; uses details to provide a context for the incident; reveals personal attitude towards the incident; presents details in a logical manner)			
Ch 10	prompt 1	prompt 1	prompts 1, 2

Benchmark Chapter(s)	Diagnostic Writing Test	Practice Writing Test 1	Practice Writing Test 2
9. Writes biographical sketches (e.g., illustrates the subject's character using narrative and descriptive strategies such as relevant dialogue, specific action, physical description, background description, and comparison or contrast to other people; reveals the significance of the subject to the writer; presents details in a logical manner)			
Ch 10	prompt 1	prompt 1	prompt 1
10. Writes persuasive compositions (e.g., engages the reader by establishing a context, creating a persona, and otherwise developing reader interest; develops a controlling idea that conveys a judgment; creates and organizes a structure appropriate to the needs and interests of a specific audience; arranges details, reasons, examples, and/or anecdotes persuasively; excludes information and arguments that are irrelevant; anticipates and addresses reader concerns and counter arguments; supports arguments with detailed evidence, citing sources of information as appropriate)			
Ch 7	prompts 3, 5	prompts 3, 5	prompts 3, 4
11. Writes compositions that address problems/solutions (e.g., identifies and defines a problem in a way appropriate to the intended audience, describes at least one solution, presents logical and well-supported reasons)			
Ch 8	prompt 3	prompt 3	prompts 3, 5
12. Writes in response to literature (e.g., responds to significant issues in a log or journal, answers discussion questions, anticipates and answers a reader's questions, writes a summary of a book, describes an initial impression of a text, connects knowledge from a text with personal knowledge, states an interpretive, evaluative, or reflective position; draws inferences about the effects of the work on an audience)			
Ch 11	prompts 4, 5	prompts 4, 5	prompts 4, 5
13. Writes business letters and letters of request and response (e.g., uses business letter format; states purpose of the letter; relates opinions, problems, requests, or compliments; uses precise vocabulary)			
Ch 12	prompt 5	prompt 5	prompt 5
14. Writes technical text, such as bylaws for an organization (e.g., identifies essential steps in a logical sequence; lists materials or equipment needed; describes all factors and variables that need to be considered; uses appropriate formatting)			
Ch 12	Not tested		

Benchmark Chapter(s)	Diagnostic Writing Test	Practice Writing Test 1	Practice Writing Test 2
McREL Standard 2: Uses the stylistic and rhetorical aspects of writing			
1. Uses descriptive language that clarifies and enhances ideas (e.g., establishes tone and mood, uses figurative language, uses sensory images and comparisons, uses a thesaurus to choose effective wording)			
Ch 2, 9	All prompts	All prompts	All prompts
2. Uses paragraph form in writing (e.g., arranges sentences in sequential order, uses supporting and follow-up sentences, establishes coherence within and among paragraphs)			
Ch 1	All prompts	All prompts	All prompts
3. Uses a variety of sentence structures to expand and embed ideas (e.g., simple, compound, and complex sentences; parallel structure, such as similar grammatical forms or juxtaposed items)			
Ch 5	All prompts	All prompts	All prompts
4. Uses explicit transitional devices			
Ch 4	All prompts	All prompts	All prompts

Benchmark Chapter(s)	**Diagnostic Writing Test**	**Practice Writing Test 1**	**Practice Writing Test 2**
McREL Standard 3: Uses grammatical and mechanical conventions in written compositions (For more detailed coverage of grammar, usage, and mechanics benchmarks, please see *Basics Made Easy: Grammar and Usage Review* available from American Book Company.)			
1. Uses pronouns in written compositions (e.g., uses relative, demonstrative, personal [i.e., possessive, subject, object] pronouns; uses pronouns that agree with their antecedent)			
Ch 6	All prompts	All prompts	All prompts
2. Uses nouns in written compositions (e.g., forms possessives of nouns; forms irregular plural nouns)			
Ch 6	All prompts	All prompts	All prompts
3. Uses verbs in written compositions (e.g., uses linking and auxiliary verbs, verb phrases, and correct forms of regular and irregular verbs)			
Ch 6	All prompts	All prompts	All prompts
4. Uses adjectives in written compositions (e.g., pronominal, positive, comparative, superlative)			
Ch 6	All prompts	All prompts	All prompts
5. Uses adverbs in written compositions (e.g., chooses between forms of adverbs such as positive, comparative, superlative degrees)			
Ch 6	All prompts	All prompts	All prompts
6. Uses prepositions and coordinating conjunctions in written compositions (e.g., uses prepositional phrases, combines and embeds ideas using conjunctions)			
Ch 6	All prompts	All prompts	All prompts
7. Uses interjections in written compositions			
Ch 6	All prompts	All prompts	All prompts
8. Uses conventions of spelling in written compositions (e.g., spells high frequency, commonly misspelled words from appropriate grade-level list; uses a dictionary and other resources to spell words; uses common prefixes and suffixes as aids to spelling; applies rules for irregular structural changes)			
Ch 6	All prompts	All prompts	All prompts

Benchmark Chapter(s)	Diagnostic Writing Test	Practice Writing Test 1	Practice Writing Test 2
9. Uses conventions of capitalization in written compositions (e.g., titles [books, stories, poems, magazines, newspapers, songs, works of art], proper nouns [team names, companies, schools and institutions, departments of government, religions, school subjects], proper adjectives, nationalities, brand names of products)			
Ch 6	All prompts	All prompts	All prompts
10. Uses conventions of punctuation in written compositions (e.g., uses colons, quotation marks, and dashes; uses apostrophes in contractions and possessives, commas with introductory phrases and dependant clauses, semi-colons or a comma and conjunction in compound sentences, commas in a series)			
Ch 6	All prompts	All prompts	All prompts
11. Uses appropriate format in written compositions (e.g., uses italics [for titles of books, magazines, plays, movies])			
Ch 13	All prompts	All prompts	All prompts

Benchmark Chapter(s)	**Diagnostic Writing Test**	**Practice Writing Test 1**	**Practice Writing Test 2**
McREL Standard 4: Gathers and uses information for research purposes			
1. Gathers data for research topics from interviews (e.g., prepares and asks relevant questions, makes notes of responses, compiles responses)			
Ch 13	prompts 3, 4, 5	prompts 1, 3, 4, 5	prompts 1, 3, 4, 5
2. Uses library catalogs and periodical indexes to locate sources for research topics			
Ch 13	n/a	n/a	n/a
3. Uses a variety of resource materials to gather information for research topics (e.g., magazines, newspapers, dictionaries, schedules, journals, phone directories, globes, atlases, almanacs, technological sources)			
Ch 13	prompts 3, 4, 5	prompts 1, 3, 4, 5	prompts 1, 3, 4, 5
4. Determines the appropriateness of an information source for a research topic			
Ch 13	prompts 2, 3, 4, 5	prompts 3, 4, 5	prompts 1, 3, 4, 5
5. Organizes information and ideas from multiple sources in systematic ways (e.g., time lines, outlines, notes, graphic representations)			
Ch 13	prompts 3, 4, 5	prompts 1, 3, 4, 5	prompts 1, 3, 5
6. Writes research papers (e.g., asks research questions, defines a topic, organizes information into major components and examines relationships among these components, addresses different perspectives on a topic, achieves balance between research information and original ideas, integrates a variety of information into a whole, draws conclusions)			
Ch 13	prompts 2, 3, 4, 5	prompts 1, 3, 4, 5	prompts 1, 3, 4, 5
7. Uses appropriate methods to cite and document reference sources (e.g., footnotes, bibliography)			
Ch 13	prompts 3, 4, 5	prompts 1, 3, 4, 5	prompts 1, 3, 4,5

BASICS MADE EASY:

WRITING REVIEW

(Revised June 2009)

Authors: Brian Freel, Dr. Frank J. Pintozzi, Maria Struder

Editor: Mallory Grantham
Project Coordinator: Zuzana Urbanek

American Book Company
PO Box 2638
Woodstock, GA 30188-1383
Toll Free: 1 (888) 264-5877 Phone: (770) 928-2834
Fax: (770) 928-7483 Toll Free Fax: 1 (866) 827-3240
www.americanbookcompany.com

ACKNOWLEDGEMENTS

The authors would like to acknowledge the production coordination and formatting expertise of Marsha Torrens in the preparation of this book.

We also thank Jason Kirk for writing and editing contributions toward the revision of this book.

Basics Made Easy

Table of Contents

Chapter 4 Drafting the Essay 67

Chapter 5 Revising the Essay 95

Chapter 6   Proofreading the Essay   117

Chapter 7   Persuasive Writing   151

Basics Made Easy

Preface

Basics Made Easy Writing Review is one of several books in American Book Company's Basics Made Easy series. This book will help students develop or review writing strategies and writing applications (essays) for improvement of writing skills. This book will also assist students who are preparing or reviewing editing (proofreading) tasks. Each chapter contains concise lessons and frequent practice exercises. Each chapter ends with a chapter review to practice skills learned.

The materials in this book are based on the fourth edition of *Content Knowledge*, an online collection of standards and benchmarks created by McREL (Mid-continent Research for Education and Learning), writing standards for Level III. The benchmarks are based on extensive research and explain what a student should know and be able to do at a certain level in a given subject. This database is available online in a searchable format on the McREL Web site: **www.mcrel.org/standards-benchmarks**.

Appendix A contains many additional writing prompts for further practice. Appendix B offers additional writing resources. Students and teachers can use the Essays Progress Chart in Appendix C to record student grades on each essay. The Diagnostic Test also includes a Writing Evaluation Chart which can be used to evaluate both the Diagnostic Writing Test and the Practice Writing Tests at the end of this book. A separate key includes answers to tests and exercises as well as interactive writing activities.

We welcome comments and suggestions about this book. Please contact the Project Coordinator at

American Book Company
PO Box 2638
Woodstock, GA 30188-1383

Toll Free: (888) 264-5877
Phone: (770) 928-2834
Toll Free Fax: 1 (866) 827-3240
Visit us online at
www.americanbookcompany.com

About the Authors

Brian Freel has a Bachelor of Arts degree from Amherst College in Amherst, MA, and a Master of Arts degree from St. Mary's University in Baltimore, MD. He's a writer specializing in language arts and history and has taught students at middle school, high school, and adult levels.

Dr. Frank J. Pintozzi is a former Professor of Education at Kennesaw State University. For over twenty-eight years, he has taught English and reading at the high school and college levels as well as in teacher preparation courses in language arts and social studies. In addition to writing and editing state standard-specific texts for high school exit and end of course exams, he has edited and written several college textbooks.

Maria L. Struder received a BA in English and an MA in Teaching English from Kennesaw State University. She has taught writing skills at the college level and home-schooled her two children. She currently teaches English as a Second Language at the middle and high school levels.

About the Editor

Mallory Grantham is an ELA writer and copy editor at American Book Company. She completed her Bachelor of Arts in English at Kennesaw State University. As a teaching assistant, she led lectures, created lesson plans, graded and edited papers, and evaluated student progress. In addition, Mallory has taught sign language and tutored students in English and mathematics.

About the Project Coordinator

Zuzana Urbanek serves as ELA Curriculum Coordinator for American Book Company. She is a professional writer with twenty-five years of experience in education, business, and publishing. She has taught a variety of English courses since 1990 at the college level and also taught English as a foreign language abroad. Her master's degree is from Arizona State University.

Basics Made Easy

Diagnostic Writing Test

For assessment purposes, this diagnostic test consists of five writing prompts. Your teacher will tell you how many essays to write and which prompt(s) to use. Make sure you understand what each prompt is saying and respond correctly.

Test-Taking Tips

Complete the chapters and practice tests in this book. This text will help you review as thoroughly and specifically as possible key writing concepts you will need to learn for middle school, high school, and college.

2. **Be prepared.** Get a good night's sleep the day before an exam. Eat a well-balanced meal, one that contains plenty of proteins and carbohydrates, prior to your exam.

3. **Arrive early.** Allow yourself at least fifteen minutes to find your room and get settled. Then you can relax before the exam, so you won't feel rushed.

4. **Think success.** Keep your thoughts positive. Turn negative thoughts into positive ones. If you have put in good study and preparation time, you will reap the benefits of that.

5. **Practice relaxation techniques.** Some students become overly worried about exams. Before or during the test, they may perspire heavily, experience an upset stomach, or have shortness of breath. If you feel any of these symptoms, talk to a close friend or see a counselor. They will suggest ways to deal with test anxiety. **Here are some quick ways to relieve test anxiety.**

   - Imagine yourself in your favorite place. Let yourself sit there and relax.
   - Do a body scan. Tense and relax each part of your body starting with your toes and ending with your forehead.
   - Use the 3-12-6 method of relaxation when you feel stress. Inhale slowly for three seconds. Hold your breath for twelve seconds, and then exhale slowly for six seconds.

1

6. **Read directions carefully.** If you don't understand them, ask your teacher for further explanation before the exam starts.

7. **Write Legibly.** Write your responses clearly so that those who will grade your writing can give you the best score for your effort.

8. **Proofread your work.** After you have written your essays, check over your responses, making corrections in grammar, punctuation, capitalization, and spelling as neatly as possible.

How to Use Your Time

To use your time wisely, you may want to follow the suggestions below. These suggestions are based on sixty minutes to complete a writing test.

Planning/Prewriting: 10 minutes

Read each writing prompt carefully, make brainstorming lists of your ideas, and organize those ideas into a clustering diagram or outline.

Drafting: 20 minutes

After organizing your ideas, write them in complete sentences and develop them into well-formed paragraphs.

Revising: 20 minutes

Now is the time to read over each draft and make improvements. You want to make sure all of your ideas are developed in a logical order and supported by relevant reasons and examples. You also want to eliminate unrelated ideas and unnecessary words. This is a good time to improve your word choice as well. Make sure all of your corrections are neat and legible.

Proofreading: 10 minutes

Take advantage of the last few minutes of the testing time to review your essay one more time. This time look for errors in capitalization, punctuation, and grammar. These small corrections can make a big difference.

Review your paper using the **Checklist for Your Writing** listed at the end of your prompts.

At the end of your essay, you or your teacher should complete the **Writing Evaluation Chart**. It will help you identify your areas of strength and areas for improvement in writing essays. You can also use the **Scoring Guides** in **chapter 14** to help you evaluate your essays.

Diagnostic Writing Test

This diagnostic writing exam will allow you to demonstrate your writing capability.

There are five prompts, each of which reflects a different writing mode. Your teacher will tell you how many essays to write as a practice for the test. Successful responses to the prompts focus on the topic, reflect a discernible organizational structure, use appropriate language conventions, and contain pertinent supporting material such as ideas, examples, and/or commentary.

When you take an actual writing test in your state, you may be asked to write in a slightly different mode. However, practicing writing in the four modes mentioned will help you develop most of the skills you will need for any type of writing.

Diagnostic Writing Test

Following are five **writing prompts** that give you instructions about writing an essay. Read each prompt carefully so you understand the topic and the purpose of each essay. Then, use the **Checklist for Your Writing** to make sure you write an effective and interesting essay based on each writing prompt.

Use your own paper for your planning, drafting, and final copy. Your instructor will tell you when to begin and when to stop writing. Do your best, and remember, this is just your first attempt. As you study the chapters in this book, you will have more time for improvement.

Writing Prompt 1

In the past, schools hired their own cafeteria staff to provide nutritious, home-cooked lunches at a low price. Today, private food service companies are claiming that they can provide better school lunches at lower prices. Your local school board is considering a proposal which would allow several food service companies to set up operation in the school cafeteria. Some parents are concerned that students will eat nothing but "fast food." Decide what you think about private companies providing school lunches.

Writing Prompt 2

One of your friends has just told you a story about his or her experience playing a sport which you found very interesting. After getting your friend's permission, you agree to write down your friend's experience and publish it on the school Web site. Write down your friend's story as carefully as possible.

Writing Prompt 3

> Do you think athletes should be dismissed from a team for breaking the law? Why? Why not? Support your opinion from your observations or experiences.

Writing Prompt 4

> Choose a character that is memorable from a book or story. In addition to what the character does or says, what is important about how the author builds this character? Explain what makes this character special.

Writing Prompt 5

> Is there too much homework at your school? Should you be given time to do some of it (or all of it) during the school day? The school board is opening the discussion to teachers, parents, and students. Write a letter to the school board stating your position. Be sure to support it with convincing reasons.

Checklist for Your Writing:

The following checklist will help you do your best work. Make sure you

- Read the description of the task carefully.
- Use specific details and examples to fully support your ideas.
- Organize your writing with a strong introduction, body, and conclusion.
- Choose specific words that are appropriate for your audience and purpose.
- Vary your sentences to make your writing interesting to read.
- Check for mistakes in grammar, spelling, punctuation, and sentence structure.

WRITING EVALUATION CHART

Keep all of your essays in one folder. As you practice writing essays, you can use the Writing Evaluation Chart on the next page to help you assess your progress.

For each essay, work with your teacher or tutor to assign a grade in each category listed. If you have an excellent grasp of the skill, write **E** for **Excellent**. If you use the skill well enough to pass, write **P** for **Passing**. If you need to practice a skill more in order to master it, write **NP** for **Needs Practice**. The number listed next to each skill indicates the chapter which discusses that skill. Read and review the chapters you need to improve each concept and skill. Your teacher may also use the 6-point scale from chapter 14, Scoring the Essay.

Writing Evaluation Chart

Writing Skills	Chapter	Essay 1	Essay 2	Essay 3	Essay 4	Essay 5
Writing Paragraphs	1					
Diction	2					
Planning the Essay	3					
Drafting the Essay	4					
Revising the Essay						
Proofreading the Essay	6					
Persuasive Writing	7					
Expository Writing	8					
Descriptive Writing	9					
Narrative Writing	10					
Writing about Literature	11					
Writing Technical Texts	12					
Writing Research Reports	13					
Scoring the Essay	14					

Basics Made Easy

Chapter 1
Writing Paragraphs

This chapter covers the following McREL standard and benchmark for Level III:	
Standard 2: Uses the stylistic and rhetorical aspects of writing	Benchmark **2**

The goal of this book is to help you produce essays that are clearly focused, well-supported, and effectively written. Each chapter in this book will help you with different aspects of this task. You will begin by writing well-organized paragraphs because these are the building blocks of an effective essay. In this chapter, you will learn about the following aspects of writing paragraphs.

• Paragraph Structure	• Supporting Details
• Writing a Topic Sentence	• Writing a Concluding Sentence
• Improving a Topic Sentence	• Organizing Paragraphs

PARAGRAPH STRUCTURE

A **paragraph** is a series of related sentences that make a single point about one subject.

Choose one subject: A paragraph is too brief to discuss more than one subject.

Make a single point: To "make a point" is to tell readers something that you want them to know. Usually, you will state your point in the **topic sentence** of your paragraph. The topic sentence often begins a paragraph, though it may also be at the end or in the middle.

Relate other sentences to the topic sentence: Though you *state* your point in the topic sentence, you must *make* your point by providing **supporting details**. Other sentences in the paragraph provide readers with information and evidence to explain your topic sentence. If the topic sentence does not end the paragraph, a **concluding sentence** can bring the paragraph to a close, and if appropriate, lead into the next paragraph.

An easy way to understand the structure of a paragraph is to compare it to a table. The topic sentence is like the table top. Just as the table top's purpose is to provide a flat surface for writing or eating, the topic sentence's purpose is to give the reader a broad view of the topic. Of course, without legs, the table top will not stand.

In a similar way, the topic sentence must be supported by details, examples, and explanations.

Finally, a table that rocks on an uneven floor makes people wonder if objects they place on it will fall off. Similarly, a paragraph that does not provide a clear conclusion may leave the reader wondering if the writer has left out some important ideas.

Writing a well-organized paragraph may seem difficult, but do you realize that you talk in paragraphs every day? Here is an example of a paragraph spoken by a cheerleading coach at the season's first practice.

Gather around here and listen up! If you really want to be cheerleaders, you have to be ready to stretch yourselves to the limit! Be sure you really want to do this, people! You will need to be at practice every day after school. There will be no time for any other extracurricular activities! All of you must be ready to give of yourselves and endure pain as you never have before! You will also need to rely on each other. Some of you will be learning how to trust someone else for the first time in your lives. Above all, this job will bring out your character and show you what you're made of. Now, if you still feel up to the task, I want to see you here tomorrow evening at five o'clock, ready to work hard.

Though spoken, the coach's instruction is like a well-written paragraph. It states the main idea in a topic sentence (indicated in bold) and then supports that idea by describing how the cheerleaders will need to "stretch themselves." The coach concludes by challenging the cheerleaders to action. The speech has overall **coherence** in that all the ideas and sentences relate to one another.

Structure of a Paragraph

Topic Sentence (Introduction)

↓

Supporting Details (examples, reasons, testimony, observations)

↓

Concluding Sentence (Summary)

Practice 1: Paragraph Structure

All of the sentences in each series make a paragraph, but they may not be in order. For each sentence, write T if the sentence is the topic sentence, S if the sentence supports the topic sentence, and C if the sentence concludes or summarizes the paragraph.

1. A. Constantly surrounded by beeping faxes, ringing cell phones, and flashing computer screens, many business people are sitting down at the end of the day to enjoy some quiet time with knitting needles and a big ball of yarn.

   B. Men and women with fast-paced, high-powered careers are turning to knitting as a way to unwind.

   C. So, as you speed through modern society, remember, knitting isn't just for Grandma anymore!

   D. Besides the peace and quiet, these knitting professionals say they find it refreshing to focus on the process of creating something, instead of looking only at deadlines and finished products.

Sentence A _____	Sentence C _____	
Sentence B _____	Sentence D _____	

2. A. As she climbed the stairs, her nose was filled with the musty smell of old things.

   B. She walked to the door of her old refuge: the attic.

   C. Times at home had always been happy, but now Sheila needed a break.

   D. The memories of good times made the present situation seem bearable.

   E. Sheila dusted off an old picture frame and found a picture of her mother, smiling.

Sentence A _____	Sentence C _____	Sentence E _____
Sentence B _____	Sentence D _____	

3. A. With the sale of each bike, he offered a monthly maintenance program.

    B. These regular check-ups kept the bikes in good working condition and brought customers back to the store where they could see new products he was selling.

    C. The success of Alek's young business shows the importance of keeping the customer happy.

    D. His work in other bicycle shops had shown him that a successful business is based on quality products and good service.

    E. With several years experience under his belt, Alek Siegers established a successful bicycle shop in Aspen, Colorado.

Sentence A _____	Sentence C _____	Sentence E _____
Sentence B _____	Sentence D _____	

4. A. While Brad, Katya, and Willy were strolling down Eighth Street, they heard a disturbing noise.

    B. Within minutes, police officers arrived and commended the teens for their quick thinking.

    C. The woman could not speak but brought them to the kitchen where her husband lay on the floor.

    The look on the woman's face propelled the three teens up the stairs to her door.

    E. Immediately, Katya called 911, while Brad checked the man's pulse, and Willy tried to reassure the woman.

    F. They looked up and saw an elderly woman calling out from a second floor win-

Sentence A _____	Sentence C _____	Sentence E _____
Sentence B _____	Sentence D _____	Sentence F _____

dow, "Help me, please."

5. A. Training involves many hours of lifting weights and running sprints.

    B. Without this preparation, performance will drop and injuries are more of a risk.

    C. Like the other athletes you see at the Olympics, javelin throwers deserve respect.

    D. The javelin is not a very heavy object, but throwing it long distances requires great arm and leg strength.

    E. Javelin throwing may look easy on TV, but in reality, it is a very demanding sport.

Sentence A _____	Sentence C _____	Sentence E _____
Sentence B _____	Sentence D _____	

WRITING A TOPIC SENTENCE

The previous section shows that a paragraph is organized around a single idea that is stated in the **topic sentence**. The topic sentence tells the reader two important pieces of information:

- the subject of the paragraph
- what the author wants the reader to know about that subject

As a writer, you can use these statements to help you develop a topic sentence. Begin by answering the following two questions:

- What is the subject of the paragraph?
- What do I want the reader to know about that subject?

Then, use the answers to these questions to form a topic sentence. For example, look at the following:

Subject:	fuel-efficient cars
Want the reader to know:	help the environment
Sentence:	Buying a fuel-efficient car is one way you can help the environment.

This simple method of forming a topic sentence can help you stay focused in your writing. The topic sentence is like your compass while you write. It tells you what direction you want to go. Then, if you feel yourself getting lost in your writing, you can return to your topic sentence to get your bearings. For each sentence in a paragraph, ask the two questions above. If the sentence doesn't relate in some way to the subject and what you want the reader to know about the subject, it doesn't belong in the paragraph.

> The topic sentence states the subject of the paragraph and what the author wants the reader to know about that subject.

Practice 2: Writing a Topic Sentence

For each of the following, write a topic sentence based on the subject and what you want the reader to know.

1. **Subject:** baseball cards

   Want the reader to know: collecting them is an interesting hobby

Topic Sentence: _____

_____

2.   **Subject:** computers in classrooms

   Want the reader to know: provide learning opportunities

Topic Sentence: _____

_____

3.   **Subject:** refugees in the United States

   Want the reader to know: struggle without knowledge of English

Topic Sentence: _____

_____

4.   **Subject:** exercise

   Want the reader to know: important for good health

Topic Sentence: _____

_____

5.   **Subject:** school uniforms

   Want the reader to know: decrease learning distractions

Topic Sentence: _____

_____

IMPROVING A TOPIC SENTENCE

The previous exercise may make writing a topic sentence
seem easy, but writing a *good* topic sentence is a little more
challenging. It is like deciding the best way to begin a
conversation. Some people are very good at starting a
conversation and keeping it going. They have a talent for
inviting others into dialogue by picking a good topic and
introducing it in an interesting way. When you write, you are
starting a conversation with the reader. The topic sentence
provides the basis for this conversation. A good topic
sentence should present a **single idea** that is **broad enough** to
invite discussion.

Rule 1. Single Idea

Because a paragraph is focused on one idea, the topic sentence also should be limited to a single idea. The sentence should have only one subject and one verb.

Incorrect	Baseball players and lawyers get paid too much for the work they do.
This sentence has two subjects, baseball players and lawyers. The support needed for this sentence requires more than one paragraph. Choose one subject for one paragraph.	
Correct	Professional baseball players get paid too much for the work they do.
Correct	Lawyers get paid too much for the work they do.

Incorrect	The Internet provides computer users with a vast resource of information and creates worldwide marketing opportunities for businesses.
The Internet is a single subject, but the sentence describes two services provided by the Internet. Either service provides the basis for a good paragraph.	
Correct	The Internet provides computer users with a vast resource of information.
Correct	The Internet creates worldwide marketing opportunities for businesses.

Incorrect	Young children bring parents great joy as well as tremendous responsibility.
This sentence introduces two ideas. One idea is that young children bring parents great joy. The other is that young children are a big responsibility for parents. Both ideas should not be in the same topic sentence.	
Correct	Young children bring great joy to parents.
Correct	Young children bring parents tremendous responsibility.

Rule 2.	Broad Enough
The topic sentence must be broad enough so that it can be supported by details. A topic sentence that is really just a detail has no place to go.	
Detail	Baking soda absorbs household odors in carpets and kitchens.
Detail	Lemon juice lightens stains and cuts grease.
Topic Sentence	Natural household products can be used for effective cleaning.

The third sentence is broad enough to be supported by the details of the first two sentences. However, the first two sentences are too specific to be discussed in a paragraph.

The same is true of the next example.

Detail	Genetic engineers have succeeded in cloning farm animals.
	Cloned Sheep Dolly
Detail	Lawyers use DNA tests in criminal court cases.
Topic	In recent years, genetic research has produced astounding, yet practical, results.

Rule 3.	Invites Discussion
A good topic sentence makes the reader want to continue reading. It usually begins the paragraph and should invite the reader to consider the writer's topic.	
Weak	I went to Florida last year.
Good	Florida is the ideal place to go for a winter vacation.

The weak topic sentence doesn't have any energy or movement. There's no clear direction to go in writing, and the reader may not want to follow anyway. A good topic sentence makes the reader ask questions and want to read more.

Weak	My uncle drives a black Nissan 300 ZX.
Good	People often choose a particular car as a reflection of their personality.
Weak	Autumn leaves are often multi-colored.
Good	I love how the leaves on the trees explode into color each fall.

14

> A good topic sentence must be a single idea that is broad enough to invite discussion.

Practice 2: Choosing a Topic Sentence

For each group of sentences, decide which is a good topic sentence. Then, describe why the others are not as effective.

1. A. Dealing with how to dispose of all our trash can be a dilemma.

    _____

    B. The trash began piling up.

    _____

    C. Last summer, I worked for a trash collection company.

    _____

2. A. It's time to plant the garden and start watching baseball again.

    _____

    B. Irises and azaleas are beginning to bloom in the garden.

    _____

    C. The fresh smell of a newly planted garden is the best part of spring.

    _____

3. A. Mark Richt is appreciated by fans and has led the Georgia Bulldogs to two conference championships.

    _____

    B. Mark Richt is a respected personality in college football.

    _____

    C. Before coaching the Georgia Bulldogs, Mark Richt was a coach in Florida.

    _____

4. A. This has been a dry summer.

    _____

    B. Rainfall in the metro region is two inches below normal.

    _____

    C. This summer's drought may put water supplies in danger.

    _____

5. A. Modern rap is rooted in traditional African music.

_____

B. Modern rap has led to creative innovations in music.

_____

C. My brother listens to rap music all the time.

_____

SUPPORTING DETAILS

An effective topic sentence starts your conversation with the reader, but it is up to you to
continue the conversation by providing a clear, logical explanation of the main idea.
Supporting details are specific statements that are related to the topic of the paragraph, but
they do more than just restate the main idea.

Supporting details are more than restatements of the topic sentence. They provide
reasons and examples that show why the main idea is true. Look at the following two
examples.

Example 1: Researchers have proved that
smoking is bad for your health.
Many researchers have
determined smoking is unhealthy.
In addition, researchers have
publicized smoking's harmful
components.

In Example 1, the underlined topic sentence is *not* supported
with details. Instead, the next two sentences simply restate the
topic sentence in different words.

Example 2: Researchers have proved that smoking is bad for your health.
The American Medical Association has issued several warnings
about the increased risk of lung cancer linked with smoking. In
addition, the *New England Journal of Medicine* has issued its
own separate findings verifying this same link between smoking
and lung cancer.

In Example 2, the same underlined topic sentence is supported by details. The writer cites the
American Medical Association and the *New England Journal of Medicine* as providing
examples of research that have shown the relationship between lung cancer and smoking.

Supporting details are related to the topic. If the details digress from the topic, these
unrelated ideas can weaken the coherence of the paragraph and confuse the reader.

Example 3: It is easier than ever to learn a new language. Sometimes it's
hard to find someone who speaks another language. It's also fun
to learn martial arts. Sometimes I just can't learn how to
memorize things.

Each of the sentences in Example 3 may have one or two words in common, but they all refer to different topics. Each sentence should relate to the main idea, "It is easy to learn a new language."

> **Example 4:** It is easier than ever to learn a new language. Right now, you can learn a language by taking an elective course in high school. If you go to college, you may have the opportunity to live in a foreign country as an exchange student. All along, you can join chat rooms on the Internet or conversation meetings in your area that will help you practice speaking your new language.

In Example 4, the supporting sentences in the paragraph explain and relate to the underlined topic sentence. The sentences provide specific examples of ways you can learn a foreign language.

Supporting details are specific, not general, statements. The topic sentence is a general statement, but you should explain it in detail. Be as specific as you can.

> **Example 5:** Opinion polls question small samples of the population in order to indicate larger trends. An important part of polling is making sure that different kinds of people are represented. Even though this country is made up of many different kinds of people, opinion polls are pretty accurate.

All of the sentences in Example 5 discuss opinion polls, but each one is general enough to be a topic for its own paragraph. They are related to the same idea, but they don't focus on one aspect of that idea.

> **Example 6:** Opinion polls question small samples of the population in order to indicate larger trends. Pollsters must be careful to select people of different ages, genders, occupations, locations, and ethnic backgrounds. In this way, a sample of as few as two hundred people can give a good indication of public opinion throughout the country. Despite the small sample, the margin of error is usually between four and six percent.

The author of Example 6 chose one general statement as the topic sentence (underlined) and supported it with specific details that emphasize the accuracy of polls based only on small samples of the population. Each supporting sentence elaborates on this one idea.

Supporting details are specific statements that are related to the topic of the paragraph, but they do more than just restate the main idea.

Practice 4: Supporting Details

Read each group of sentences below. If the group forms a well-developed paragraph, write "Correct." If the group restates the topic sentence, contains unrelated ideas, or uses general statements instead of specifics, state the problem, and rewrite the paragraph on a separate sheet of paper.

1. Swimming is really the healthiest exercise anyone can do. Jumping rope is also healthy and it's a lot of fun. Sometimes just talking on the phone with friends can be fun, but you don't get much exercise. Going to the movies can be amusing, and if you walk there, it might be healthy. Just don't get butter on your popcorn because that's not healthy.

2. Something should be done about the cafeteria food because it tastes bad. Every time I gobble a mouthful, the taste is foul. Everyone agrees that the food tastes bad, and they bring in sack lunches instead. The food just does not taste good.

3. Scientists have a new theory to explain the mass extinction of aquatic life 180 million years ago. Using chemical analysis, researchers have determined that a large amount of methane gas was released from ocean floor sediment about that time. The methane combined with oxygen in the ocean and formed carbon dioxide. Without oxygen available, marine life could not breathe. Researchers believe this was the cause of death for many ancient underwater creatures.

4. I enjoy the smell of the air after a good rain. The air smells very good when the rain ends. After the water comes down from the clouds, the air smells very clean. Everyone enjoys the smell outside after a long soaking downpour. Nothing refreshes the air like a spring rain.

5. Many people wonder whether there is life on other planets in the universe. All around the world, people claim to see UFOs. The idea of creatures from other planets visiting Earth has been the topic of many books and movies. Science fiction clubs are very popular and often have large annual meetings.

DEVELOPING SUPPORTING DETAILS

A good way to develop a list of details to support your main idea is to consider what questions a reader might ask about your topic sentence. Here is an example:

Topic Sentence:	Florida is the ideal place to go for winter vacation.
Reader May Ask:	Where in Florida?
	How do you know it's ideal?
	What makes it ideal?
	What kinds of things can you do there?
	What if I like to go snow skiing?

By answering these questions, you can develop a list of supporting ideas for your topic.

Possible Answers:	Panama City
	went last year for annual vacation
	good seafood, great night life, beautiful beaches
	swimming, snorkeling
	water skiing

From this list, you can develop a paragraph like the following:

Florida is the ideal place to go for a winter vacation. Last year, our family spent its annual vacation on the white beaches of Panama City. During the day, we snorkeled, swam, and water skied in the clear, warm waters of the Gulf of Mexico. In the evenings, we enjoyed fresh seafood at the small local restaurants. At night, we joined other vacationers from around the world in various festivities sponsored by our hotel. Every year we travel to a new vacation spot, but the beauty and excitement of Florida will bring us back next year.

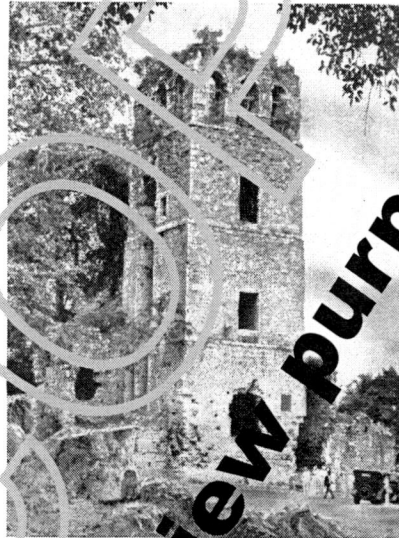

St. Augustine, Florida

Supporting details provide answers to questions the reader may have about a topic sentence.

Practice 5: Developing Supporting Details

For each of the following topic sentences, develop a list of at least 3 supporting details. The first topic is completed as an example.

1. The fresh smell of a newly planted garden is the best part of spring.

   A. The smell of new growth contrasts the long months of dead winter.

   B. Early budding flowers have a gentle fragrance.

   C. The freshly tilled earth has a unique smell.

2. Parents have a tremendous responsibility in raising young children.

   A. _____

   B. _____

   C. _____

3. Computers in classrooms provide a wide range of learning opportunities.

   A. _____

   B. _____

4. Professional baseball players get paid too much for the work they do.

   A. _____

   B. _____

   C. _____

5. You can get so much done when you manage time wisely.

   A. _____

   B. _____

   C. _____

ORGANIZING PARAGRAPHS

Now that you have a topic sentence and a list of supporting details, you must decide how you want to organize your paragraph. Just like the table we discussed in the beginning of this chapter, a paragraph is not put together haphazardly. It has a **sequential order**: the sequence depends on what you want to point out. This structure and organization help it stand up. And just like there are different types of tables, there are different ways to organize paragraphs, such as **time order**, **spatial order**, **order of importance**, and **contrasting ideas**. Each of these patterns has a different sequence.

TIME ORDER

Time order is especially important when you are writing a narrative. A story doesn't make sense when the events are not presented in the proper sequence. Here is an example:

> I arrived after the speaker had begun her presentation. As I was running down the hill, I remembered that I had left my car keys on the kitchen table. When I started the car, I saw the clock, and I knew I was going to be late. I had to go back and get my keys.

The lack of organization in this paragraph makes it very difficult to follow the story. Now, see how organizing the passage in a time sequence makes it much easier to read and understand.

> As I was running down the hill, I remembered that I had left my car keys on the kitchen table. I had to go back and get my keys. When I started the car, I saw the clock, and I knew I was going to be late. I arrived after the speaker had begun her presentation.

You can also use time order to organize other types of writing, including writing to explain why. Review the paragraph on page 19 about vacationing in Florida. Notice how the details are organized according to time order.

SPATIAL ORDER

When you describe a scene or a location, you can sometimes use **spatial order** to arrange your ideas in a paragraph. Imagine yourself holding a camcorder and moving it in every direction. You can order your observations from top to bottom, left to right, clockwise, near to far, front to back, inside to outside, east to west, north to south, etc., and all of these directions reversed (e.g., bottom to top). Read the following description which is organized in spatial order.

> When I saw the horse, I knew I was looking at a creature of great athletic beauty and ability. The horse's head was finely shaped, as if sculpted by an artist. On either side of its head, the eyes were alert and far-seeing. The ears were pointed and moved attentively to the slightest sound. The horse's neck was crested in a proud arch, and its muscular shoulders tapered down to powerful legs. The spine of the horse was perfectly aligned, and the back legs were unblemished and moved freely. The hindquar-

ters of the horse were well rounded, and the horse's tail flowed like silk in the wind. In short, this horse was a magnificent animal.

Look at the picture of the horse on the previous page. Does it make sense from the description you just read? If not, what additional details or observations would improve the description?

In the passage, the details of the horse are organized in a front-to-back order. First, the writer discusses the horse's head, along with the eyes and ears. Second, the writer provides details about the neck, shoulders, and front legs. Third, the writer describes the spine and the back legs. Finally, the author tells us about the horse's hindquarters and tail.

Spatial order can also be an effective way to organize other kinds of writing, as you can see in the following example of persuasive writing.

It's time for the city to clean up Zenith Park. As visitors enter the park, they are greeted by a broken sign that is smeared with graffiti. Next, they pass the pond where they must hold their noses because of the smell of decaying trash. If visitors make it past all of this, they reach the playground in the middle of the park. Here they find swings with ripped seats hanging limp beside slides with broken steps. The park, in its current state, is a hazardous waste area that must be cleaned up.

ORDER OF IMPORTANCE

The most common way to organize a paragraph is in **order of importance**. All of the details you include in your paragraph should be relevant to the topic and important to the reader. Some details, however, you will want to emphasize more than others. You can emphasize a certain idea by placing it either at the beginning or at the end of a paragraph. The following letter provides a good example.

Dear Aunt Jenny,

I would really like to spend the summer with you because I have never spent much time in Oregon. Also, I am interested in earning some extra money for my college savings, and many jobs are available in your area. Most importantly, I really enjoy our short visits when we get together over the holidays, and I want to spend more time with you so we can be closer.

Please write back soon, and let me know what you think.

Love,

Sandra

In this letter, Sandra begins with a simple wish that may be of some interest to her aunt. Aunt Jenny would be more likely to respect Sandra's second reason. However, Sandra's desire for a closer relationship will make the greatest impression upon her aunt's decision.

Of course, the letter could be arranged so that the most important idea comes first.

> *Dear Aunt Jenny,*
>
> *I would like to spend the summer with you because I really enjoy our short visits which we get together over the holidays, and I want to spend more time with you so we can be closer. I am also interested in earning some extra money for my college savings, and many jobs are available in your area. Besides, I have never spent much time in Oregon.*
>
> *Please write back soon, and let me know what you think.*
>
> *Love,*
>
> *Sandra*

Sometimes you will want to start off with the most important idea. Other times you will want to "save the best for last." The decision is yours based upon your audience, topic, and personal preference.

CONTRASTING IDEAS

Sometimes writing assignments require that you choose one side of an issue or topic and convince the reader of the validity of your position. One good way to do this is to **contrast** your position with its opposite. In this kind of contrasting, you will point out differences and show why your position is better. For example, look at the paragraph below in which the writer is trying to convince his or her family to get a cat as a pet, instead of a dog.

> Since our family spends a lot of time traveling, a cat is definitely a better choice than a dog for a family pet. Dogs need to be let outside several times a day, while a cat knows how to use a litter box. Dogs also need to be fed regularly, whereas a cat can snack on one bowl of food for a few days. Dogs are very social animals and get lonely if they don't have people or other dogs to play with. Cats, on the other hand, are affectionate sometimes, but they can also get along just fine by themselves. A dog would not be treated well enough in our busy household. A cat would be much happier.

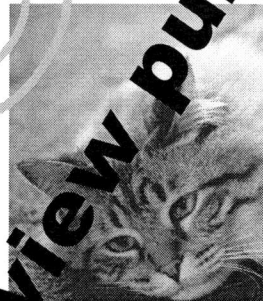

In this example, the writer contrasts the qualities of a dog with those of a cat. The writer points out the reasons why a cat would fit better in the family that likes to travel. Someone with a different family situation could write a paragraph like the one below.

For our young family, a dog would be a much better choice for a family pet than a cat. Dogs are social animals who love to be around people, especially kids. Cats, on the other hand, avoid crowds and often run from children. Dogs require regular feeding, which is a great opportunity to teach children responsibility. Cats require much less regular care. A dog offers great security to a home and family by barking when strangers approach. A cat can do little more than hiss at someone it doesn't like. A cat just doesn't offer our family the benefits a dog would offer.

This second paragraph shows how **awareness of audience** is important in writing. The writers know that each of their families have different needs and interests. Therefore, the writers choose reasons and examples that are appropriate for each family's unique situation.

Paragraphs can be organized according to space, time, importance, or contrasting ideas.

Practice 6: Organizing Paragraphs

Return to the list of supporting details you developed in Practice 5 on page 20. Put each list in order according to time, space, importance, or contrasting ideas. Save these lists for Practice 8.

WRITING A CONCLUDING SENTENCE

As you learned in the last section, the beginning and end of a paragraph are very important. Sometimes a topic sentence will end a paragraph, but often it comes at the beginning, in order to alert the reader to the main idea. In this case, the paragraph will end with a **concluding sentence**. The concluding sentence brings closure to the paragraph by providing a summary of the topic and the supporting details. It may also suggest what action the reader should take. If another paragraph follows, the concluding sentence serves as a link between the two paragraphs.

As we compare a paragraph to a table, we see that the concluding sentence is like the floor which provides a stable base on which the table can stand. A paragraph that lacks a concluding sentence may leave the reader hanging, as if in midair, wondering if the author left out something. Read the example below to understand the importance of concluding sentences.

Example: The federal government should continue to increase spending for defense. Now that the war on terrorism has started there is a need to keep this country well-armed. Currently, the United States spends more for defense than all other countries in the world combined! Congress continues to approve larger amounts of money for defense.

This paragraph lacks an ending. The paragraph begins with an opinion about the amount of money spent for defense, and supporting details follow to back up this point. However, the lack of a conclusion leaves the reader wondering whether the paragraph is finished.

The addition of a concluding sentence like the following would make a big difference.

Concluding Sentence: Write to your representatives to say the terrorist attacks have justified every penny spent on defense and more.

This one sentence ties the paragraph together by summarizing the main idea and supporting details and urging the reader to take action. The reader may agree or disagree with the writer's ideas, but the reader has no doubt that the writer has brought the paragraph to a close.

> A concluding sentence may achieve one or more of the following:
>
> - Emphasize an important point
> - Provide a summary of the topic and details
> - Suggest a response for the reader
> - Link one paragraph to another

Practice 7: Concluding Sentences

Read the following paragraphs. In the space after each, write a concluding sentence that best completes the topic. If the paragraph has a concluding sentence, write "Correct."

1. The global economy is moving toward the East. By 2020, China is projected to have an economy that is roughly eleven times as large as the economy of the United States! In addition, Japan, India, and Indonesia will have production levels that rival the United States. Only four nations in Europe will even make the top twenty list of the world's largest economies.

_____

2. The dancing craze is back in full force in the United States. After years of obscurity, swing music has made a rapid comeback. Also, the Latin rhythms of salsa, merengue, and cumbia can be heard in many cities. Two-stepping in clubs playing country music is also popular with the younger generation. In addition, the clubs playing techno, hip hop, and R&B music continue to draw larger crowds.

_____

3. At the church potluck dinner each family competes to bring in the best entree and dessert. Mrs. Collin's chicken cacciatore was a fierce challenge to Mr. Ewing's homemade barbeque. Miss Laramie brought in two scrumptious apple pies that were gone in seconds, and everyone marveled at Miss Jenkin's homemade ice cream. This potluck dinner was deliciously serious business.

_____

4. Lifting weights is both mentally and physically demanding. It takes a great amount of concentration to lift large weights safely. Every lifter knows that form is crucial. The lifter must understand and visualize what he or she is doing during every second of a lift. People who do not exercise their mind in this manner end up with strains, sprains, and back and neck injuries.

_____

5. The National Public Radio station in your city is a great educational resource. Because it receives funding from listeners, not big businesses, the station can offer diverse programming. You can hear informative and entertaining presentations about science, history, cultural movements, business trends, and film. In addition, the news programs provide longer, in-depth reports about major issues. Best of all, you can listen to all these great programs without those annoying commercials. Tune in to public radio today, and feed your mind with some high quality programs.

_____

Practice 8: Writing Paragraphs

Use the topic sentences and supporting details from Practices 5 and 6 to write four well-organized paragraphs. Be sure each paragraph has a concluding sentence.

CHAPTER 1 SUMMARY

Using well-organized **paragraph structure** is essential to building an effective essay.

- A paragraph should make a **single point** about **one subject**.
- State the point in the **topic sentence**, and use additional sentences to offer **supporting details** to clarify and defend that point. In the **concluding sentence**, bring the paragraph to a close. This sentence can also lead into the next paragraph, if there is one.

Paragraphs should follow a logical **sequential order**.

- **Time order** tells events in the order that they happen.
- **Spatial order** can be used to describe a scene or location.
- **Order of importance** emphasizes key points. Details can be given from most important to least important or the other way around.
- **Contrasting ideas order** is a good way to present the differences between two things or ideas.

CHAPTER 1 REVIEW: WRITING PARAGRAPHS

On a separate piece of paper, rewrite each unorganized group of sentences (1–5) in the form of a well-organized paragraph. Each group contains an unrelated idea that you must eliminate. Also, each group is missing a topic sentence, so you will need to create one and include it in your re-written paragraph.

1. A. Neither the Republicans nor the Democrats are eager to tackle this issue.

    B. When considering the environment, most people think only about their own little world.

    C. They have to start going beyond the "What's in it for me?" attitude.

    D. The decisions we make have a big impact on the rest of the world.

    E. Citizens of this country need to realize that we are all part of a global community.

2. A. The owner of the resort had breakfast ready downstairs.

   B. To our right, three deer were drinking out of a small stream.

   C. Straight ahead, the colorful valley opened up for us.

   D. To our left, the sun pierced through the tall trees.

   E. We were deeply impressed with everything we saw from our cabin.

3. A. Our friends took the day off with us, so we could go to the mall.

   B. The editors also warned us that we would need to find some place else to work if we ever did that again.

   C. Unfortunately for us, we did not know that ACME motors advertised in our newspaper.

   D. The editors pulled every copy from the newsstands before the public saw them.

   E. The story concerned the bad performance of ACME transmissions.

4. A. Something needs to be done, and soon.

   B. The problem is that costs keep skyrocketing while service is plummeting.

   C. Doctors used to make house calls.

   D. Meanwhile, patients spend more and more time waiting, and less and less time talking with the doctor.

   E. Doctors order more and more high-tech tests that increase medical bills.

5. A. In addition, you are the first person to be unhappy with our product.

   B. We found, however, that the product you sent to us was in perfect working condition.

   C. The letter you sent said that the product was broken.

   D. Have you ever considered selling those gadgets yourself?

   E. Based on these reasons, I am sure you can understand why there is no possibility of a refund.

On a separate piece of paper, rewrite each group of sentences (6–10) in the form of a well-organized paragraph. For each group, you will need to eliminate one unrelated idea and create a <u>concluding sentence</u>.

6. A. Donna aimed the shot high and swished the basketball through the hoop.

   B. She passed the ball to Jenna the first chance she had.

   C. Donna and Jenna want to go to the same college.

   D. Jenna certainly gave Donna an assist on the first play of the game.

   E. Next, Jenna shielded the other players from Donna as she took her shot.

7. A. Calligraphy is one of the most difficult forms of art I know.

   B. Each stroke of the pen has to be perfect.

   C. Because of the precision required, it can take many months to master a single alphabet in calligraphy.

   D. Also, the letters have gaps if the stroke is too fast.

   E. For example, the ink runs if the stroke is too slow.

   F. I hope to open a business selling calligraphy pens and ink supplies.

8. A. Some parents don't have time to coach sports for children.

   B. They said the boy wasn't getting enough playing time.

   C. This may be extreme, but how often do some parents start screaming at officials who make a bad call?

   D. Recently, the father and uncle of a football player in California beat up the boy's coach.

   E. Sometimes parents get carried away by the competition of children's sports.

9. A. The dome's shape is especially resistant to storms and earthquakes because the foundation supports all portions of the structure.

   B. A few nonconformists are building dome-style homes because of their stability and energy efficiency.

   C. The lack of walls in a dome-shaped house allows more equal distribution of heating and cooling, making it more energy efficient.

   D. Other people enjoy traditional four-sided brick homes.

10. A. This move brings Nuke-Clean closer to one of its big customers—the nuclear plant down the river.

    B. It also brings Nuke-Clean closer to my neighborhood.

    C. Some people in the neighborhood don't mind, but I think we should take action now.

    D. Nuke-Clean wants to move its operation to Smith County, so it can clean clothes that are contaminated with radiation.

    E. The nuclear plant in Chernobyl was shut down recently.

The paragraphs below (11–15) may be missing a topic sentence or a concluding sentence. Also, they may contain supporting details that restate the topic or describe unrelated ideas. For each paragraph, identify the problem. Then, on a separate piece of paper, rewrite the paragraph to make it complete.

11. Getting the right tennis shoe for school can be an important decision. Getting blue jeans to fit is difficult sometimes. Whenever I try to tie-dye my T-shirts, they always turn out brown. My skin feels better after a long dip in the swimming pool. In summary, comfortable tennis shoes are vital for school survival.

12. Exercising will improve blood flow to the brain and condition the muscles and bones to support the body under stress. In addition, a proper diet will ensure that the brain and other parts of the body are supplied with the proper nutrients. Third, a proper amount of sleep will keep the receptors in the brain connected for maximum efficiency. These three life activities in proper balance will keep the body and mind in shape for each day.

13. Misha Patel enjoyed his visit to Disney World in July. The July visit to Disney World was very enjoyable for Misha. Disney World provided Misha with many interesting experiences. In conclusion, Misha was very happy experiencing many of the attractions offered at Disney World.

14. Global warming is a very real and measurable phenomenon. Over the past century, glaciers near the poles have receded. In addition, the polar ice caps have thinned up to 40 percent from their previous thickness. Finally, air temperatures have warmed over 1° Celsius.

15. The world now produces more than enough food to feed every man, woman, and child currently living. However, land useful for farming is not evenly distributed. Another challenge lies in lack of transportation to areas where there is no arable land. Furthermore, many nations lacking the arable land also lack the resources necessary to purchase the food they need. Together, these factors point to a problem in food distribution, not a lack of food.

ADDITIONAL ACTIVITIES: WRITING PARAGRAPHS

TOPIC SENTENCES

1. Review photographs, advertisements, paintings, or cartoons in books or magazines or on the Internet. Make copies of four of these visual expressions. Then, write topic sentences based on these examples. Seek feedback on your topic sentences from your teacher or from other students. Do the topic sentences focus on a single idea? Are they broad enough to be supported by details and examples? Do they invite discussion?

2. Write four topic sentences based on topics of your choosing. You can also use any of the following topics to help you get started.

boyfriend	girlfriend	nose rings
have a cold	gossip	pet peeves
drinking	ideal job	school buses
favorite entertainer	losing weight	tattoos
favorite food	my dream	worst job

Exchange your topic sentences with your teacher or with other students. Do the topic sentences focus on a single idea? Are they broad enough to be supported by details and examples? Do they invite discussion?

SUPPORTING DETAILS AND ORGANIZING PARAGRAPHS

3. Choose four of your best topic sentences from the first or second activities listed above. Write four to six sentences that support these topic sentences. Make sure your details relate to the topic, are specific, and avoid restating the topic sentence.

Use a different way to organize each paragraph. In other words, use time order for one paragraph, spatial order for your next paragraph, order of importance for another paragraph, and contrasting ideas for your last paragraph.

CONCLUDING SENTENCES

4. Write a concluding sentence for each of your four paragraphs. Make sure that your concluding sentence summarizes the topic sentence and supporting details in each paragraph.

FINAL ACTIVITY

5.   Turn in your completed paragraphs for feedback from your teacher or tutor. Revise them as needed. For further practice in writing paragraphs, repeat steps 1–4, using different topics.

Note: For more instruction and practice for various aspects of writing, visit the Web sites or check out the books listed in Appendix B (pages 326).

Basics Made Easy

Chapter 2
Diction

This chapter covers the following McREL standard and benchmark for Level III:	
Standard 1: Uses the general skills and strategies of the writing process	Benchmark **5**
Standard 2: Uses the stylistic and rhetorical aspects of writing	Benchmark **1**

Diction often refers to the way a person pronounces certain words while speaking. In writing, however, diction involves the author's choice of words, especially regarding correctness, clearness, or effectiveness. The words you choose to describe and explain your ideas greatly influence how readers receive your ideas. To choose the best words, you need to consider your purpose for writing and the audience who will read your work. Then, you can choose a language and tone that is appropriate for your readers. This chapter will help you choose correct, clear, and effective words by discussing the following topics:

• Author's Purpose	• Audience	• Language and Tone

AUTHOR'S PURPOSE

Everyone who writes is an author, and each author writes for different reasons. Think of the reasons why you write: you write essays for English class because the teacher requires it; you may write a note in a birthday card to your mother to express your love; or you may send e-mails to Internet friends just to say "hello." Every author writes for a specific purpose. Often, the **author's purpose** is revealed in the way the author writes. See if you can determine the author's purpose in the following two paragraphs.

Example 1: The common opossum is the only kind of opossum found in the United States. This species grows about as big as a house cat. It has rough grayish-white hair, a long snout, dark eyes, and big hairless ears. This opossum has a long tail that does not have much hair on it. The animal can hang upside down by wrapping its tail around a tree branch. Its teeth and claws are sharp.

Example 2: One warm fall evening, our son, Tom, went out to the garage to feed the cat. Suddenly we heard him yell out, "A rat! A Texas-sized rat!" His older brother, Joey, went to investigate and reported back, "Sure enough, Mom. It is a rat." Finally, Barb and I went to look at this "rat." When the little critter turned around to see us gawking, we realized that it was a 'possum . . . a fat 'possum.

Both paragraphs discuss opossums, but they do so in very different ways. Example 1 provides basic information about the physical features of one type of opossum. Though the paragraph contains descriptive words, there is no dialogue and no action. This paragraph would fit well in a science textbook. The author's purpose is **to inform**.

Example 2, on the other hand, describes characters and events with expressive words and interesting dialogue. It is part of a brief story about a surprising and funny event. Perhaps you would find it in a book of short stories. The author's purpose is **to entertain**.

Examples 1 and 2 show how authors can use a different style of writing depending on the purpose of their writing. The words they choose reflect a certain feeling or direction. The ability to determine the author's purpose for writing enhances your reading comprehension. In addition, being clear about your purpose as an author will make your writing more effective. Become familiar with the following list of purposes for writing so that you may better understand the reasons why authors write.

Purpose	Definition	Reading Selection
To inform	To present facts and details	"Ocean Fishes"
To entertain	To amuse or offer enjoyment	"How My Cat Turned Purple"
To persuade	To urge action on an issue	"Raise Penalties for Polluters"
To explain why	To provide clear reasons	"How Plants Grow"
To instruct	To teach concepts and facts	"Mastering Exponents"
To create suspense	To convey uncertainty	"Will Gnats Rule the World?"
To motivate	To inspire to act	"You Can Make a Difference!"
To cause doubt	To be skeptical	"Is Chocolate Health Food?"
To introduce a character	To describe a person's traits	"First Look at Captain Nemo"
To create a mood	To establish atmosphere	"Gloom in the House of Usher"
To relate an adventure	To tell an exciting story	"Lost in a Cave"
To share a personal experience	To tell about an event in your life	"The Time I Learned to Share"
To describe feelings	To communicate emotions through words	"When My Dog Died"

Your purpose for writing affects your diction, or the words you choose.

Practice 1: Author's Purpose

Based on the list of author's purposes, identify the author's purpose for the following reading passages. Then, discuss your choices with your class or with your instructor.

1. The fire crackled musically. From it swelled light smoke. Overhead the foliage moved softly. The leaves, with their faces turned toward the blaze, were colored shifting hues of silver, often edged with red. Far off to the right, through a window in the forest, could be seen a handful of stars lying, like glittering pebbles, on the black level of the night.

   – Stephen Crane, *Red Badge of Courage*

   A. to describe an event   C. to persuade

   B. to create a mood   D. to instruct

2. Columbus' own successful voyage in 1492 prompted a papal bull (a directive from the Pope) dividing the globe between rivals Spain and Portugal. But the Portuguese protested that the pope's line left them too little Atlantic sea room for their voyages to India. The line was shifted 270 leagues westward in 1494 by the Treaty of Tordesillas. Thus, wittingly or not, the Portuguese gained Brazil and gave their language to more than half the people of South America.

   A. to introduce a character   C. to relate an adventure

   B. to describe feelings   D. to instruct

3. Twelve-year-old Nadia told us a seemingly unbelievable story about her family's journey to the United States. In Romania, her father was involved in the politics of Romania, opposing the communist regime of Ceausescu. Because of death threats made against her family, Nadia and her family had to leave the country in the middle of the night. They had arranged for a boat to meet them so they could sail the Black Sea to freedom in Bulgaria. Because they left in a hurry, they took nothing with them except their clothes. The boat never came, so they swam into the sea until a boat from Bulgaria discovered her family swimming. All of them survived the swim except for Nadia's little brother, Dimitry. From that country, they obtained refugee status and traveled to the United States. Nadia is very grateful to be living here, and after hearing her story, so are we.

   A. to describe feelings   C. to relate an adventure

   B. to explain why   D. to persuade

4. Hand grippers can help give your arms those bulging biceps you're after, but only if they offer enough resistance. If you can squeeze them repeatedly for one to two minutes, and your hands don't get tired, they're too weak for you. You can keep buying stronger ones or make something at home that can do the same job.

   A. to inform

   B. to persuade

   C. to describe an event

   D. to entertain

5. My family came to America in 1985. No one spoke a word of English. In school, I was in an English as Second Language class with other foreign-born children. My class was so overcrowded that it was impossible for the teacher to teach English properly. I dreaded going to school each morning because of the fear of not understanding what people were saying and the fear of being laughed at.

   –Yu-Lan (Mary) Ying, a personal account about learning English

   A. to cause doubt

   B. to entertain

   C. to share a personal experience

   D. to create suspense

Practice 2: More Author's Purpose

A. In a group or on your own, clip six articles from newspapers or magazines. Using the list of purposes for writing from this section, identify the author's purpose in each selection. Exchange your passages with a classmate to see if he/she identifies the same purpose. Then, discuss your findings with the class or with your teacher.

B. Choose two or more purposes listed in the chart of purposes for writing. Write paragraphs that emphasize each purpose. Without revealing your purposes, share your paragraphs with your classmates or teacher. See if they can identify your intended purposes.

AUDIENCE

Once you are clear about your purpose for writing, you must consider your audience—the person(s) who will read what you write. Unless you are writing in your journal or taking notes in class, you are always writing for a particular audience. It may be your teacher, a friend, your parents, or a manager at work. Knowing your audience gives you important information including the following:

- the audience's interest: what topic or information is of interest to the audience (so you can capture the interest of your readers),

- the audience's prior knowledge: what the audience already knows (so you don't tell the readers something they already know, and you can draw on that prior knowledge),

- the audience's vocabulary: words that the readers understand (so you don't use words that are too easy or too difficult),

- what the audience needs to know: information or explanations that you want the audience to know (so you can make a unique presentation for each audience).

This valuable information helps you write more effectively.

Read the following two paragraphs written by the same person. Try to develop a picture of the audience that the writer had in mind.

Example 1: Have you noticed the decrepit state of some of the city buses? Some that are riding around town spew smelly gases. They rattle down the street. The doors stick, so sometimes you have to wait until the driver wrestles with controls before you can get on or off. It's a disgrace. There's just got to be some money in the budget. After all, a new fountain was installed a few months ago. If the city can afford that, it had better be able to get a new bus or two. After all, we need to get around more that we need to hear trickling water! Write to the city council to insist they do something.

Example 2: As a citizen and user of public transportation, I have an urgent request. The city needs to replace some of its oldest buses. Several times in the past few months, I have personally witnessed some troubling issues. First, there are several buses that are very noisy and seem to have mechanical issues. They vibrate tremendously when in motion, and sometimes when idling. Second, these old buses emit a large amount of smoke and odorous fumes. This is not only frustrating, but is also a danger to safety, as doors that will not open may prevent passengers from exiting in an emergency. Please address the critical need for new buses at the next budget meeting.

In both paragraphs, the author is talking to someone about the city buses. However, each paragraph includes very different details, language, and tone. Based on these differences, how would you describe the intended audience of each one? What evidence is there for your ideas?

> When considering how to convey what you think your audience needs to know, consider the audience's interests, prior knowledge, and vocabulary skill.

Practice 3:   Audience

For each of the following topics, describe the interest, knowledge, and vocabulary of the given audience, as well as what you think the audience should know. The first one is done as an example.

1.   Topic: parental advisory stickers on music CDs   Audience: parents

Audience Interest   *interested in the welfare of their children*

Audience Knowledge   *familiar with specific artists, but aware of rude music*

Audience Vocabulary   *some knowledge of teen vocabulary, but mostly not*

Audience Should Know   *parents, not record companies, need to take responsibility*

2.   Topic: parental advisory stickers on music CDs   Audience: students

Audience Interest

Audience Knowledge

Audience Vocabulary

Audience Should Know

3.   Topic: high salaries of professional athletes   Audience: baseball players

Audience Interest

Audience Knowledge

Audience Vocabulary

Audience Should Know

4. Topic: high salaries of professional athletes   Audience: stadium worker

Audience Interest _____

Audience Knowledge _____

Audience Vocabulary _____

Audience Should Know _____

5. Topic: using lottery to fund public education   Audience: church pastor

Audience Interest _____

Audience Knowledge _____

Audience Vocabulary _____

Audience Should Know _____

6. Topic: using lottery to fund public education   Audience: governor of state

Audience Interest _____

Audience Knowledge _____

Audience Vocabulary _____

Audience Should Know _____

7. Topic: importance of a high school diploma   Audience: high school dropout

Audience Interest _____

Audience Knowledge _____

Audience Vocabulary _____

Audience Should Know _____

8. Topic: importance of a high school diploma   Audience: employer

Audience Interest   _____

Audience Knowledge   _____

Audience Vocabulary   _____

Audience Should Know   _____

LANGUAGE

In regard to writing, **language** refers to the words that a writer uses to present ideas. From your own experience, you know that the way you speak to your friends is different from the way you speak to a teacher or a parent. Also, the words you use in a conversation with a teacher are different from the words you would write in a composition for that teacher. See two different types of language in the examples below.

Example 1:   An honest man has hardly need to count more than his ten fingers, or in extreme cases he may add his ten toes, and lump the rest. Simplicity, Simplicity, Simplicity! I say, let your affairs be as two or three, and not a hundred or a thousand: instead of a million count half a dozen, and keep your accounts on your thumbnail. In the midst of this chopping sea of civilized life. . . he must be a great calculator indeed who succeeds. Simplify, Simplify. Instead of three meals a day, if it be necessary eat but one, instead of a hundred dishes, five, and reduce other things in proportion.

– Henry David Thoreau, *Walden*

Example 2:   Sometimes life gets so crazy. You've got cell phones ringing, T.V.s blaring, cars honking, and everybody talking at the same time. You've got to simplify these days, or you just won't make it. Do you really need three beepers and two cell phones? One cell phone is <u>more</u> than enough—trash the rest. When things are getting out of control, try to focus only on the important things. Forget everything else. Take one day at a time, and use the KISS principle: Keep It Simple, Stupid.

The authors of the two examples above use very different words to describe similar ideas. Example 1 uses formal language which includes complex sentence structure and a higher level of vocabulary. Example 2 uses informal language, including simpler vocabulary and sentence structure.

The differences between formal and informal language are sometimes small, but often very important. These differences are presented in the table below.

Formal Language	Informal Language
Characteristics	
broader vocabulary	simple words
more complex sentence structure	simple sentences
strict attention to proper grammar	loose following of grammar rules
Appropriate Uses	
written assignments for school	conversations with friends or relatives
business letters	personal letters, e-mail

As indicated in the table above, you should use formal language for any writing assignments in school or for any standardized tests. Formal language is also appropriate for business letters or letters to people who hold a particular office, such as superintendent, mayor, or editor of a newspaper.

Formal

Each pair of sentences below uses different language to express the same idea. Read each sentence, and decide whether the sentence uses formal or informal language.

Example 3: Danny's mom told the other kids to go away.

Example 4: Danny's mother told the other children to leave.

Example 5: He did not like our offer.

Example 6: He didn't like our deal.

Example 7: I've just about finished my homework

Example 8: I have almost finished my homework.

Examples 3, 6, and 7 contain contractions and other simple words, which are characteristic of informal language. Examples 4, 5, and 8 are somewhat different, and they do not contain contractions. They also replace words like *mom, kids,* and *deal* with *mother, children,* and *offer*. These changes make the language formal, which is more appropriate for most writing assignments.

Informal

While informal language can be grammatically correct, formal language is more appropriate for writing assignments, including standardized tests that require written responses.

41

Practice 4:   Language

Read each sentence below. On the line next to the sentence, write F if it contains formal language or I if it contains informal language.

1. You must consider the feelings of each person before making your decision. _____

2. How long has he been having trouble with his wrist? _____

3. The Web is a great place to get lots of cool information. _____

4. Would you like to join me in seeing a movie Saturday night? _____

5. Make sure you stop by while you're in town. _____

6. We anticipate future success due to our investment strategy. _____

7. Stay on the right track, and you'll be a winner. _____

8. She's never gonna go for that. _____

9. The principal presented an unusual award to one member of the faculty. _____

10. We'll have a great trip, as long as the RV doesn't break down. _____

TONE

While growing up, you have probably heard a parent or other adult say, "Don't use that tone of voice with me!" And you have probably responded, "What tone?" **Tone** is the attitude or feeling that underlies words. You know that the same words can be said in many different tones. Just think of the many different ways you can say "No" or "Hi." In writing, tone is the way a writer uses words to present a certain attitude or feeling to the reader. A writer can use the same type of language to convey very different tones. For example, compare the following letters.

Mrs. Barbara Jones
15 Oak Lane
New York City, NY 10020

Acme, Inc.
Customer Service
10 Main Street
Bedford, NY 1050

March 16, 20

To Whom It May Concern:

I am very displeased with the service I have received from your company. In fact, it would be more accurate to say the "disservice" which I have received from your company. On three separate occasions (March 11, 14, and 15) I have dialed your so-called "Helpline" and been left on hold for over twenty minutes. You may find it hard to believe, but I have much better ways of spending my time than listening to sleep-inducing music while I'm waiting for your service personnel.

Therefore, I am writing this letter so that you may waste your time contacting me at the phone number below. If I do not hear from a representative by the end of this week, I will cease doing business with your company.

Sincerely,

Barbara Jones

Barbara Jones (1-555-IAM-MADD)

Acme, Inc
10 Main Street
Bedford, NY 10506

Mrs. Barbara Jones
15 Oak Lane
New York City, NY 10020

March 27, 2009

Dear Mrs. Jones

Please accept our apology for the inconvenience you suffered because of our Helpline. In general, we try to respond to customers within 45 seconds of their call. At times, the volume of calls we receive prevents us from doing that. I am sending this letter to let you know that I have asked one of our representatives to call you this afternoon. If you do have not received this call by the time you receive this letter, please use the number below to reach me directly, and we will solve your problem immediately. Thank you for working with Acme, Inc., and we look forward to serving you in the future.

Sincerely,

Zhong Li

Zhong Li
Customer Service Director (1-800-IAM-SORI)

The authors of both letters use formal language to express their ideas. However, the tone which each author uses is very different

In Example 1, the author is clearly frustrated about being left on hold. She states directly that she is "displeased with the service" she has received. She adds a slightly sarcastic twist in the second sentence by calling the company's service "disservice." The author states her problem and uses stronger sarcasm in the sentence which begins "You may find it hard to believe . . ." The last sentence is called an ultimatum, that is, a challenge for someone to do something or else suffer certain consequences. This shows that the author is ready to take serious action. Therefore, the author's tone could be described as angry, sarcastic, or serious. However, frustrated is the most accurate description of the author's tone.

The author of the second letter is responding to a frustrated customer. The author wants to solve the customer's problem and make her feel better so that she will still be a customer. He begins his letter by apologizing. He tries to offer an explanation without making excuses. He states the action he has taken and gives the customer direct access to his phone. This action shows that he, too, is serious about solving her problem. The tone of his letter may be called apologetic, expressing sorrow for his part in doing something wrong.

There are many different tones which you can use in your writing. Some tones are listed in the following table. Use a dictionary to learn what these words mean.

Different Types of Tone

angry	dramatic	horrified	optimistic	sarcastic
anxious	excited	humorous	pessimistic	satirical
apologetic	expectant	hysterical	relaxed	serious
calm	fearful	lighthearted	relieved	sympathetic
cynical	frustrated	lofty	rude	threatening
doubtful	happy	neutral	sad	tragic

> In your writing, pay attention to tone—the feeling or attitude you present with your words.

Practice 5: Tone

Based on the list of types of tone, identify the author's tone for the following passages. Then, discuss your answers with your class or teacher.

1. Doctors are a regular set of humbugs, and most of them are quacks. They go off to school and learn some recipes for curing diseases. Then they manage in one way or another to get the teachers in their school to give them a certificate, and then they'll go out into some town or village or city and rent some space over a drugstore and get some bones and an old skull and a lot of books and spread them around the room and call it an office. They put up a sign and call themselves doctors. Then they guess what your illness is and collect their money.

– John S. Draper, *Shams*

A. happy   B. neutral   C. sympathetic   D. cynical

2. I ain't never seen nothin' like it all my life. There we was just walkin' down the street when two guys came runnin' out of Joe's Store shootin' up everything in sight. We hit the pavement fast as we could. Thank God nobody got killed or nothin'. It's not like I ain't seen it before, but this time was too close for comfort. Ya know what I mean. That's the last time I'm takin' that short cut home from school. I'll take the long way next time. I bet you should do the same.

   A. relieved   B. rude   C. anxious   D. threatening

3. During Napoleon's war with England, both England and France seized neutral ships and goods. In addition, they were conscripting United States merchant sailors into their navies, enraging the people of the United States. In August 1810, Napoleon publicly repealed his previous decrees and declared that neutral ships could freely trade in France without risk of confiscation or conscription. President Madison believed Napoleon's words. When Britain refused to promise the same thing, Congress declared war on England and began invading Canada, starting the War of 1812.

   A. cynical   B. expectant   C. ironic   D. neutral

4. Suddenly, the boat capsized. "Felix, where are you?" I screamed. All I could see was the overturned boat and pieces of our shattered picnic lunch being tossed on the waves. I swam around to the other side of the boat, but there was no sign of him. "He's gotta be under the boat!" I thought as panic began to grip me. I dove under the boat and found Felix. His eyes were closed, but his arm was wrapped around the seat of the boat. I grabbed him and pulled him up for air. As I tried to get him breathing again, I kept shouting, "Wake up, Felix! Wake up!" Luckily, I was able to get him breathing again. Our picnic was ruined, but it wasn't a tragedy. Thank goodness.

   A. pessimistic   B. dramatic   C. humorous   D. relaxed

5. The traffic began moving again. Josh was glad to be finished building houses in Washoe county. Now he was ready to relax for a couple of weeks in the Great Basin National Park. The drive home would take about two hours on the interstate. When Josh got home, he'd pack the tent, sleeping bags, food, and cooking gear in the truck. Then he'd pick up his son, David. They'd be together for the whole weekend in a secluded woodland with no one around for miles. They'd fish the streams and lakes with fly rods. The cool air and water would refresh his mind and spirit. Josh could already smell the freshly caught fish sizzling over an open fire.

   A. expectant   B. sad   C. sarcastic   D. humorous

CHAPTER 2 SUMMARY

Diction includes an author's choice of correct, clear, and effective words. The words he or she will choose depend on the **author's purpose** for writing. Purposes for writing include to inform, to entertain, to persuade, and so on.

To choose the right words, an author must consider the **audience** for the writing. This includes thinking about the audience's interest, prior knowledge, vocabulary, and need for information. The author must also choose the appropriate **language** and **tone** for the chosen purpose and audience.

CHAPTER 2 REVIEW: DICTION

Read the following two articles. Then, on your own paper, answer the questions, using complete sentences.

Article 1

The results of a recent survey conducted by the NIH (National Institutes of Health) indicate that substance abuse had increased in the Manhattan area since September 11. During the months of October and November, researchers randomly phoned residents of New York City, carefully screening for those living in the Manhattan area. Answers to questions about alcohol, cigarette, and marijuana use before and after September 11 revealed a 25 percent increase in alcohol consumption, a 10 percent increase in tobacco use, and 30 percent increase in marijuana use.

The data collected during this survey will help researchers find more effective ways to treat substance abuse in people coping with severe stress. This research has revealed that people who admitted to an increase in substance abuse were most likely suffering from post-traumatic stress disorder and depression. Substance abuse did not differ significantly among ethnic groups or gender. Age, marital status, and income seemed to play a more integral role in determining whether the trauma of September 11 caused an increase in substance abuse.

Article 2

Did you know that you could die from smoking that cigarette or taking that last drink for the road? You are killing your children right now with that cancer stick, and you could kill them or someone else by drinking and driving. Smoking causes lung cancer and heart disease: there ain't no butts about it. Alcohol causes cirrhosis of the liver and birth defects: go ahead and toast to *that*. Smoking and drinking aren't cool: they are a subtle form of terrorism that kills you and your family. Don't look to the HOMELAND SECURITY POLICE to protect you. You have got to protect your own home and your family against this threat. So, go home and be a hero—lose the booze and the smokes!

1. What is the purpose of each report?

2. Examine the language of each report. What kind of tone is used in each?

Read the following excerpt, and complete the writing exercise that follows.

> There was a proposition in a township there to discontinue public schools because they were too expensive. An old farmer spoke up and said if they stopped the schools they would not save anything, because every time a school was closed a jail had to be built. It's like feeding a dog on his own tail. He'll never get fat. I believe it is better to support schools than jails.

– Mark Twain, *Speeches*

3. Write a paragraph, on your own paper, analyzing the effectiveness of this passage. Discuss the use of language and tone.

Mark Twain

Read the following two letters which discuss censorship in the public school libraries. Then, complete the writing exercise that follows.

Dear Fellow Students,

There is a quiet, hush-hush censorship happening in our schools that administrators were hoping we wouldn't notice. Did you know that the library won't order certain books they think we shouldn't read? Do they think we're too young to understand the facts of life, such as the prejudice against the immigrants who helped build this country or the social problems of the "haves" versus the "have-nots" with political double dealing and business scandals? Are they afraid we'll be brainwashed by the authors? Do they think that we are a second generation of slackers and just don't care! Many of these books are considered to be classics, and we should be required to read them, not restricted from reading them. I am really insulted by the heavy-handed censorship happening in our very own school. Help me take a stand against this ignorance forced on us by school officials, and write to your school board telling them how ticked off you are about this whole thing.

Thanks,

Ricky Mondego

Dear Members of the School Board,

I am writing to express my disappointment that the library will not order books they deem too controversial for our school. As a member of the 11th grade and a soon-to-be contributing member of this community, I should be encouraged to read quality literature and to think critically about the issues these books represent. I feel that my right to access information of my choice has been violated by this censorship.

Allowing, and even encouraging, the students of this school to read this material will help us to develop the kind of analytical skills that we need to become productive citizens. Through reading these books, we will be reassured that the very issues we face today have been plaguing the minds of great writers for centuries. Sheltering us from these issues accomplishes nothing. I ask that you reconsider your decision to ban these books from the school library and renew your faith in the developing minds of the younger generation.

Sincerely,

Ricardo Mondego

4. Although the same student wrote these letters to accomplish the same goal, the tone and language are very different. Write a paragraph explaining how the audience has influenced the author of these letters. Discuss the differences in tone, language, and audience.

5. Look at the first letter on the previous page. Notice the vocabulary differences in this letter. Is it more informal than the second letter? Why? Change some of the vocabulary in the letter to sound as though it were aimed at an adult audience. How did you choose the words to change, and what did you change them to?

ADDITIONAL ACTIVITIES: DICTION

1. Put yourself in someone else's shoes. Imagine you are running for mayor of your town. Write three paragraphs: one a press release for the local paper, one a letter to your opponent, and one to your best friend. Here are some possible topics with which you can agree or disagree.

school vouchers	school uniforms
new licensing laws for ATV operators	restricted internet use
amusement park safety	hybrid cars
mandatory community service	restriction on concerts

Share these paragraphs with your teacher or classmates. Is the language effective for the audience? Why? Why not?

2. Your younger brother or sister has the school's toughest math teacher this year. In one paragraph, offer him or her advice on passing the class.

3. Write two letters from a pet's point of view. The first should be a list of demands; the second a thank you note for the things your owner does for you. Don't reveal what kind of animal you are; let your audience guess.

4. Compare the language on the front page of your local paper to the language in one of your textbooks. Both are intended to inform, but the audience for each is different. Discuss how this affects the language.

5. You just bought a CD by your favorite band, and you can't wait to listen to it. Once you open it, you discover there is a huge scratch in the disc. Write a letter of complaint to the company. Once you are finished with the letter, exchange complaint letters with a classmate. Now write a response to your friend's letter of complaint as if you were the president of the company.

Basics Made Easy

BME
Writing Review

Chapter 3
Planning the Essay

This chapter covers the following McREL standard and benchmark for Level III:	
Standard 1: Uses the general skills and strategies of the writing process	Benchmarks **1** and **5**

In the last two chapters, you practiced writing paragraphs. In this chapter, you will expand your writing skills to compose a five-paragraph essay. You will learn about the following:

- The Basic Structure of an Essay
- The Writing Process
- Generating Ideas

- Focusing Ideas
- Making a Plan for Your Essay

BASIC STRUCTURE OF AN ESSAY

A five-paragraph essay should include three main parts: **introduction**, **body**, and **conclusion**.

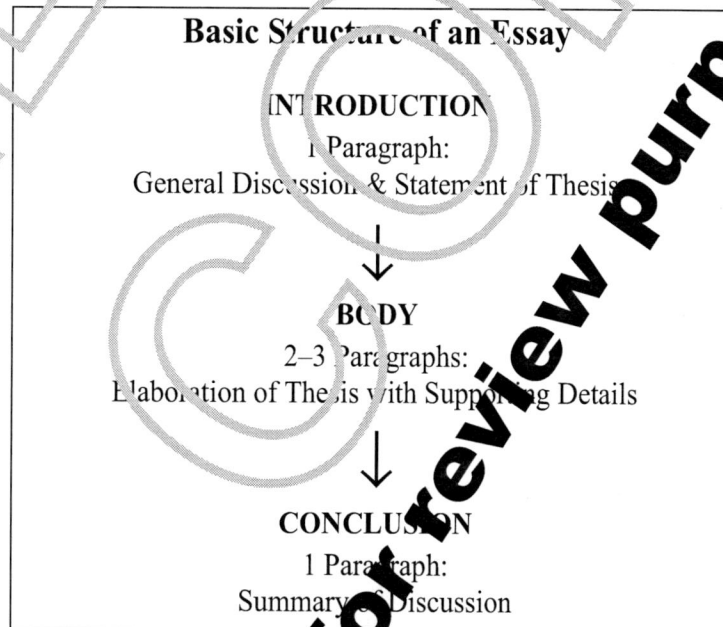

Basic Structure of an Essay

INTRODUCTION
1 Paragraph:
General Discussion & Statement of Thesis

↓

BODY
2–3 Paragraphs:
Elaboration of Thesis with Supporting Details

↓

CONCLUSION
1 Paragraph:
Summary & Discussion

The **introduction** is the first paragraph of your essay. It gets the reader's attention, prepares the reader for what will follow, and states the **thesis** of the essay. The thesis of an essay is much like the main idea of a paragraph.

The **body** consists of three paragraphs which support the thesis. Each paragraph is focused around a topic sentence which can be drawn from the key points of the thesis. In turn, the topic sentence of each paragraph is supported by the details explained in the rest of that paragraph.

The **conclusion** is the last paragraph of your essay. It reinforces the thesis of your essay with a vigorous summary of your argument. It ties everything together and convinces the reader of the rightness of your position.

THE WRITING PROCESS

Whether you are composing a letter, an in-class essay, or a lengthy homework assignment, your writing does not appear magically. You must follow a process. You have to **think**, **write**, **review**, and then repeat these steps. Study the writing process described below.

The Writing Process

Think

1. **Read the writing prompt carefully.** Make sure that you understand what question the writing prompt is asking and who your audience is.

2. **Generate ideas.** Make a list of every idea that comes into your head regarding the topic. Don't judge the ideas as good or bad yet.

3. **Focus your ideas.** From your list, choose some ideas that you can use for your essay, and make a plan for how you will present them.

Write

4. **Write.** Write a draft based on your plan. Use complete sentences to develop your ideas into paragraphs.

Review

5. **Revise.** Check over your draft for coherence, transitions, and sentence variety and structure. Delete any unnecessary words, phrases, or sentences.

Think

6. **Think** about any other ways you can improve your essay.

Write

7. **Write** the final copy of your essay clearly on the lined paper.

Review

8. **Proofread.** Neatly correct punctuation, spelling, capitalization, word choice, grammar, and sentence formation.

It may seem like there are many steps to follow when you only have a limited amount of time to write an essay. For now, go through the steps slowly, learning each one thoroughly. As you practice, these steps will become like second nature to you. Then, you will be well prepared for any writing assignment you face, including timed essays on exams.

> Practice the writing process: think, write, and review.

READ THE WRITING PROMPT CAREFULLY

The first step in writing a good response is to **read the writing prompt carefully**. Make sure you understand the question you are to answer. It is also important for you to identify the audience to whom you are writing, such as the principal, other students, or readers of the local newspaper. Read the following sample writing prompt carefully.

> A recent survey has shown that teens aged twelve to seventeen watch an average of eleven hours of television each week. However, children between the ages of two and five watch an average of thirteen hours of television each week. Your teacher has given you the homework assignment: discuss with your family the amount of television watched in your home. Decide what you think about young children watching nearly two hours of television each day.
>
> As a way of introducing the topic of children watching television, you will write an essay answering the following question: "Does television affect young children positively or negatively? Explain your answer." Once you finish the essay, you will give it to your parents to "look over." This will start your family's discussion.

1. What question does this writing prompt ask?

> "Does television affect young children positively or negatively?"

The writing prompt does not ask you to address whether your family watches too much television, or why teens watch less television than younger children. The prompt asks whether television affects young children positively or negatively. Stick to this issue.

Watching television may affect young children in both positive and negative ways. You must decide if, overall, the effects are positive or negative. For persuasive writing, it is important to choose one side of an issue. Though it is helpful for you to acknowledge and/or answer possible objections to your position, don't try to argue both sides of the issue at the same time. Since your purpose is to persuade readers, you must first be clear about your own position.

2. Who is the audience?   **Your Parents**

Of course, the teacher will be reading your essay, but you will also share it with your parents. This dilemma of a dual audience is similar to testing situations or writing homework assignments in which you are asked to address a certain audience, but the essay will be graded by a teacher or professional reader. In response to this sample writing prompt, you must use more formal language and tone for your teacher, while at the same time being aware of comments or objections your parents may have.

> Answer the correct question for the proper audience.

GENERATING IDEAS

Once you clearly understand what the writing prompt is asking, you can begin generating ideas to use in your response. You may have many good ideas, but they aren't useful until you get them out of your head onto the paper. **Brainstorming** and **freewriting** are two methods of getting your ideas out of your head so you can work with them.

BRAINSTORMING

One way to explore possibilities for your essay is through **brainstorming**. Begin writing down whatever comes to mind regarding the topic and questions provided by the writing prompt. Do not worry about grammar or spelling, and don't make any decisions about the ideas as you write them. Just let them flow freely from your thoughts. Your purpose is to create a list of ideas and details that you can use to develop your essay. For example, look at the brainstorming list below which is based on the following prompt.

> Does television affect young children positively or negatively? Explain your answer.

What's wrong with television?   what if parents aren't home

learn new information   kids watch too much TV

kids are quiet   kids like TV

kids need exercise   Too many hours in front of the tube

they should be out playing   tv is violent

safe places to play?   sitting around playing video games

educational programs   see lots of commercials!

Hannah Montana, Sesame Street, CSI   sex is used in commercials

As you can see from the list above, the process of brainstorming helps you generate ideas for your essay, but it also can help you clarify your thoughts. As the ideas flowed freely onto the page, the student who wrote the above brainstorming list developed an opinion about the effects of television on young children.

Practice 1: Brainstorming

Create a brainstorming list for each of the following topics.

1. Should prayer be allowed in public schools?

2. What are the effects of having metal detectors at the doors of your school?

3. Agree or disagree with the following statement: "All teenagers should be required to complete a driver's education course before they are approved for a driver's permit."

4. Air pollution is increasing in your area. How should your community respond?

FREEWRITING

Freewriting is another way to write down ideas that you can use for an essay. When some people are asked a question, they just start talking to help them think out loud. Sometimes, this is how people find out what their thoughts are. When you freewrite, you simply start writing and see what happens. Don't worry about grammar and spelling. If you get stuck and don't know what to put next, write "I don't know what to write." Just keep writing, and let the ideas flow. Look at the following freewriting sample about the topic of school uniforms.

> School uniforms are stupid. I want to wear what I want to wear. Can you see me in one of those silly skirts? Those colors are always so bad. Who would want uniforms anyway? How much do they cost. I couldd never get a date if I were wearing a uniform. I don't know what to write. School uniforms stifle student individuality. Everyones an individual we don't need to look the same. What are the benefits? As long as clothing is clean and respectable, why do we all have to wear the same thing? Think of the added expense of buying two sets of clothes. Clothes that can conly be worn at school and closthes at home, I wouldn't be caught dead in one of those school uformns otuside of school

Obviously, the student who wrote this has some strong opinions that could lead to a good essay.

> To generate ideas for your essay, write down whatever you think, without making judgments about it.

Practice 2: Freewriting

Try freewriting about each of the following topics.

1. The need for improved public transportation in your area.

2. Life contains many joyful moments. What was the happiest day of your life?

3. School activities such as field trips, plays, and concerts can be fun and educational. What was your favorite school activity last semester?

4. Cheating in school is the wrong way to get an education. How should students who are caught cheating be punished?

FOCUSING IDEAS

Obviously, you cannot create an essay directly from a brainstorming list or a freewriting sample. The ideas don't follow any logical order. Also, there are too many ideas. You can't use them all. You need to choose a group of related ideas that you can develop into a coherent, well-organized essay.

CLUSTERING

Clustering is one helpful way to start organizing your ideas by grouping related thoughts together. In the clustering process, you put the main question of the writing prompt in the center of the page, and draw a circle around it. Then, you draw branches off from this circle to add topics and supporting details.

Sample Clustering for Effects of Television on Young Children

The clustering process can help you narrow your ideas, but these ideas still need to be limited further. You can choose only one portion of your cluster to develop your essay. For example, in the cluster diagram above, there are more ideas grouped around the negative effects of television. This indicates interest, enthusiasm, and support for this idea, and would, therefore, make a good focus for an essay.

Practice 3: Clustering

Choose four of the topics from Practice 1 or Practice 2, and create a clustering diagram for each one. (You will use these diagrams for Practice 5, so keep them in a safe place, like your portfolio or writing folder.)

THESIS

Your response to each writing prompt will be focused around the **thesis** or controlling idea of your essay. The thesis is the main point—the idea you are trying to prove. It is what *you* want to say. The thesis must be broad enough to invite discussion but narrow enough to be manageable in four to five paragraphs. It summarizes the topic and purpose of your essay in one sentence and includes the general topic, your focus, and supporting points. Look at the example below.

General Topic	Focus	Supporting Points
Television affects young children	in a negative way	• showing them adult programs • commercials make kids want things • takes from playtime activities

A sentence which states the thesis would look like this:

> Television has a negative effect on young children because they can watch programs that are not meant for their age, see commercials for products they don't need, and miss out on playtime they need.

The statement of the thesis for your essay is similar to the topic sentence of a paragraph. It provides the reader with valuable information about what is to come and it gives you a kind of compass to keep your essay on track. As you will see in the next section, you can use each of the supporting points from your thesis to form topic sentences for the body paragraphs.

> Use clustering to help you develop the thesis for your essay.

57

Practice 4: Thesis

A. Below are three topics that have been focused in a specific way. Choose another way to focus each topic, and provide three supporting points.

General Topic	Focus	Supporting Points
1. School uniforms	not good idea	look bad
		limit individuality
		more expensive
School uniforms	*good idea*	*less distracting dress*
		promote professional attitude
		large families pass down to younger kids
2. Doing homework in school	not a good idea	not enough time, distractions
		projects and reading too long to finish at school
Doing homework in school	_____	_____
		_____
3. Guest speaker at school	fire chief	explain how to become firefighter
		tell about exciting work
		teach fire safety
Guest speaker at school	_____	_____
		_____

B. For 2 and 3 above, choose the position you support. Then, write a statement of the thesis for three different essays in which you will defend your position.

1.
_____

_____

2.
_____

_____

MAKING A PLAN

Your thesis is like the destination you have chosen for a journey. The ideas you have gathered in your clustering diagram are the stops you want to make along the way. You still need to decide how you will get to your destination, putting your steps in the proper order. An **outline** helps you plan your journey.

OUTLINE

An **outline** lays out the plan for your essay in a very structured way. It is the road map you will follow in writing your draft. You will get to your destination more easily if your road map looks like the following:

I. Introduction: General discussion including thesis statement

II. Body

    A. Paragraph 1: Topic 1 (from thesis statement) and supporting details

    B. Paragraph 2: Topic 2 (from thesis statement) and supporting details

    C. Paragraph 3: Topic 3 (from thesis statement) and supporting details

III. Conclusion: Summary of discussion

An outline for the essay about the effects of television on young children might look like this:

I. Introduction: Television affects young children negatively because they can watch programs that are not meant for their age, see commercials for products they don't need, and miss out on playtime they do need.

II. Body

    A. Television exposes children to adult programs.

        1. Theft

        2. Murder

        3. Sex

    B. Commercials increase children's wishes for needless products.

        1. Children find it difficult to tell reality from pretend

        2. Products bring happiness

    C. Television takes away from children's playtime.

        1. Lack of play with others

        2. No fresh air and movement

III. Conclusion: Young children should watch less television.

OUTLINE SHORTCUT

An outline can be very helpful for organizing an essay when you have more than ninety minutes to complete the assignment. However, sometimes you must complete writing assignments within a class period or other limited testing time.

One way to save time is to use your clustering diagram to create an **outline shortcut** in place of a complete outline. You can look at the clustering diagram you have already produced, and write "T" next to the circle that will be your thesis. Then, choose two or three circles from which you can form your body paragraphs, and put them in order by writing 1, 2, or 3 next to them. You may even want to group a few ideas for one paragraph by circling them. With this shorthand notation, you have made a kind of outline that will help you write your introduction around the thesis and support it with the body paragraphs according to the order you have chosen. Then, you can summarize your key ideas in your conclusion.

See below how the clustering diagram from page 56 can be used in this way.

Sample Outline Shortcut for Effects of Television on Young Children

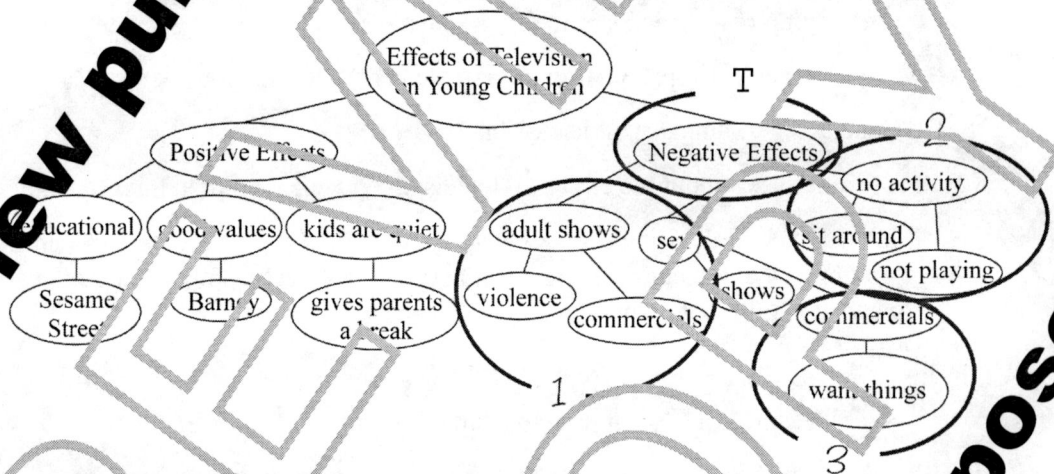

> Use an outline or your clustering diagram to make a plan for your essay.

Practice 5: Making a Plan

A. Choose two of the topics for which you have generated ideas, and develop outlines for each one.

B. Choose two of the clustering diagrams you have made, and organize each one into an outline shortcut.

CHAPTER 3 SUMMARY

In **planning the essay**, remember the basic structure of a five-paragraph essay:

- 1 Paragraph: Introduction
- 2–3 Paragraphs: Body
- 1 Paragraph: Conclusion

Practice the steps of the **writing process** using "**think, write, review**" to complete the following tasks.

- **Read the writing prompt carefully** to be sure you understand what you need to write.
- **Generate ideas** using methods such as **brainstorming** and **freewriting**.
- **Focus ideas** by organizing what you generated. **Clustering** can help group related thoughts.

Create a **thesis** statement that summarizes the topic and purpose of your essay.

- Make an **outline** to lay out the plan for your essay. You can also make an outline shortcut by labeling ideas in your clustering. Follow the outline like a roadmap to keep you on course as you write.

CHAPTER 3 REVIEW: PLANNING THE ESSAY

Note: Keep your papers from this chapter review in your portfolio. You will use the work you have done here in the review for other chapters in this book.

A. Read the sample brainstorming list for the next writing prompt. Then, on a separate sheet of paper, write down your brainstorming ideas surrounding the topics in prompts 1, 2, and 3.

Sample Writing Prompt:

> This year, the Parent Teacher Association (PTA) is planning an extended field trip for your grade. The parents and teachers want to make sure the trip is educational, but they also want it to be entertaining. In order to make a good choice, the PTA is seeking input from the students. What do you think would be a good place for an entertaining and educational field trip?

Sample Brainstorming List:

Disney World	Innovations	Parade of Lights
Epcot Center	Living Seas	Disney Quest
exhibits	technology displays	computer simulators
cultural showcases	unlimited video games	interactive exhibits
native food	Spaceship Earth	computer software
native workers	bumper cars	custom-designed roller coaster
native animals	Disney characters	Magic Kingdom

Prompt 1:

> People receive inspiration in different ways. Think about a person, place, or idea that fills you with emotion and excitement. What are you motivated to do? Describe who or what inspires you and how it changes what you do or plan to do.

Prompt 2:

> Many school districts are now considering the idea of school vouchers. In the voucher system, parents who do not want to send their children to public schools will receive a voucher which can be used to pay for tuition at any accredited private school. Is this initiative a good idea or not? Why?

Prompt 3:

> Your local newspaper is sponsoring a contest with a $1,000 prize. The contestants must write a two-page essay which answers the question, "If you were granted one wish to change the world, what would you change?" Write a convincing essay for the judges.

Note: If you would rather brainstorm about a different topic, choose one or more from the several writing prompts in Appendix A (pages 311–325).

B. Read the freewriting example below that creates ideas about the sample prompt for Part A. Then, on your own paper, freewrite your ideas surrounding prompts 4 and 5.

Sample Freewriting:

Members of the PTA, I think we should go to Orlando, Florida, to have our field trip. We would have a great time. I remember going into Disney Quest, we could play video games for free all day. In Epcot, you can tour many important countries of the world and eat their food, too. I remember going to the Magic Kingdom. You see, at night they do this special show called Parade of Lights. It's pretty fun. Of course, they have the Disney characters over there too, Oh yeah, did I forget to mention that Epcot has all of these special attractions where you get to explore and experience some great technological innovations. They seem to have new attractions there every year!

Prompt 4:

> Your parents have informed you that they will be moving to another state during the middle of your senior year in high school. One of your relatives, however, lives in the area of your school. Write a letter to your parents either convincing them to let you stay on at the high school or convincing them that you would be better off moving with them to another state.

Prompt 5:

> Your school district is considering changing to a year-round school schedule with month-long breaks in December and July. Many students are in an uproar because they enjoy having a long summer vacation to take extended trips. However, many teachers and parents support the proposal because students would remember more information. Which do you think is a better school calendar? Why?

Note: If you would rather freewrite about a different topic, choose one or more of the several writing prompts in Appendix A (pages 311–326).

C. On a separate sheet of paper, take each of the ideas from Parts A and B, and organize them by clustering. Be sure to include your thesis. From these clusters, notice common details, and write a controlling idea. See the sample below taken from the sample brainstorming list in Part A.

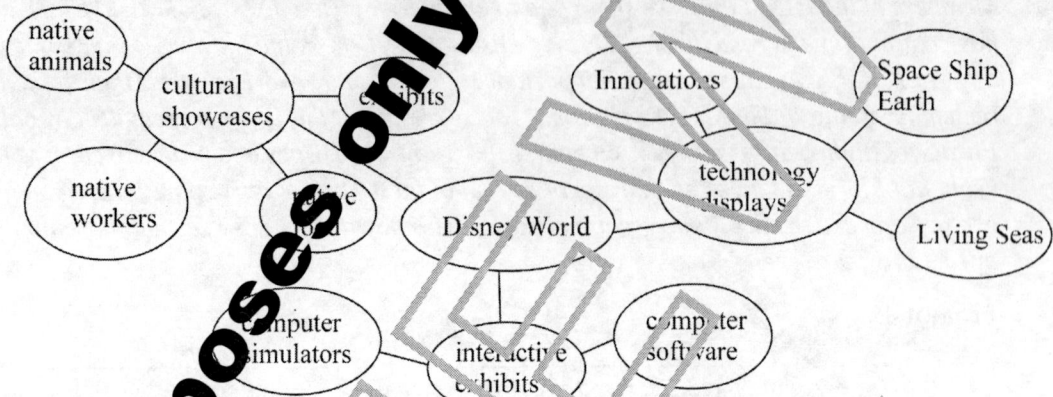

native animals — cultural showcases — exhibits — Innovations — Space Ship Earth — technology displays — native workers — native food — Disney World — Living Seas — computer simulators — interactive exhibits — computer software

Thesis: Walt Disney World will provide the best educational and entertainment opportunities because of its cultural showcases, technology displays, and interactive exhibits.

D. Use your clustering diagrams from Part C to create outline shortcuts for prompts 1, 2, and 3.

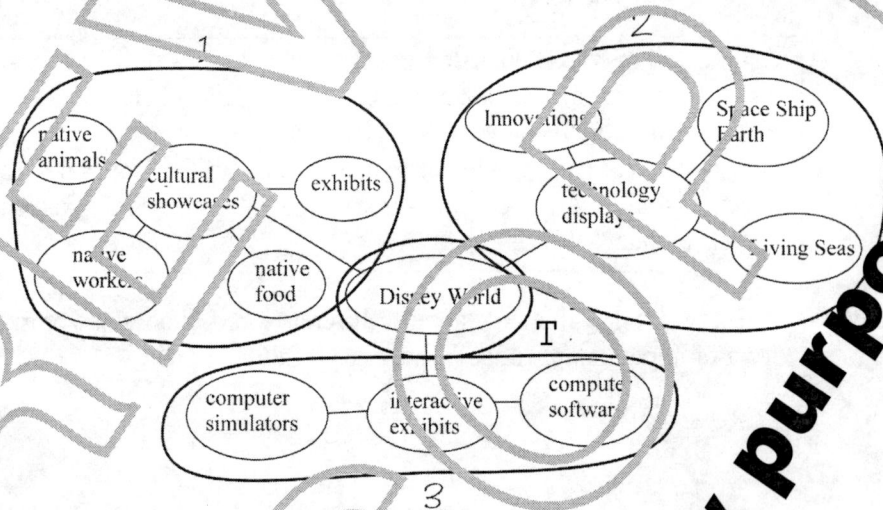

1 — native animals — cultural showcases — exhibits — native workers — native food — Disney World — T

2 — Innovations — Space Ship Earth — technology displays — Living Seas

3 — computer simulators — interactive exhibits — computer software

E. On a separate sheet of paper, create an outline for prompts 4 and 5 based on the clustering diagrams you designed in Part C.

Example:

I. Introduction: Walt Disney World will provide the best educational and entertainment opportunities because of its cultural showcases, technology displays, and interactive exhibits.

II. Body

   A. Cultural showcases

      1. Exhibits and food

      2. Native workers

      3. Native animals

   B. Technology displays

      1. Innovations

      2. Spaceship Earth

      3. Living Seas

   C. Interactive exhibits

      1. Computer simulators

      2. Computer software

III. Conclusion: Disney World is the best place for this special field trip.

Note: Keep your papers from this chapter review in your portfolio. You will use the work you have done here in the reviews for other chapters in this book.

ADDITIONAL ACTIVITIES: PLANNING THE ESSAY

1. As a class, choose one of the following topics to discuss.

raising the driving age to 18	offensive bumper stickers
voting on the Internet	sex before marriage
using cell phones while driving	praying in school
no homework policy for high school students	race prejudice in school
benefits of studying a foreign language	your favorite cars

Once your class has chosen a topic, each student should create a brainstorming list of ideas regarding that topic. Then, students should gather in small groups to share, compare, and further develop their lists. The class should then create a large brainstorming list by writing ideas on the board. Finally, the class should choose which ideas would make the strongest essay.

2. Choose another topic from #1. On your own, freewrite on this topic for about ten minutes. Then, gather in small groups to share, compare, and further develop your freewriting. Finally, as a class, create one extensive freewriting sample on the board or overhead projector. Then, choose the ideas that would make the best essay.

3. In #1, you developed a brainstorming list, and in #2, you created a freewriting sample. Now, choose either one and develop a clustering diagram. Then, discuss your clustering in a small group. Finally, contribute your best ideas to a clustering diagram for the entire class.

4. Review your clustering diagram from #3. Then, circle and label the part of your cluster that would be an outline shortcut. Use the sample outline shortcut on page 00 as a guide.

5. Based on your outline shortcut from #3, create a thesis for your essay. Write it down, and then compare it with the thesis from other students in the class. Make sure it includes your topic, your focus, and your supporting ideas.

Basics Made Easy

Chapter 4
Drafting the Essay

BME
Writing Review

This chapter covers the following McREL standard and benchmark for Level III:	
Standard 1: Uses the general skills and strategies of the writing process	Benchmark **2**
Standard 2: Uses the stylistic and rhetorical aspects of writing	Benchmark **4**

Once you have generated ideas, focused the ideas, and made a plan for your essay, you are ready to start writing a **draft**. A draft is an attempt to put all of your ideas and planning onto paper in the form of an essay. You develop this draft by organizing complete sentences into paragraphs.

Some people like to write several drafts, changing and improving each one significantly. Other writers spend more time being precise the first time and may write only two or three drafts. For in class writing assignments, you usually have only enough time to write one draft, revise it, and proofread it. That is why it is important for you to practice writing essays now, so it will be easier for you to do when you only have a limited amount of time like on an exam.

This chapter will help you improve your writing skills by providing practice in the following areas:

• Improving Word Choice	• Using Transition Words
• Developing Coherence	• Writing the Draft
• Writing Introductions and Conclusions	

IMPROVING WORD CHOICE

Your draft is an attempt to convey your ideas accurately and in an interesting way to the reader. Once you have identified your audience and decided which tone and language would be appropriate, you will select certain words and phrases to reflect these decisions. Your **word choice** is an important way to interest the reader, accurately convey your ideas, and provide convincing reasons for your position on a topic. Improving word choice involves **selecting specific words, using a dictionary and thesaurus, being aware of connotations and denotations**, and **avoiding clichés and sweeping generalizations**.

SELECT SPECIFIC WORDS, NOT GENERAL WORDS

One aspect of good word choice is selecting specific and concrete words rather than general or abstract words. Avoid vague, overused words like *thing*, *nice*, *great*, *bad*, *good*, and *a lot*. These words have many meanings, but none is very clear or specific. Specific words provide the reader with a clear image of what you are describing. For example, compare the two passages below which describe the same event.

> **Example 1:** As we rode down away from the hill, the lightning kept flashing and flashing. One thunderclap followed right after another, but each sounded very strange. The lightning made it hard to see, and hail hit the windshield as I continued to drive.

> **Example 2:** A moderate incline runs towards the foot of Maybury Hill, and down this we clattered. Once the lightning had begun, it went on in as rapid a succession of flashes as I have ever seen. The thunderclaps, treading one on the heels of another and with a strange crackling accompaniment, sounded more like the working of a gigantic electric machine than the usual detonating reverberations. The flickering light was blinding and confusing, and a thin hail smote gustily at [the windshield] as I drove down the slope.

> – H. G. Wells, *The War of the Worlds*

As you can see from Example 1, general words provide a bland description, while in Example 2, concrete words paint a vivid picture. A good way to improve your word choice is to try to answer the questions *who?*, *what?*, *where?*, *when?*, *why?*, and *how?* in as much detail as you can. Take, for example, the following sentence:

> **Example 3:** When he hit the home run, the crowd cheered.

The sentence tells the basic facts, but it could be improved significantly with a more detailed description. Consider the following questions: Who hit the ball? How did he hit it? Where did it go? How did it get there? In what way did the crowd cheer? To answer these questions, one might write the following sentence:

> **Example 4:** When John's mighty swing sent the ball hurtling over the right field fence, the crowd leapt to its feet and burst into wild cheers.

In this sentence, the writer gives detailed answers to the above questions and provides a vivid picture of what happened. Good descriptions are more interesting and more persuasive.

Practice 1: Using Specific Words

A. Fill in the blanks with the appropriate words. The first two are completed as examples.

General	More Specific	Very Specific
1. athlete	football player	wide receiver
2. food	fruit	banana
3. animal	_____	cocker spaniel
4. _____	lake	Lake Erie
5. car	SUV	_____
6. _____	pop music star	David Cook
7. _____	below freezing	12° F
8. young	school age	
9. tree	_____	pine
10. government official		Barack Obama

B. On your own paper, rewrite the following sentences using specific words to create more vivid descriptions.

1. The dog barked all night long.

2. The strong wind caused a tree to fall on our house.

3. It was so hot, we had to jump into the pool.

4. He almost cried when he saw his son graduate.

5. That book was boring.

USE A DICTIONARY OR THESAURUS

A dictionary and thesaurus are valuable tools to help you improve your writing. Even if you are not allowed to use them for in-class writing assignments, using them for your practice essays will greatly improve your vocabulary and your writing skills.

When you are unsure of the meaning of a word, look it up. A good **dictionary** will provide you with the most exact meaning of the word. For example, try looking up the words *flammable* and *inflammable*. You may be surprised at what you find.

When you can't find just the right word to express the idea or picture you want to convey, go to a **thesaurus**. A thesaurus provides many different words that have similar meanings. For example, if you look up the word *see*, you will find many interesting alternatives such as *observe*, *behold*, *examine*, *inspect*, *stare*, *notice*, *scan*, *spy*, *catch sight of*, *survey*, or *contemplate*.

Practice 2: Using a Dictionary or Thesaurus

In a thesaurus, look up these common words: *eat*, *sleep*, *drink*, *short*, *big*. For each word, list three similar words that you find in the thesaurus. In a dictionary, look up the definitions for each of the words you found in the thesaurus. How are the words similar to and different from each other?

BE AWARE OF CONNOTATIONS AND DENOTATIONS

One important part of word choice is knowing the difference between the **denotations** (dictionary meanings) and the **connotations** (emotional associations) of words. For example, the words *slender* and *skinny* both mean "thin." However, if you called a person *slender*, that compliment might get you a date. On the other hand, calling the same person *skinny* might be offensive. In a similar way, the words *determined* and *stubborn* both refer to persistence and an unwillingness to be moved from a particular position. However, *determined* carries a positive connotation, while *stubborn* is usually considered a negative word.

Practice 3: Connotations and Denotations

Use a dictionary to help you describe the connotations and denotations of the following words.

1. watch, glance, stare

2. walk, stroll, meander

3. run, sprint, scurry

4. shivering, trembling, quaking

5. strong, sturdy, tough

AVOID CLICHÉS AND SWEEPING GENERALIZATIONS

Avoid using **clichés** in your writing. These overly familiar expressions include popular phrases such as "busy as a bee" and "to make a long story short." These dull, overused expressions interfere with your message. Simple, straightforward language is often more effective. Look at the examples in this table.

Clichés	Simple Language
busy as a bee	very active
to make a long story short	to summarize
cute as a button	endearing
stop beating around the bush	get to the point
save it for a rainy day	save it for when you need it

Also, avoid **sweeping generalizations** like the following: "No one ever calls me." Unless used for dramatic effect in a story, words like *always, never, ever, no one, everybody,* and *everywhere* are most often not true and show an overly simple understanding of the topic being discussed. Replace these unrealistic claims with accurate descriptions. Look at these examples.

Sweeping Generalization	Accurate Description
No one ever calls me.	I rarely get phone calls.
It always rains on my birthday.	It seems like every year it rains on my birthday.
Everybody knows that Boston has the best team.	Many people believe Boston will win the championship again.

> Improve your word choice by using specific words, using a dictionary and thesaurus, being aware of connotations and denotations, and avoiding clichés and sweeping generalizations.

Practice 4: Clichés and Sweeping Generalizations

The passage below expresses strong patriotic feelings, but the writer has weakened the impact of the argument by using sweeping generalizations and worn out phrases. Rewrite the passage by improving the language used.

The United States has always been the most patriotic country. From the beginning, people worked day after day to do the right thing and make this country free. Everyone knows that the United States is the best place in the world to live. You'll never see the good life until you come to the Land of the Free and the Home of the Brave. Nobody can ever deny that our country is Number One.

Practice 5: Word Choice

On your own or with others, review some of your previous written responses, looking for inappropriate word choices. Revise them, using more effective word choices. (This is a good opportunity to use a dictionary and a thesaurus.)

Practice 6: Sweeping Generalizations

On your own paper, rewrite the following sweeping generalizations with a more accurate description.

1. Today's movies are better than movies of the past.

2. I always get up early on Saturday mornings.

3. I never get to watch the shows I want to watch.

4. We always laugh at every joke.

5. Airplanes are not safe anymore.

6. All people like to play basketball.

7. That dog follows me everywhere I go.

8. None of the people in wheelchairs can ever play sports again.

9. No one here can ever get a phone call because Mary is always on the Internet.

10. Old people always complain about their aches and pains.

WRITING INTRODUCTIONS

In chapter 1, you learned that the beginning and the end of a paragraph are important. The same is true of an essay, where the **introduction** and the **conclusion** should each consist of one paragraph. In this section, you will learn how to write an introduction and about different types of introductions. In the next section, you will learn to write conclusions.

HOW TO WRITE AN INTRODUCTION

The **introduction** is the first paragraph of your essay. Usually it is shorter than the body paragraphs, but it serves an important purpose. It tells readers where you are going and invites them to join you. It should catch the readers' interest and clearly describe the thesis of the essay. The introduction may also inform readers of the order of support for the thesis.

You probably have seen stores that try to attract customers by placing a huge, fluorescent sign outside, advertising an incredible sale. This catches the interest of potential buyers and leads them into the store. Then, the salespeople can show the customers other merchandise that is of higher quality, but is also higher priced. This is what the store managers really want to sell.

This approach to sales is somewhat similar to how you want to lead readers into your essay. You want to catch the readers' attention, lead them into your essay, and then, explain the purpose of your essay. A simple way to build an introduction is by using the following three components: **lead**, **tie-in**, and **thesis**.

LEAD

Sometimes you can start your essay by stating the thesis of your essay, but, often, that type of beginning is too abrupt. You need to grab the reader's attention first, and make the reader want to read further. You can do this with the first sentence, called a **lead**. The lead may be one of the following:

• **statement of your position on the topic**	• **brief story**
• **problem or riddle**	• **quotation**
• **surprising statistic or fact**	• **catchy remark**
• **question**	• **general, thought-provoking statement**

TIE-IN

Once you have captured the readers' attention with your lead, you need to draw their attention to the thesis of your essay. You need to consider the audience, the topic of your essay, and your personal preference in developing a creative link between the lead and the statement of your thesis.

THESIS

You practiced developing a thesis in the last chapter. The first paragraph is a good place to state the thesis because it lets the reader know the topic of the essay, your position on the topic, and how you are going to order your supporting points.

DIFFERENT TYPES OF INTRODUCTIONS

Here, you will find examples of introductions that use different types of leads followed by a tie-in and a statement of the thesis. The first example is labeled for you. For the other examples, circle the lead, [bracket] the tie-in, and underline the statement of the thesis.

1. State Your Position on the Topic

Panama City, Florida, is the ideal place to go for a winter vacation. [You may want to ski the snow-capped peaks of the Rocky Mountains, but I have enough cold weather all winter long. When Christmas break arrives, I want a taste of the warm summer sun. A wool blanket and a roaring fire may do it for some people, but I want more than a cup of hot cocoa to warm my chilled bones.] I want to go someplace where I can choose from a wide assortment of water sports, enjoy the mouth-watering taste of fresh seafood, and run through the cold waves hitting the shoreline at night.

Here, the writer's position is stated directly and emphatically in the first line. This emphatic declaration is an attention-getter. As discussed in chapter 1, this topic sentence invites discussion. The author briefly comments on a possible objection to the topic sentence, and then states the thesis in the last sentence of this brief introduction.

2. Problem or Riddle

Dentists recommend brushing your teeth with it. House cleaners use it to scour counter tops. You can add it to your laundry detergent to freshen your clothes. And, of course, it is an essential ingredient for many baking recipes. Sodium bicarbonate, popularly known as baking soda, is the most useful item in your household. It is especially helpful for cleaning, eliminating odors, and maintaining personal hygiene.

Unlike the introduction that states your purpose right off, the "riddle" introduction holds back one piece of information while teasing the reader to guess what it might be. Notice how this introduction gives examples that support the thesis, even before stating that idea in the final sentence. More examples are needed for the body paragraphs, but these are good starting places.

3. Surprising Statistic or Fact

In one year, firearms killed 0 children in Japan, 19 in Great Britain, 57 in Germany, 109 in France, 153 in Canada, and 5,285 in the United States. In the "land of the free and the home of the brave," we cling to our right to bear arms. However, the frightening numbers that result should make us reconsider the effects of this "right." If I could change any law in the United States, I would make a sensible gun law that includes licensing of handgun owners, registration of handguns, and limiting gun purchases to no more than one a month. A law like this would protect children, make society safer, and secure liberty for those who want guns and those who fear guns.

A statistic or fact is only surprising if it contradicts common views or beliefs. Regarding gun violence, people who read or watch the news know that people using firearms often tragically kill children. What they may not know is that the United States is unique in this area among its primary political allies. This statistic will catch the attention of readers and make them want to continue reading.

4. Question

Isn't coin collecting for nerds, old people, or wealthy investors? Coin collecting stirs up images of shy, lonely people locked away in a room seeking comfort from some shiny coins. When I tell people that my favorite hobby is collecting coins, they ask if it isn't really old-fashioned and boring. Well, maybe it used to be boring, but not since the United States mint began circulating the new state quarters. They are full of history, fun to collect and trade, and they are not expensive.

Beginning an essay with a question automatically engages readers and makes them start thinking. It also creates curiosity about how you will answer the question, making the readers wonder if you will agree or disagree. In the example above, notice that the answer the author gives is surprising.

5. Brief Story

When I walked into the Fairlawn Nursing Home for the first time, I had an uneasy feeling in my stomach. I didn't know what to expect when I entered the circular Activities Room. I found a dozen elderly people, each staring out the floor-to-ceiling picture windows that framed a variety of unique bird feeders. The Activities Director had assured me that my visit would be a great help, but I didn't know what to do. I walked over to one of the windows and spotted a small, dark gray bird with white underparts and black on top of its head. I whispered to myself, "I wonder what kind that is?" Next to me, a gray-haired, frail-looking woman smiled and said in her gravelly voice, "That's a nuthatch, my dear." Our conversation continued from there and continues each Tuesday when I visit Mrs. Joblanski. I consider my time at the nursing home to be my most rewarding after-school activity because the staff is happy to have some help, I have a new friend in Mrs. Joblanski, and I learn so much from the wisdom she has gained during her years of life.

The key to beginning an essay with a short story is to keep it brief. The story is not the focus of the essay, it is only a lead-in to your topic. You can increase the effectiveness of this type of introduction by including details in the story that relate to the thesis. Notice in the story above that the author describes examples of a resident who loves to see visitors, a welcoming staff person, and the wisdom of an older person. These details not only help introduce the thesis but also help to support it.

6. Quotation

"April is the cruelest month," wrote T. S. Eliott. Most people wonder why he wrote this, but I don't. Many people spend the winter months longing for the tiny buds and lengthening days of spring. Others consider the summer the high point of the year because they can escape to their cabin on the lake for fishing and mosquito dodging. Some people spend all year waiting for the fall foliage to explode in brilliant color. These people are missing the best season of the year. For me, winter could last all year long, and I would be happy. So what if you can't swim in the lake, and you have to go to school everyday. When else can you enjoy unique outdoor sports, warm, cozy nights by the fire, and the wonderful holiday season?

Any interesting quote that can be easily related to your topic will make a good lead for your introduction.

7. Catchy Phrase

For some students, taking a standardized test is almost as daunting as fighting a major economic depression, but as Franklin D. Roosevelt said in 1933, "We have nothing to fear but fear itself." With these words, the president encouraged the people of the United States not to despair of the bank closings and job losses. He believed the American people, with the help of their government, had the resources and talent to restore their economic well-being if they did not let fear stop them. In a similar way, students must overcome "test anxiety" in order to succeed. Through adequate preparation, good health practices, and simple relaxation techniques, students can improve their performance on standardized tests.

Franklin Roosevelt

This introduction uses a catchy phrase followed by a quotation. The striking contrast between taking a test and fighting a Depression sparks interest, and the quote from Roosevelt continues the metaphor. The writer may choose to use allusions to fighting panic later in the essay to help connect the ideas.

8. General Thought-Provoking Statement

Almost 40 years since Martin Luther King's "I Have a Dream" speech and nearly 140 years after Abraham Lincoln's Emancipation Proclamation, the scourge of racism still undermines the great principles of this nation. It has become obvious that legislation cannot erase the fear that prevents people from seeing their common humanity. Racism is the biggest problem in the United States precisely because many people don't think it's a problem, it contradicts the very principles upon which this country is founded, and it is an international embarrassment in an age of increasing global diversity.

Martin Luther King

Large issues attract large audiences. By stating a general principle, idea, or situation at the beginning of the essay, you allow readers to connect with a familiar idea. Then, you can direct them to the specific issue or approach you want to discuss in your essay.

> Build your introduction with a lead, tie-in, and statement of the thesis.

Practice 7: Writing Introductions

For four of the topics listed below, use brainstorming or freewriting to develop a thesis and three supporting points. Next, write an introduction. Use a different type of lead for each introduction. (Save your work for other practices in this chapter.)

1. What is your favorite type of weather, sunny and fine or stormy and dramatic? Explain why you like this type of weather.

2. What do you think is the best way to deal with the energy crisis? Why is your solution the best one?

3. If cost were not an issue, what music concert would you want to attend, and why?

4. How do your dreams affect your life? Give reasons why dreams are important to you or why they are not.

5. What class would you choose if you could pick any elective for the next semester? Why?

6. What play would you want your school to perform with you in the lead role? Why?

7. What way do you prefer to communicate with your friends when you are not with them: letter, phone, cell phone, e-mail, Facebook, or some other way? Why?

8. If you could choose whatever you wanted, how would you want to celebrate your birthday? Why?

WRITING CONCLUSIONS

The ending of a composition is just as important as the beginning. You don't want to end your composition by running out of ideas. You want to bring your essay to a logical **conclusion**. You can imagine your essay is like taking someone for a ride in a taxi. When you get to your destination, you don't want to slam on the brakes and tell your passenger, "Get out!" You want to announce that you are nearing the destination, ease on the brakes, and say "good-bye" when your passenger steps out of the car. This increases your chances of a good tip. The concluding paragraph should be similar. You want to let the readers know that they have reached the end of the composition. Then, remind them about the points you have discussed along the way, but don't restate the thesis. Finally, leave the readers with a thought to ponder. In writing the conclusion, you can use many of the same strategies as you do for writing the introduction, but instead of saying "hello," you are saying "good-bye."

SUMMARIZE YOUR THESIS

The last thing you want to do in a conclusion is to introduce a new idea. Instead, summarize the information and reasons that you have already provided. This does not mean to repeat the introduction or to restate the thesis. Before you say "good-bye," remind the reader of some highlights you've covered along the way, as in this example.

> In summary, collecting the new state quarters has provided me with hours of enjoyment. I have been researching the history of the states, collecting and trading the coins with my friends, and enjoying this hobby without hurting my bank account. The value of these coins may never reach an out-of-sight amount, but the personal satisfaction, learning, and friendship that I have found through this hobby is invaluable to me.

CONCLUSION AS INTRODUCTION IN REVERSE

One effective way to write a concluding paragraph for an essay is to write an introduction in reverse. In other words,

1. briefly remind the readers of your topic sentence,

2. tie in the thesis to your final "good-bye," and

3. instead of a lead, use a "good-bye" statement.

The following conclusion uses this model.

> Panama City gives me everything I want in a vacation spot, and more: exhilarating water sports, fresh seafood, and moonlit beach walks. Year after year, my family escapes the cold northern climate by traveling south, but we never tire of the fun, the food, and the relaxation that this great vacation spot provides. However, in case you still have questions about where to go for your next winter vacation, just consider your packing list: bathing suit, towel, sun screen. Sounds good to me!

GIVE THE AUDIENCE A QUESTION TO PONDER

In the conclusion, you want to summarize the information and reasons that you have already provided. Though you don't want readers to have questions about your position or choice, you may want to leave readers with a question that invites them to ponder their own positions. The following conclusion is an example.

> Citizens of the United States fiercely protect their right to individual freedom. Independent-minded people formed this country telling Great Britain to leave them alone and to stop interfering in their lives. This rich tradition of liberty should be protected, but not at the expense of our children. Sensible gun laws place reasonable limitations on the purchase of firearms. These laws do not abolish the "right to bear arms." They simply protect our children. How many more children must die before we make reasonable laws to protect them?

> In your conclusion, summarize your main points and say "good-bye" to the readers.

Practice 8: Writing Conclusions

Using your ideas from Practice 7 on page 77, write conclusions to match the introductions you wrote. Experiment with different types of conclusions. (Save your work for Practice 13.)

USING TRANSITIONAL WORDS

In chapter 3, you saw how an outline is like a road map guiding you as you write your essay. As you write your draft, remember that your readers do not have a road map. It is not enough for you just to write a series of ideas. You need to lead the readers through your composition by showing how the ideas are related to each other. **Transitional words** help the readers see the relationship between your ideas. These relationships include **time order**, **order of importance**, **cause and effect**, **comparison**, and **contrast**.

TIME ORDER

You can use transitional words to show **time order**, that is, when events happen in relation to each other: one event before another, one after another, or both at the same time. Read the following example to see what happens when transitional words are missing.

> **Example 1:** Our family has a daily routine to get us to work and school. My father leaves the house. He wakes up my brother and me. I get up and take a shower. My brother takes a shower. I get dressed. My mother gets our lunches ready. We eat breakfast. We jump in the car and drive to school. Mom drops us off on her way to work.

Example 1 is choppy because it is missing transitional words to clarify the order of events. Without these words, the reader wonders how the father can leave the house, and then wake up his sons. Below is a corrected example with transitional words underlined.

> **Example 2:** Our family has a daily routine to get us to work and school. <u>Before</u> my father leaves the house, he wakes up my brother and me. I get up <u>first</u> and take a shower. <u>Then</u>, my brother takes a shower <u>while</u> I'm getting dressed. <u>Meanwhile</u>, my mother gets our lunches ready. <u>After</u> breakfast, we jump in the car for the drive to school. <u>Lastly</u>, Mom drops us off on her way to work.

Using transitional words is a simple and effective way to present your ideas and descriptions clearly. The chart below provides you with examples of transitional words that show time order.

Transitional Words for Time Order			
after	again	and then	as
as long as	as soon as	at the same time	before
currently	during	eventually	finally
first	gradually	immediately	in the future
later	meanwhile	now	second
soon	suddenly	then	third
until	when	whenever	while

ORDER OF IMPORTANCE

In chapter 1, you saw how to structure ideas in a paragraph according to their **order of importance**. Transitional words help show which idea you want to emphasize as more important than others. The example below lacks these transitional words.

Example 3: You should always be aware of your surroundings in parking lots at night. Look over the lot carefully for potential danger spots, for example, areas of low visibility and areas which do not have parking attendants. Be sure you have a defensive weapon, such as pepper spray or a loud noisemaker, in your hand as you walk to your vehicle. Before entering your vehicle, look through the windows to make sure no one is hiding inside.

Notice how in Example 3 the writer did not use transitional words to indicate whether one of the steps is more important than another. Below is a corrected example with underlined transitional words showing the order of importance.

Example 4: You should always be aware of your surroundings in parking lots at night. <u>First</u>, look over the lot carefully for potential danger spots, for example, areas of low visibility and areas which do not have parking attendants. <u>More importantly</u>, be sure you have a defensive weapon, such as pepper spray or a loud noisemaker, in your hand as you walk to your vehicle. <u>Above all</u>, before entering your vehicle, look through the windows to make sure no one is hiding inside.

As you can see, using these transitional words helps to rank the steps required to reduce the potential danger of parking lots at night.

Transitional Words for Order of Importance	
above all	especially
first	in fact
in particular	of highest importance
more importantly	most importantly

CAUSE AND EFFECT

Linking **causes and effects** is an important aspect of writing a convincing persuasive essay. You can use transitional words to make these connections clear. Read the example below.

Example 5: Local graffiti "artists" are becoming more brazen. Two weeks ago, they sprayed paint across three community centers. Last week, several businesses found their buildings "decorated" against their wishes. Last night, some graffiti writers took their work inside, painting the twelfth floor of the Baxton building. The city council announced a special hearing for Thursday of next week to discuss possible responses to this problem.

The cause and effect relationship in Example 5 is not clear because the paragraph is missing a crucial transition. Read example 6, and notice how just one transitional phrase (underlined) can bring clarity to this paragraph by signaling the effect of the graffiti writers' activities.

Example 6: Local graffiti "artists" are becoming more brazen. Two weeks ago, they sprayed paint across three community centers. Last week, several businesses found their buildings "decorated" against their wishes. Last night, some graffiti writers took their work inside to the twelfth floor of the Baxton building. As a result, the city council announced a special hearing for Thursday of next week to discuss possible responses to this problem.

Because the writer added one transitional phrase in Example 6, the whole paragraph is clearer. The phrase *as a result* shows that the city council's announcement is an effect of the graffiti writing.

Transitional Words for Cause and Effect	
as a result	because
for this reason	if...then
since	so
so that	therefore
thus	whenever

COMPARISON

Transitional words help a writer show **comparisons**, that is, how certain ideas or subjects are similar. Example 7 lacks these transitions.

Example 7: The United States and the USSR did not want to enter World War II. They had been forced to enter the fighting because of sneak attacks. The Soviets were caught off guard when Hitler broke his non-aggression treaty and invaded the Soviet Union on June 22, 1941. The United States suffered a surprise attack when the Japanese struck the US naval base at Pearl Harbor on December 7, 1941. From that time on, the two countries were allies in fighting the Axis powers of Germany, Italy, and Japan.

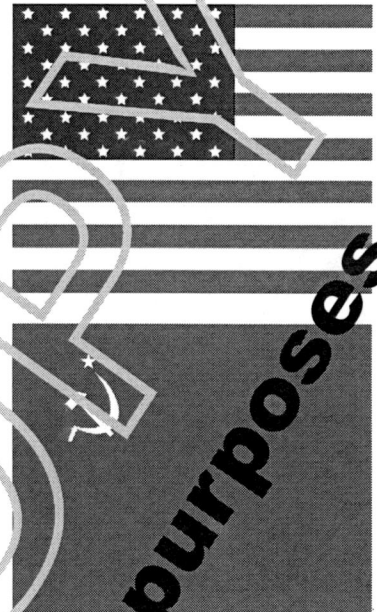

Due to the lack of transitional words in Example 7, the similarities between the United States' and the Soviet Union's entry into World War II are not as clear as they could be. In fact, the first sentence is awkward. The few well-placed transitions shown in Example 8 make the passage much more effective and easily understood.

Example 8: Neither the United States nor the USSR had wanted to enter World War II. Both countries had been forced to enter the fighting because of sneak attacks. The Soviets were caught off guard when Hitler broke his non-aggression treaty and invaded the Soviet Union on June 22, 1941. Similarly, the United States suffered a surprise attack when the Japanese struck the US naval base at Pearl Harbor on December 7, 1941. From that time on, the two countries were allies in fighting the Axis powers of Germany, Italy, and Japan.

Neither and *nor* may not sound like comparison words, but they point to negative similarity. The other underlined transitional words make the comparisons between the United States and the Soviet Union clearer.

Transitional Words for Comparison		
also	as well as	at the same time
both	equally important	in the same way
likewise	neither/nor	similarly

CONTRAST

Transitional words also help a writer make **contrasts**, or differences, clearer. Read the example below to see how a contrasting paragraph needs transitions.

Example 9: You may consider caves and mines the same kind of holes in the ground. They are really quite different. Underground streams and rivers form caves over millions of years through erosion. Humans use machines to dig mines over the course of only a few months. The rapid removal of rock during the mining process requires the use of supports to prevent a mine's ceiling from collapsing. The slow, natural formation of caves makes these supports unnecessary. The slow process of cave formation allows natural gases to escape slowly and safely. Miners must be cautious of the explosive and poisonous gases that are rapidly released as the earth is blasted open. As you can see, human development of the earth is often rapid and dangerous. Nature's development can be gradual and peaceful.

Example 9 makes sense without transitional words, but it does not flow well. The writer lists ideas but does not connect them. Read Example 10 to see how transitional words can help the flow of the ideas in the paragraph.

Example 10: You may consider caves and mines the same kind of holes in the ground, but in reality, they are quite different. Underground streams and rivers form caves over millions of years through erosion. In contrast, humans use machines to dig mines over the course of only a few months. The rapid removal of rock during the mining process requires the use of supports to prevent a mine's ceiling from collapsing. However, the slow, natural formation of caves makes these supports unnecessary. The slow process of cave formation also allows natural gases to escape slowly and safely, whereas miners must be cautious of the explosive and poisonous gases that are rapidly released as the earth is blasted open. As you can see, human development of the earth is often rapid and dangerous, while nature's development can be gradual and peaceful.

Transitional Words for Contrast		
although	and yet	but
despite	even so	even
though	however	in contrast
instead of	in spite of	nevertheless
whereas	while	rather than
still	on the one hand	on the other hand

> Use transitional words to help readers see the relationship between your ideas. These relationships include time order, order of importance, cause and effect, comparison, and contrast.

Practice 9: Transitional Words

Read the paragraphs below. Decide how each paragraph would be best organized, whether by *time order*, *order of importance*, *cause and effect*, *comparison*, or *contrast*. Then, rewrite the paragraph on a separate sheet of paper, inserting the correct transitional words or phrases.

1. There are many things to remember as you get ready to go back to school. Develop a positive attitude about the upcoming school year. Make sure you understand your class schedule. You know your classes. You should buy plenty of school supplies such as pens, paper, notebooks, and a calculator. Take time to inventory your clothes, and make sure you have the clothes you need. These tasks are completed. You will be ready for the new school year.

2. Both your beliefs and your actions are important in leading an exemplary life. Your beliefs should guide you to knowing how to act in all situations. If your actions do not match what you believe, people will not listen to what you say. If you act in a way that seems good to others, but you have no beliefs to explain your actions, people may label you as shallow. Be certain and careful with both your beliefs and your actions in order to be an example to others.

3. Watching television at my grandmother's house was always a family event. Her TV was so old, it didn't even have remote control! My family fought over what show to watch. We were used to watching two or three channels at the same time, while using the remote control. Grandma didn't have cable. We had to twist and turn the antenna, and our bodies, just to get a decent picture. Two of us were on the sofa watching TV, and somebody else sat in the recliner. The TV screen would get all fuzzy. We all had to pile onto the sofa. We could avoid these problems with the television and the family fights. We bought Grandma a new television (with remote control!) and a year's cable service. Our visits to Grandma's are much more peaceful, though, in a way, we miss the wrangling.

4. I like to prioritize the duties I feel towards those around me. I feel duty-bound to care for and protect my parents, brothers, and sisters. I try to take care of my extended family and close friends. I consider it necessary to serve my country in the case of foreign attack. These three circles of obligation complete the priorities I feel in my social and civic life.

5. Ordering something as simple as a pizza requires several steps. You should look through the tower of coupons that has grown from daily advertisement mailings. You must endure the arduous process of finding out what everyone wants on their pizza. Call the pizza place and wait on hold. You are ready to hang up and make your own pizza. Distract your mind from the growing hunger in your stomach by getting your money ready. The delivery person arrives, run out to the car, grab the pizza, and shove the money in the person's hand. You can enjoy the lukewarm pizza that you earned with all your hard work.

6. The preparation required for a test is quite similar to the preparation needed for a sports event. Training for any sports event requires daily practice to keep the athlete's body in good condition. Test preparation requires daily practice and review to keep the scholar's memory up to date. The night before a sporting event, the athlete must get plenty of rest. A scholar must rest his or her mind, so it will be fresh for the big event of the test. A good athlete will take pride in a nutritious diet that provides the building blocks for a strong body. A scholar must feed the mind with nutritious food to increase mental skill. Test taking may not have the same glamour as athletic competition, but both activities require preparation in order to achieve success.

Practice 10: More Transitional Words

A. On your own, or in small groups, skim through articles in newspapers, in magazines, or on the Internet. Find paragraphs that contain transitional words based on each of the following: *time order, order of importance, comparison and contrast,* or *cause and effect*. Share these paragraphs with your teacher or other students. Do the transitional words improve your understanding of the paragraph? Why or why not?

B. On your own or in small groups, write four different paragraphs. Each paragraph should include transitional words from the different categories discussed in this chapter: *time order, order of importance, comparison and contrast,* or *cause and effect*. Return to the lists of these words to help you. Then, exchange your collection of paragraphs with your teacher or with another group, and grade the paragraphs by evaluating how well the transitional words are used within each paragraph.

Here are some possible topics for each of your four paragraphs:

Time Order	Order of Importance
Describe a situation that took courage.	Prioritize your duties for today.
Tell about a change that has happened in your neighborhood or your school.	Who are the three most important people in your life? Why?

Comparison and Contrast	Cause and Effect
Do you prefer pizza or hamburgers?	Why is a high school diploma important?
Which is better on a Friday night: watching television at home or going out to a movie?	What are the effects of sports programs on high school students?

DEVELOPING COHERENCE

Coherence means to stick together. You want the ideas of your essay to "stick together," that is, to be connected and to lead from one paragraph to the next. Tying your ideas together is an important part of helping readers understand your writing. Three ways you can link the ideas and paragraphs in your essay are **planning an order**, **using transitions**, and **repeating key words and phrases**.

PLANNING AN ORDER

In chapter 1, you practiced four different ways to organize ideas: spatial order, time order, order of importance, or contrasting ideas. Organizing your ideas in a certain order is the first step to developing a coherent essay.

USING TRANSITIONS

In the last section, you saw how transitional words link ideas from one sentence to another. They also link ideas between paragraphs to make the whole essay "stick together." Without these transitional words and phrases, the writing becomes less interesting or even less understandable.

REPEATING KEY WORDS AND PHRASES

While you don't want to say the same thing over and over, repeating certain key words and phrases can improve the readers' understanding of the topic. By including key words or ideas from your thesis in the topic sentences of your paragraphs, you will make it easier for readers to follow your train of thought. These repeated words are like landmarks along the road of your essay, reminding the readers where you have been and where you are going. For example, look at the following plan for an essay in which the topic sentences repeat key words from the thesis.

Thesis:	Citizens of the United States could greatly improve the country by obeying the law, protecting the environment, and being kind to other people.
Topic Sentence:	The first and most basic step to improving the country is to obey the law.
Topic Sentence:	In addition to obeying the law, citizens can make this country even more beautiful by protecting the environment.
Topic Sentence:	A third way to make the United States a better place to live is for citizens to reach beyond their own self-interest and be kind to one another.

You can also repeat key words or phrases throughout the essay, not only in topic sentences.

> Develop coherence (link the ideas and paragraphs) in your essay by planning an order, using transitional words, and repeating key words and phrases.

Practice 1: Developing Coherence

Read the following essay. Decide how the writer ordered ideas in the essay. Then, circle transitional words, and underline repeated words.

Do Animals Have Souls?

In this era of the global community, more and more of us enjoy discussing different philosophies. Presently, there are as many different philosophies as there are cultures. One philosophic-type topic of unending interest is the question of whether or not animals have souls. Of course, most organized religions and philosophies have opinions on this question. One way to keep your balance when discussing it is to keep an open mind and heart. You never know when a new viewpoint will change your thoughts. Or at least, listening allows you to understand someone else's perspective.

A different approach to the question of whether or not animals have souls is found in the philosophy of Taoism, a Chinese belief system, which includes the concepts of the *yin* and *yang* energies. Taoism holds that embracing the natural flow of these energies, balanced and open to the path of life, creates harmony. Instead of making a definite statement about the existence of animal souls, the way of Tao would look to the natural world for instruction.

There is a story in the writings of Chuang Tzu, a spiritual leader in China, called "The Joy of Fishes," which begins with two men walking along a river, where they see fish leaping in the water. One of the men remarks on the happiness of the fish. The other man asks how, since the speaker is not a fish, can he know the fish are happy. The first man answers this way: "I know the joy of fishes in the river through my own joy, as I go walking along the same river." The concept is that all beings truly share the walk along life's river experiencing the same kinds of joys and sorrows even though they are different beings.

A tale from the city of Edinburgh in Scotland, for example, illuminates this idea. Long ago in the 1850s, a little dog, Bobby by name, devoted himself to guarding the final resting place of his master—this was a grave in Greyfriars Kirk graveyard. This he did for fourteen

Copyright © American Book Company. DO NOT DUPLICATE. 1-888-264-5877.

years. The people of the city, likewise, noticed the dog's devotion and felt a connection with the loss and sorrow the dog experienced. They recognized the sorrow that comes to us all.

In the happier days of Bobby's life, he belonged to John Gray (known as Jock), a policeman in the city of Edinburgh. Bobby, a Skye terrier, was Jock's steady companion in the city, walking up and down the cobbled streets or standing at the policeman's post. Together, they braved the infamous Scottish weather, which was often damp and freezing.

Then, sadly Jock fell ill with tuberculosis and passed away in 1858. Bobby followed his master's funeral procession. After the service, Bobby was taken to the Grays' home to stay. However, that Bobby could not do. He followed the route back to the graveyard, and for the next fourteen years, the graveyard was where he stayed.

Meanwhile, people of the city took notice. James Brown, the groundskeeper of the graveyard, took care of Bobby, while another townsman who admired Bobby's devotion to his lost master paid for the license that was needed to keep Bobby out of the pound. The news of the little dog spread through the city and beyond, bringing visitors who wanted to see and experience Bobby as the living monument to his master.

Finally, after his fourteen-year vigil, Bobby died. For the first time ever, the city leaders voted to allow a dog, Bobby, to be buried beside his master in the graveyard. Moreover, a statue of Bobby was placed at the entrance to the graveyard. We all respond to feelings of loss as well as those of joy. For many, Bobby symbolizes true gratitude. For followers of Tao, this is an important virtue. Subsequently, not only did Bobby, a mere dog, possess this virtue, in fact he brought a city to share in this gratitude to John Gray. Did Bobby have a soul? You may want to find the balance of this question soon in your own heart.

WRITING THE DRAFT

After practicing the many different aspects of drafting, you are ready to write your own draft. Remember when you write a draft, it does not have to be perfect on the first try. You have time to revise and proofread later. Focus on getting your ideas onto paper. As you write, leave wide margins, as well as space between each line, so you have room to make changes later. As you practice writing, you can develop your own personal writing process. Some writers follow their clustering directly. Other writers begin writing the body paragraphs, write a strong conclusion, and then go back and write an introduction. There are no rules for this part of writing. Find the best way for you to get your ideas on paper.

Before you get started, let's return to the essay topic about the effects of television on young viewers. As you will recall, the thesis or controlling idea was stated as follows:

Television has a negative effect on children because they watch programs that are not meant for their age, see commercials for products they don't need, and miss out on playtime they do need.

Based on this thesis and the outline that appeared in chapter 3, a student wrote the following draft.

Television has a negative effect on children because they watch programs that are not meant for their age, see commercials for products they don't need, and miss out on playtime they do need. Little kids watch a lot of television. Television can be great for teaching kids numbers and letters and sometimes even manners. Kids learn other things from television too. Besides that, they could be doing a lot of other good things other than watching television.

People get killd all the time on TV, children are watching Sesame Street or Barney or some other cartoon, and on comes a commercial for an adult show that will be on later that night. In those few seconds, children exposed to theft, murder, and sex that they shouldn't see.

Another important question to ask about TV and small children is what they are <u>not</u> doing while they are watching television. Children especially between the ages of two and five are growing very quick and need to exercise their growing muscles. They learn by doing, not by sitting. When children sit in front of a televsion, they are not running or jumping. They are not exploring the world outside or learning motor skills developed through puzzles or blocks. Further theyre not learning the social skill of playing with other children. Children may watch tv together, but it does not require them to actually play togetherr.

Commercials are another problem with television. Commercials advertise other shows with adult content in them. commercials tell kids to buy all this stuff theat they don't need. Thats how television pays for itself. Companies pay to put commercials on tv and they hope kids will buy their stuff. The commercials tell kids that they will be happy if they buy the stuff. They will be like other kids and they will be liked by other kids if they have this stuff. It is difficult enough for adults to tell the difference between reality pretending in commercials. How is a three-year-old supposed to do that?

Some shows on television may be educational or entertaining for children, but libraries and schools are much better places for kids to learn. Kids can learn a lot from computers too. Although some problems with television are the same for computers. Violence, sex and commercials are important problems with television. Little kids shouldn't watch much television. They should be outside playing.

This draft has many errors that you can detect easily as you read. These errors are typical of any draft. That is why revising and proofreading are so important. In the next two chapters, you will practice these skills. For now, let your ideas flow from your outlines onto the paper as you write your drafts for Practice.

> As you write a draft, leave wide margins, as well as space between each line, so that you have room to make changes later.

Practice 12: Writing the Draft

A. In Practice 8 and Practice 9, you created an introduction and a conclusion for four different essays. Return to your introductions, conclusions, and brainstorming lists and develop outlines for two essays on the four topics. Then, draft the body paragraphs. Remember your essays don't have to be perfect. However, pay attention to the skills you practiced in this chapter.

Use the following checklist as you write each essay.

- ☐ I used specific words.
- ☐ I avoided clichés and sweeping generalizations.
- ☐ I developed a clear introduction.
- ☐ I wrote an appropriate conclusion.
- ☐ I used transitional words to link ideas together.
- ☐ I wrote a coherent essay.
- ☐ I left wide margins and space between each line, so I can make corrections more easily.

B. Return to Practice 5: Making a Plan on page 60 in chapter 3. In this exercise, you developed outlines and clustering diagrams for four different topics. Now, use these plans to draft an essay for one or more of the topics. Use the checklist above to help you.

C. For further practice and instruction in writing, visit two of the Web sites, or consult one of the books listed in Appendix B: Writing Resources on page 326.

CHAPTER 4 SUMMARY

When **drafting the essay**, work to get all of your ideas on paper.

As you write, focus on improving **word choice** by selecting specific words, using a **dictionary** and **thesaurus** to word accuracy, being aware of **connotations** and **denotations**, and avoiding **clichés** and **sweeping generalizations**.

Create an **introduction** that captures the attention of readers. Include a good **lead**, **tie-in**, and **thesis**. Keep in mind that there are many types of introductions, including the following:

- Problem or riddle
- Question
- Brief story
- Quotation
- Catchy phrase
- Thought-provoking statement

Draft an effective **conclusion** that summarizes but does not restate the thesis. Remember that the conclusion can be an **introduction in reverse** and can give the audience a **question to ponder**.

To make your ideas clear, use the appropriate **transitional words** for the essay order you chose.

As you write your draft, remember to leave line spacing and wide margins so you can go back and make changes.

CHAPTER 4 REVIEW: DRAFTING THE ESSAY

For the chapter review in chapter 3: Planning the Essay, you prepared brainstorming lists, freewriting samples, clustering diagrams, outlines, and outline shortcuts for five different writing prompts. Based on these prewriting activities, write a draft of an essay for one or more of the writing prompts. Use the skills you practiced in this chapter.

- ☐ I used specific words.
- ☐ I avoided clichés and sweeping generalizations.
- ☐ I developed a clear introduction.
- ☐ I wrote an appropriate conclusion.
- ☐ I used transitional words to link ideas together.
- ☐ I wrote a coherent essay.
- ☐ I left wide margins and space between each line, so I can make corrections more easily.

Note: You will revise these drafts in the chapter 5 review, so keep them in a safe place, such as your portfolio.

ADDITIONAL ACTIVITIES: DRAFTING THE ESSAY

1. Rewrite the following paragraph, using vivid images and concrete words to enhance the description.

> The trees line both sides of the street, giving shade to all who pass by. The trees also shade the houses in the neighborhood. Birds play in the air and make their usual noises. Woods surround the neighborhood, and in these woods there is a small pond. Sometimes children will swim there, or sail toy boats across the pond. There is usually a breeze blowing across.

2. This paragraph below contains clichés and sweeping generalizations. Rewrite the paragraph in Standard American English.

> I have a bone to pick with Lindsey Savage. Two shakes of a lamb's tail after his election, he is raising a ruckus. "The county roads need fixing," he says, "so let's add 1 percent to the sales tax." Lindsey Savage is so crooked he has to screw on his socks. The extra money for road improvements will just go to line the pockets of his sidekicks in the road construction business. Then they'll just piddle around and waste our money. If you hate more taxes, make a beeline for the county commission meeting next Tuesday night. Voice your opinions, or we're up the creek without a paddle.

3. On your own or in a group, skim through three or four articles in magazines such as *Time*, *Newsweek*, *People*, *Sports Illustrated*, etc. Find an article that has an effective introduction and conclusion. In three or four sentences, explain why they are effective. Then share your findings with your class or instructor.

4. Use the same articles from #3, and describe how the articles develop coherence. List four or five examples of how the author uses transitional words and repeats certain key words or phrases. Also describe how the author ordered his or her ideas. Share your findings with the class or instructor.

Basics Made Easy

Chapter 5
Revising the Essay

This chapter covers the following McREL standard and benchmark for Level III:	
Standard 1: Uses the general skills and strategies of the writing process	Benchmarks **2** and **3**
Standard 2: Uses the stylistic and rhetorical aspects of writing	Benchmark **3**

Even if you plan your essays very carefully and try to write your drafts precisely, you will still have room for improvement. Your teacher or the professional readers who grade your essay will look only at your final product. You want them to see your *best* effort, not your *first* effort. Remember, writing is a process of thinking, writing, and reviewing. Once the drafts are finished, it is time for reviewing which includes **revising** and **proofreading**. This chapter will help you with revising, and the next chapter will show you how to proofread.

Revising is looking again at the drafts of your essays with the intention of making changes to improve them. Revising involves the steps shown below.

- Adding Clarifying Information
- Deleting Unrelated Sentences
- Eliminating Unnecessary Words

- Correcting Shifts in Tense or Person
- Checking for Parallel Sentence Structure
- Developing Sentence Variety

HOW TO REVISE

Before revising your drafts, you may want to take a short break of a minute or so to think about something else. Then, return to your essays, and read them as if you were the audience. Put yourself in the place of the people who will be reading them, and read as if you were seeing the essays for the first time. Make your changes by using the spaces in between the lines and in the margins. While you read your essays during the revising stage, ask yourself the following questions.

1. Is the introduction a good preview of the rest of the essay?

2. Does my statement of the thesis give my essay a clear purpose?

3. Do the body paragraphs support the thesis with logically arranged supporting details?

4. Will my audience clearly understand how my ideas fit together?

5. Is there any irrelevant or repeated information that I can cut out?

6. Is there information that I need to add to make my ideas clearer?

7. Do my sentences fall into a repetitive and uninteresting pattern?

8. Have I used transitional words appropriately?

9. How can I improve my word choice?

10. Are there unexpected shifts in person or tense?

11. Are there unnecessary words that I can delete?

12. Does my conclusion tie the essay together and leave the reader with an action or thought to consider?

Return to the draft of the essay about how watching television affects young children (pages 90–91 in chapter 4) and consider the questions above.

As you looked over the draft, you probably noticed the following:

In the **first paragraph** of the sample essay, the thesis is clearly stated. However, an introduction is stronger when it begins by getting the reader's attention and leads up to a statement of the thesis, usually in the last sentence of the first paragraph.

The **second paragraph** begins with a broad generalization that does not provide a good connection with the first paragraph. The details which follow are a good start, but they could be improved with more description.

The **third paragraph** and **fourth paragraph** both have some significant grammar and spelling errors that need to be corrected. More significantly, the fourth paragraph, which addresses commercials, should follow the second paragraph, which also deals with commercials. Rearranging ideas, even paragraphs, is appropriate for the revising step in the writing process.

The **conclusion** strays away from the topic by introducing subjects that haven't been discussed in the essay, such as libraries and computers. The conclusion should not introduce new ideas or information but tie previously developed arguments together into a strong ending. You want to leave your readers with something they can remember easily.

Considering these improvements, a revised essay might look something like this:

"Hey kids, let's count to ten! One, two, three . . ." Sure television can be great for teaching children numbers and letters. Some TV shows even teach children manners. But what else do children learn from TV? Does television harm children? And what could they be doing instead of watching TV? Television has a negative effect on children because they can watch programs that are not meant for their age, see commercials for products they don't need, and miss out on playtime they do need.

Even though children may be watching shows appropriate for their age, there is still a chance that they will see programs that are meant only for adults. A young child may be enjoying *Sesame Street*, but in changing the channel to watch *Barney*, he or she sees commercials for adult shows that will be on later that night. Two teens run up to car, throw the driver out, jump in themselves, and drive away. Next, mean looking faces shout angry words, guns flash, and a person lies dead. Finally, a man and a woman are shown taking off each other's clothes. In these few seconds, the children are shown theft, murder, and sex that children shouldn't see.

Commercials are another problem with television. As well as advertising shows with adult content, commercials persuade children to buy products that they do not need. That is how television pays for itself. Companies pay to put commercials on television, and they hope children will buy their stuff. The voice on commercials tells children that they will be happy if they buy a certain toy or cereal. They will be like other children, and other children will like them if they have those products. It is difficult enough for adults to tell the difference between reality and pretending in commercials. How is a three-year-old supposed to do that?

Another important question to ask about TV and small children is what they are <u>not</u> doing while they are watching television. Children, especially between the ages of two and five, are growing very quickly and need to exercise their growing muscles. They learn by doing, not by sitting. When children sit in front of a television, they are not running or jumping. They are not exploring the world outside or learning motor skills developed through puzzles or blocks. Further, they're not learning the social skill of playing with other children. Children may watch television together, but it does not require them to play together.

Some shows on television may be educational or entertaining for children. However, in between these shows are commercials with adult situations and violent images. In addition, other commercials teach children the false idea that buying all kinds of products will make them happy. And even if children would only watch educational shows without commercials, they would learn more and be more healthy if they went outside to play with their freinds.

In addition to revisions, the writer also corrected spelling and punctuation errors. The next chapter will address how to do this. For the rest of this chapter, you will practice some revising skills.

ADDING CLARIFYING INFORMATION

When you write your drafts, *you* know what you mean, but you want to be sure it will be clear to your audience. As you revise your essays, imagine that you are the intended audience reading the essays for the first time. You want to make sure the readers have enough information so that they have no unanswered questions. Ask yourself if added information, more details, or another example would make your writing clearer. The following sentence provides a good example.

Example 1: At its next meeting, the school board will consider the proposal.

The writer may have provided enough information for someone who is familiar with the situation described. However, another reader might ask, *"Which school board?" "What proposal?"* or *"When's the next meeting?"* The writer must add information to make the description clearer, as in the following sentence.

Example 2: Next Thursday night, the city school board will consider the proposal to expand the recycling program in all schools.

With this sentence, the readers don't have to be members of that particular school district in order to understand what the writer is describing. All the necessary information is provided. You want to write the same kind of sentences for the reader of your essays.

> Make sure you provide the audience with enough information to understand your ideas

Practice 1: Adding Clarifying Information

Revise the following sentences by adding clarifying information.

1. I went with Rafael and Scott to our favorite hangout, and we saw Priscilla.

   _____

   _____

2. The plants withered because of the drought.

   _____

   _____

3. Few people have big families these days.

   _____

   _____

4. Trees clean the air.

   _____

   _____

5. I bought a new lens to take better pictures.

   _____

   _____

DELETING UNRELATED SENTENCES

In some cases, you may want to add information, ideas, or examples to your sentence. In other cases, you will want to eliminate information, ideas, or examples if they do not relate directly to the topic of your essay. Look at the paragraph below.

> I got a lot of great deals at the Clothing Mart. All the shoes were 50 percent off, so I bought two new pairs. I bought four new shirts because they were on sale—buy one, get one free. I'm so glad my friend Chris was there to help me pick out clothes. The pants were reduced by only 10 percent, but I really liked a green pair, so I bought it. I've never seen such a great sale.

Each sentence in the paragraph relates to the writer's purchasing new clothes at a big sale. The author's appreciation of Chris' help, however, does not fit well in the paragraph. This sentence is not related closely enough to the other sentences, so it weakens the coherence of the paragraph. Deleting the fourth sentence will make the paragraph more concise and coherent.

Delete sentences or phrases that are not directly related to the paragraph or essay.

Practice 2: Deleting Unrelated Sentences

Read each of the following paragraphs, and draw a line through the unrelated sentence.

1. Out of all the classes I took in high school, it seems that social studies dealt most with real-life situations. For example, we studied current events and discussed how what's going on in the world affects us right here at home. We also learned some of the historical reasons why certain conflicts continue to this day. That teacher really knew what was going on! We were shown how to read newspaper and magazine articles about current events and evaluate them for facts versus opinions. Since having that class, I've been able to "read between the lines" much better.

2. My first day in middle school was pretty challenging. For the first time, I changed to a different class every fifty minutes. The school was huge, and I got lost during every move. I showed up to every class late. To top it all off, the combination to my locker didn't work, so I had to carry all of my books the entire day. I was not looking forward to going home, either, because I had to mow the lawn. My only consolation was that the other students in my classes were really friendly, and the teachers were understanding of what happens that first day.

3. When Leah turned the corner and entered the perfume shop at the mall, she got more than she bargained for. The most horrid smell in the world assaulted her nose. Customers and sales associates in the store were coughing and gagging! Leah quickly pinched her nose and ran for her life. After running for about fifty feet, holding her nose, she released her nose and breathed some fresh air. There's nothing like fresh air to increase your mental functioning. After that incident, Leah thought it would be best to go home. Then, the next morning, she read about someone placing a stink bomb in the store as a prank.

4. I look forward to a solution to the problem of the super-sensitive security motion sensor. Once that type of motion sensor is activated, the slightest movement can set it off. A flying moth or even my cat scratching the litter box after a large dinner can send loud sounds pulsating through my house. I know the sensor needs to detect the sounds and motions of a thief, but how many thieves are actually as small as a moth or as silent as a cat? A home security system is very expensive.

5. Jorge pulled his car over to the side of the road when he reached the bridge spanning the Ohio River from West Virginia to Ohio. This 451-mile southern boundary of Ohio which started near East Liverpool at the junction of Ohio, West Virginia, and Pennsylvania had great memories for him. As a teenager working on a tugboat, he had traveled the river to its end just west of Cincinnati at the junction of Ohio, Kentucky, and Indiana. Jorge checked his tires. He had great memories of boating, fishing, sailing, and water skiing on this river. He leaned over the railing and watched a tugboat push some coal barges upstream. The early morning sun glistened on the water below. It was exciting to be home again where his memories had their beginning.

ELIMINATING UNNECESSARY WORDS

Along with unrelated sentences, you want to eliminate unnecessary words. Good writing does not necessarily involve lengthy sentences full of big words. Good writing expresses ideas clearly through effective words—the fewer the better. As an example, read the following sentence.

> **Example 1:** As I was reflecting the other day, I thought about the very great number of people who, as of yet, have had very little experience of their own with using the Internet by going online.

This sentence includes various words that do not help readers understand the writer's intended idea. In fact, these extra words cloud the meaning. Read the following sentence without the extra words.

> **Example 2:** Two days ago, I thought about the many people who have never used the Internet.

This shorter sentence provides the same information, but it does so more directly and clearly.

As you write your drafts, don't worry too much about extra words. Let the ideas flow. However, when you are revising, eliminate unnecessary words, and replace them with a simpler way of expressing the same ideas. Use the following chart to help you.

Unnecessary Words	Simple Language
due to the fact that	because
with respect to	about
hurried quickly	hurried
at that point in time	then
conduct an investigation	investigate
circular in shape	circular
there are many students who join	many students join
has a preference for	prefers
it is my belief that	I believe that
she is the kind of person who doesn't tolerate rudeness	she doesn't tolerate rudeness
In Nathaniel Hawthorne's novel *The Scarlet Letter*, he writes about	In *The Scarlet Letter*, Nathaniel Hawthorne writes about

Good writing expresses ideas clearly through effective words—the fewer the better.

Practice 3: Eliminating Unnecessary Words

Rewrite the following sentences, and eliminate the unnecessary words.

1. I received various and many compliments while attending the cast party due to the fact that the peers of my own age have a preference for acting that is less formal in style.

   _____

   _____

2. At this point in time, the county commissioners are taking into consideration the reasons for or against pursuing formal and official charges against the sheriff.

   _____

   _____

3. These are the issues that will determine who will be elected president.

   _____

   _____

4. In my mind, I was thinking that the class's poor results on the tests that were administered in physics class were due in large part to the short amount of preparation time.

    _____

    _____

5. There are many people who have homes in the urban downtown area due to the fact that they can live in close proximity to work.

    _____

    _____

CORRECTING SHIFTS IN TENSE OR PERSON

Remember the image on page 78 of giving the reader a taxi cab ride through your essay? While you are "driving" you don't want to shift gears abruptly. You want to keep the ride smooth, not giving the readers any unexpected surprises. One way to do this is to avoid shifts in **tense** or **person**.

SHIFTS IN TENSE

It is important to keep one **verb tense** throughout your essay. Once you choose present or past tense, stay with it. Read the following passage, and notice how the underlined verbs shift from present tense to past tense.

Example 1: It is the last game of the championship. Tamara, the girl who <u>is</u> always picked last when forming teams, <u>sits</u> on the bench and <u>cheers</u> her team, the Rockets, against the visiting team, the Panthers. Earlier in the game, Louise, the star pitcher of the Rockets, <u>sprained</u> her arm in the opening pitch. Now, in the last inning with one run Rockets advantage and bases loaded, her replacement, Jenny, also <u>sprained</u> her arm. In a desperate move, Dalia, the coach of the Rockets, <u>told</u> Tamara, "Try your best, honey. Just try not to break your hand when you throw the ball."

The shifts in tense make the readers unsure about how the narrator is related to the action. See how much more smoothly the passage below reads because it keeps the same tense.

Example 2: It was the last game of the championship. Tamara, the girl who <u>was</u> always picked last when forming teams, <u>sat</u> on the bench and <u>cheered</u> her team, the Rockets, against the visiting team, the Panthers. Earlier in the game, Louise, the star pitcher of the Rockets, <u>sprained</u> her arm in the opening pitch. Now, in the last inning with a one run Rockets advantage and bases loaded, her replacement, Jenny, also <u>sprained</u> her arm. In a desperate move, Dalia, the coach of the Rockets, <u>told</u> Tamara, "Try your best, honey. Just try not to break your hand when you throw the ball."

Example 2 reads much more smoothly because the tense is consistent. The last sentence contains a quotation which creates a situation where a shift to present tense is appropriate. Also consider the following example.

Example 3: When the teacher said, "We will now turn to page 103," we all laughed because of the funny picture we knew was there.

In this sentence, the shift in tense is clear and appropriate. The quotation marks the shift in tense, so it does not come as an unexpected surprise to the readers. Be sure to pay attention to verb tense in order to improve your writing.

SHIFTS IN PERSON

Person refers to the point of view of the writer, as outlined in the chart below.

Point of View		
Person	**Use**	**Pronouns**
first person	the writer speaks	*I* or *we*
second person	the writer speaks to the reader	*you*
third person	the writer speaks about someone	*he*, *she*, *it*, or *they*

Shifts in person have a similar effect to shifts in tense. They can cause confusion by making the readers unsure of the writer's perspective. Consider the following passage.

Example 4: When I saw the water bubbling up from the ground, I knew there was a pipe leaking under there. I started digging slowly because you never know if you might hit the pipe or an electrical cord. You just have to be careful. As I dug deeper, I found the leak. You can just imagine how happy I was to find it.

In everyday speech, shifting from *I* to *you* is quite common. However, this practice does not follow the rules of Standard English. In Example 4, the writer tells a personal story about an underground water leak. The writer begins speaking from the perspective of the first person, then shifts to the second person, then back to first and finally, back to second. These shifts interfere with the clarity and flow of the passage. Compare the revised passage below.

Example 5: When I saw the water coming up from the ground, I knew there was a pipe leaking under there. I started digging slowly because I knew I might hit the pipe or an electrical cord. So, I dug carefully. As I dug deeper, I found the leak. I was very happy to find it.

Example 5 gives the readers a clear sense of where the narrator stands in relation to the story. The narrator maintains the first person point of view, rather than shifting points of view.

> Keep person and tense consistent in your writing.

Practice 4:   Shifts in Tense or Person

Rewrite the following sentences, making sure that tense and person are consistent.

1. A person who wants to learn how to play piano must be dedicated because you have to practice every day.

    _____

    _____

2. I was walking to the laundromat when I saw Philip, and I would talk with him.

    _____

    _____

3. Typically, first-year students have trouble adjusting to a new schedule, but after a while, you learned your schedules.

    _____

    _____

4. I went to the bank to make a deposit, but I couldn't because you know how long the line gets.

    _____

    _____

5. Students need to take out huge loans since it takes a lot of money for you to finish college.

    _____

    _____

6. It was the first of October, and I am planning on driving into the mountains to see the leaves change color.

    _____

    _____

7. I am an athlete who trains hard, but you never knew when an injury can happen.

_____

_____

8. So many children go hungry every day, while other people threw food in the trash.

_____

_____

9. People don't think it will happen, but a bad illness can made you lose your job.

_____

_____

10. Because a growing baby is so small, any drugs a pregnant mother took affected the baby greatly.

_____

_____

PARALLEL SENTENCE STRUCTURE

Parallel sentence structure means that the parts of the sentence which are equally important are then similarly expressed. In other words, verbs match with verbs, adjectives with adjectives, prepositional phrases with prepositional phrases, and so on. Note the parallel structure in the following famous sentences.

I came; I saw; I conquered.

– Julius Caesar

Ask not what your country can do for you, ask what you can do for your country.

– John F. Kennedy

For I was hungry and you gave me food; I was thirsty and you gave me something to drink; I was a stranger and you welcomed me.

– Jesus Christ

These sentences have a rhythm and power because they are written in parallel structure. Writing that is not parallel can be difficult to read, and it is not Standard English. Carefully read the following examples, listening to the flow and logic of the words.

Not Parallel: Billy knows how to play basketball, sing opera, and can even cook gourmet meals.

Parallel: Billy knows how to play basketball, sing opera, and cook gourmet meals.

Not Parallel:	The three best things about summer are eating ice cream, swimming at the pool, and no school.
Parallel:	The three best things about summer are eating ice cream, swimming at the pool, and not going to school.
Not Parallel:	Sarah likes pole bending, to barrel race, and to rope calves.
Parallel:	Sarah likes pole bending, barrel racing, and roping calves.

Parallel sentence structure means matching verbs with verbs, adjectives with adjectives, and so on.

Practice 5: Parallel Sentence Structure

Rewrite the following sentences using parallel sentence structure.

1. The coach told us to go to bed early, to eat a good breakfast, and don't arrive late for the game.

   _____

   _____

2. The school lunches need more fresh fruit, less fried food, and there should be more choices.

   _____

   _____

3. We searched for Tiger upstairs, downstairs, and crawled under the house.

   _____

   _____

4. My hobbies include reading books, watching movies, and stamp collecting.

   _____

   _____

5. In this class, we will learn to blend various colors, to use different types of paper, and how to draw realistic portraits.

   _____

   _____

6. Did you make your bed, wash your clothes, and cleaned your room today?

    _____

    _____

7. Statistics show that the world's population will increase rapidly while the world's resources are declining at an alarming rate.

    _____

    _____

DEVELOPING SENTENCE VARIETY

Sentence variety involves writing sentences of different structures and lengths. It includes using different types of words and phrases. These variations make your writing more interesting to readers. Three ways to develop sentence variety are by **combining simple sentences into longer ones, starting a sentence with something other than the subject,** and **using a question or exclamation occasionally.**

COMBINING SIMPLE SENTENCES

Simple, direct sentences are often the best way to convey ideas. However, if these simple sentences become repetitive, they make the writing uninteresting. Compare the two examples below.

Example 1: We went to the basketball game. We were late. There was a huge crowd of cheering fans. The team won. Everybody celebrated in the parking lot. Then, some jubilant fans had parties at their houses. It was a great night.

Example 2: After arriving late to the basketball game, we joined the huge crowd in cheering our team to victory. Hundreds of people continued the celebration into the parking lot and then on to the homes of jubilant fans. What a night!

Example 1 is a list of simple sentences, and the repetition is boring. In Example 2, the writer has combined several of these simple sentences into a few longer ones. Both passages tell the same story, but the second one is more interesting to read because of sentence variety.

STARTING A SENTENCE WITH DIFFERENT BEGINNINGS

Most sentences begin with a subject, continue with a verb, and end with an object. Adjectives and adverbs may appear along the way. This pattern works well, but your writing could get repetitive and boring. Therefore, from time to time, start a sentence with something other than the subject. Look at the following examples.

Begin with an adverb:
Replace "I found myself suddenly in a bad situation." with "<u>Suddenly</u>, I found myself in a bad situation."
Begin with a prepositional phrase:
Replace "We stopped at the ice cream stand on the way home." with "<u>On the way home</u>, we stopped at the ice cream stand."
Begin with a participial phrase:
Replace "The children ran into the candy store, screaming with joy." with "<u>Screaming with joy</u>, the children ran into the candy store."

The examples above show different ways of forming sentences. They also show how a modifier is best understood when it is placed near the noun or verb it is modifying.

USING A QUESTION OR EXCLAMATION

Finally, using a question or exclamation occasionally can provide a welcome change of pace for the reader. Compare the following two examples:

Example 3: I didn't like it when my best friend told me he was going out with my ex-girlfriend. It was the worst feeling I've ever experienced.

Example 4: How would you like it if your best friend told you he was going out with your ex-girlfriend? Well, I know. It's the worst feeling I've ever experienced!

Examples 3 and 4 show how to use a question or exclamation to add variety to your writing. Example 4 also shows how a shift in person can be used effectively.

> Vary your sentences by combining simple sentences into longer ones, starting a sentence with something other than the subject, and using a question or exclamation occasionally.

Practice 6: Sentence Variety

On your own paper, rewrite the following paragraphs by varying the sentences.

1. My friends and I went to the Great Western Forum to see professional wrestling. There was a huge crowd. Everybody was screaming and yelling. All the fans were cheering for their favorite wrestlers. My favorite wrestler won all her matches. She flipped one of her opponents off the mat. She flew into the crowd. I was scared that she was going to land on me. She fell right next to me. I saw her up close. I saw that she was very big.

2. My best friend is a boy. We've known each other forever. Other girls ask me about him. They ask me why we are good friends. I tell them he is funny. He thinks of weird stuff. He tells me his stuff to hear me laugh. Sometimes I just tell him that he is too strange. He will listen to my opinion. He says that he is glad that he knows someone who will both laugh and tell him different.

3. You never know what effect you can have on other people. Sometimes it can be a big effect. Our school held a talent show. My friends and I did a lip sync to a song by the Jonas Brothers. The crowd cheered. Everyone thought it was great. After the show, everyone wanted to tell us how great we were. I shook everybody's hand. I had a little fever that day. I found out later that I had strep throat. A lot of students were out sick the next week.

4. There's a new student in our school. His name is Omar. Most of his friends are in the chess club. He wasn't very popular. He wanted to run for student council. There was another student who was coming up for re-election. Her name is Theresa. Omar's friends were excited about his campaign. They put up a lot of posters all around the school. Omar gave a good speech. He had some good ideas. This was the first time he did something like this. He won by a small margin.

Practice 7: Revising

A. Based on the skills you learned in this chapter, revise the following paragraphs.

1. The first and primary duty and responsibility of an American citizen is to support and uphold the government, the United States, and the Congress. In particular, a citizen can become a member of the local school board. I enjoy eating that old American favorite, the hot dog. You could be an active part of public education. You could influence the lives of children in your community. Another way to support the government is to serve on a jury in a public trial. We could keep criminals out of society. You must be an active citizen. Then our government will be stronger because of the active participation and involvement of all citizens.

2. At first, do not be scared when people in public tried to communicate with you. We Americans are much more outgoing than I saw in Britain. They are the kind of people who are more subdued. They put smile on their face that is polite. People were very emotional here in the United States. When Americans are happy and cheerful, they will show it. When they are unhappy and sad, they are not embarrassed to cry in front of the other many people.

3. Becoming popular in life has one big part of people getting into groups. To become popular may cause a person to join a group because they want to prove themselves to someone. This happens usually to new students at a new school. Becoming popular and well known in the working area is about the same as school. This happens when someone gets a job they would like to keep. They try to impress the boss. People also join groups to become popular to be cool so other people around them will like them.

B. Return to Practice 12: Writing the Draft, on page 91 in chapter 4. In this practice exercise, you wrote two essays on some topics. Based on what you have learned in chapters, revise these essays to make them better. Then, share your essays with other students, seek their input, and incorporate their suggestions to improve your essays.

Use the following checklist to help you.

☐ I added clarifying information.

☐ I corrected any shifts in tense or person.

☐ I deleted any unrelated sentences.

☐ I checked for parallel sentence structure.

☐ I eliminated any unnecessary words.

☐ I used sentences of different lengths and structures.

Note: You will proofread these essays in chapter 6, Proofreading the Essay.

CHAPTER 5 SUMMARY

Revising means reading your draft and making changes to improve it. Specific ways to improve the draft include the following:

- Add clarifying information
- Delete unrelated sentences
- Eliminate unnecessary words
- Correct shifts in tense or person
- Check for parallel sentence structure
- Develop sentence variety

CHAPTER 5 REVIEW: REVISING THE ESSAY

Using the skills you practiced in this chapter, revise the essay on the following page. It was written as a response to the following writing prompt.

> Write a letter to your school counselor explaining what career field you wish to enter and why you have chosen that field. Include details and convincing information to show your counselor that you are serious about your career choice.

Dear Counselor Billings,

I would like to show you why I am now choosing to pursue a medical career. While I have been growing up I have had many doctors to inspire me. When I was diagnosed with cancer as a young four-year-old, I was very scared. However, the doctors and nurses took the time to explain how they would help me. In the end I would like to be a doctor to help others in an important way, provide an income for my family, and make important contributions to the medical field.

Most importantly, I want to be in a profession where I can help people in the way I was helped. Being a doctor would give me the ability to touch the lives of people because being there for some one when their health is at risk and being able to give them the advice they need is a great feeling. I look forward to looking at my patients as people. not cases. I want to make them laugh, as well as give them the medicine they need. I want to make their lives better by giving them real support and lending them my expertise. The best kind of knowledge to have is the kind that you can share with the world.

Secondly, providing an income for the family I will one day have concerns me. I don't want to have to work sixty hours a week in a job I hate so that I can bring in enough money, to keep my family taken care of. I want to have time to spend with my family instead of being with a company that becomes my family because I spend so much time there. I want to be able to earn enough in a regular work week to not need to work overtime hours. Being a doctor will give me the opportunity to work the hours I want while still being able to provide for my family.

Thirdly, I want to pursue a career in medicine so that one day I can make important discoveries to help patients. I believe there are other cures to cancer waiting out there in the world. I find it hard to believe that the only way today to cure people from cancer is to inject them with poisonous chemicals. I was really scared when I was a kid and all my hair fell out. Those chemicals do things to your body that nature didn't intend. And they damage you. I want to find cures for diseases from the natural world. Our bodies are natural, so we shouldn't be surprised to find cures for diseases coming from nature. I would like to be at the front of efforts to find natural remedies to many of the diseases afflicting the people.

To tell you the truth, I want to be a doctor because I can help people in an important way, provide a good income for my future family without having to work too hard, and contribute important natural discoveries for cures for diseases. Being able to work my own hours will help have balance between future family responsibilities and work. Helping people is why I feel I have been put on this earth, and I want to help someone in the way someone else helped me. In addition, producing natural cures for diseases will help me to leave this earth feeling I have made a lasting difference while I was here.

Sincerely,

Felix Lee

B. For the review in chapter 4: Drafting the Essay, you wrote drafts for several different essays based on your prewriting activities from chapter 3: Planning the Essay. Return to those essays now. Revise them based on the skills you practiced in this chapter. You may also use the checklist below.

☐ I added clarifying information.

☐ I corrected any shifts in tense or person.

☐ I deleted any unrelated sentences.

☐ I checked for parallel sentence structure.

☐ I eliminated any unnecessary words.

☐ I used sentences of different lengths and structures.

Note: You will proofread these essays in the chapter 6 Review, so keep them in your writing folder (portfolio).

ADDITIONAL ACTIVITIES: REVISING THE ESSAY

1. Revise the essay below. It was written in response to the writing prompt below.

> Your school board is planning to require all people entering the school to pass through a metal detector and wants to know how the students feel about this decision.
>
> State how you feel about the use of metal detectors in school, and give specific reasons why you feel this way. Give enough details so that your readers will understand your ideas.

Now that the year is winding down, we be confronting an important issue. Do we want metal detectors in our school next year or not? This issue is complex because, you know, we have had a lot of problems with student violence on campus. At this moment anyone can walk on campus with a knife or gun in their pocket and no one would know until the person decided to display or use the weapon. At the same time, having metal detectors inhibits our freedom. Every time we want to enter the school would be having to submit to an electronic search. I believe however that the benefits of having metal detectors far outweigh the costs. Every time we have something metallic on, we will have to remove it and display it to the public. This interferes with our constitutional right to privacy. We need to protect ourselves from our own student body, visitors to campus, and adults; in the school in order to make the school a truly safe environment.

Firstly, the metal detectors will protect us from ourselves. As students, we know how easy it is for us to get our emotions up on any number of issues. It doesn't take much arguments be starting all of the time over boyfriends and girlfriends. More often than not on campus these days, students is fighting about these problems instead of discussing them. Another thing, people starting vicious rumors cause people to get angry. We have had two people on campus arrested already for assault and battery in separate incidents. As violence increases, the numbers show that the potential for weapons to come into play be increasing to. Weapons, unlike a fist, has a much higher potential to permanently disable or kill. Weapons be causing all kinds of tragedy among the student body. Needless to say, I understand how students would feel hassled by going through machines and having to remove metallic items because some of you people will probably need to change your whole wardrobe! However, students need to realize it is for their own safety that this is becoming necessary.

Secondly, metal detectors will protect us from visitors that may want to harm us on campus. Currently, people may come on campus with the permission of the administration, but they do not get searched for weapons beforehand. Let's say some intelligent, crazy person convinces to administration to let him on campus for snow and tell or something, then he pulls out a handgun while we're changing classes and kills ten of us. Now who here wants that. No one of course. If visitors get offended about being having to go through a metal detector, maybe they have something to hide.

Third, metal detectors would protect us from adults within the school as well. Remember, teachers and administrators would have to go through the metal detectors just like us. Sometimes in class I have seen the students get out of control. I can just imagine how tough it is to be a teacher. There are times I imagine that if I had a gun in my desk, I just might be tempted to let off a round at some kid whose throwing spit wads or throwing balls of paper across the classroom. I'm not saying the teacher would shoot a student they might just shoot up in the air but you have to imagine that the bullet could kill somebody on the second floor. It is for our safety and for the safety of every those obnoxious jerk kids that we have metal detectors for the teachers and the administrators.

To make it short, the safety of the student body, visitors, and the school faculty is at stake in this decision. We need to complete our education in a safe environment for all, so please support the installation of metal detectors starting next fall.

2. Choose either writing prompt 2 or 3 below, and write an essay about it. Then complete activity 4.

Prompt 2:

> You are entering a contest to win a new Lexus convertible. You must write a composition that addresses the following question: "Who is your all time favorite entertainer?" Brainstorm about this topic, and write your draft. Try to convince the judges that your choice is the best one. Then, use the skills you learned in this chapter to revise your composition. Share the composition with the class or with your instructor.

Prompt 3:

> One of your friends lies about everything from how much money his family has to all of the parties he goes to every weekend. Persuade him that lying is wrong and will hurt him in the long run. Do prewriting activities (brainstorming, freewriting, clustering, outlining) on this topic. Then, write a draft for a composition. Revise this composition based on the tips and strategies you practiced in this chapter. Compare your revision with those of others in the class.

Activity 4:

> With a partner or in a small group, exchange your compositions from prompts 2 or 3 above. Provide oral or written feedback to each other. Use the checklist on page 114 as a guide. If you agree with your peers, incorporate their suggestions into an improved revision of your composition. Then, share it with the class or with your teacher.

Basics Made Easy

Chapter 6
Proofreading the Essay

This chapter covers the following McREL standard and benchmarks for Level III:
Standard 3: Uses grammatical and mechanical conventions in written compositions	**Benchmarks 1–10**

You've written and revised your essays, and now you are ready to hand them in to your teacher, right? Well, they are almost ready, but not even the best writers turn in a piece of writing before they do a careful **proofreading**. Proofreading is the process of checking your essays for errors in capitalization, punctuation, spelling, and grammar as well as for repeated words or omitted words. Before turning in your final copies, take time to look for these small, but costly, errors.

The essays require you to demonstrate knowledge of Standard American English through grammar and usage, punctuation, and sentence formation. Proofreading the final copies of your essays will help you demonstrate these skills. In this chapter, you will review proofreading notation, and then practice proofreading for errors in the following areas of writing:

• Capitalization	• Spelling
• Internal Punctuation	• Sentence Formation
• Grammar and Usage	

If you or your teacher feels more practice or review of grammar would be beneficial, read the text and complete the exercises in American Book Company's companion resources, *Basics Made Easy: Grammar & Usage Review* book and software.

PROOFREADING NOTATION

Handwriting quality is not graded on writing assessments, but if your paper cannot be read, it will not be graded. So, write neatly and clearly even for your proofreading corrections. **Proofreading notation** refers to a set of standard correction markes. The following example shows how the author made corrections to the third paragraph from the essay about the effects of children watching television (from page 97).

117

Commercicals are another problem with television. As well as advertising shows with adult situations, commercials persuade children to buy products theat they do not need. ~~Thats~~ ^{That is} *how television pays for itself. ~~C~~ompanies pay to put commercials on television and they hope children will buy* ^{their} ~~there~~ *stuff. The voice in commercials tell children that they will be happy if they buy a certain toy or cereal. They will be like other children ∧ and other children will like them if they have those products. It is difficult enough for adults to tell the difference between* ^{and} *reality ∧ pretending in commercials. How* ^{is} ~~are~~ *a three-year-old supposed to do that?*

Notice how the proofreading marks are written neatly and clearly, so they don't interfere with reading the passage. Develop standard abbreviations and notations for editing your writing.

EDITING AND PROOFREADING CHART

Symbol	Meaning	Example
sp	spelling error	^{They're} Their back from vacation. (sp)
cap	capitalization error	I live in the e^East, but my sister lives in the we^Wst. (cap)
. ? !	end marks	Where are you going/(?)
∧	comma	Hello ∧' Mr. Ripley (,)
∧	add	Ray went to ∧ store ^{the}
/	change	Television teaches kids manners. ^{children}
frag	fragment	Near Kokomo. (frag)
RO	run-on	He tripped he fell. (RO)
t	tense error	Yesterday I walk to school. (t) ^{ed}
s-v	subject-verb agreement	Keisha and I loves to shop. (s-v)
mod	misplaced modifier	Quickly, Sam ate the sandwich. (mod)

CAPITALIZATION

Capitalization involves the practice of using a mixture of capital letters (*A*) and lower case letters (*a*). In the early development of English, writers used only capital letters. Now, in modern English, there are rules for capitalizing certain words in order to emphasize their importance. One example is the first word of a sentence, like the word *One* which began this sentence. Another example of words that are capitalized is proper nouns, like *Ely, Minnesota*. There are many other examples of words that should be capitalized. Think for a moment about the examples that you know.

Looking for errors in capitalization is an important proofreading skill. You will practice this skill in the following exercise.

> Certain words are capitalized to emphasize their importance. These words include the first word in a sentence, proper nouns, words in titles, and so on.

Practice 1: Capitalization

Carefully read the letter below, proofreading for errors in capitalization. Circle all of the words with capitalization errors, including words that should have been capitalized and were not, and words that should *not* have been capitalized but were.

Hint: There are forty-seven words with capitalization errors to find.

> july 24, 2008
>
> dear mr. Golden,
>
> My Family and i finally went on our vacation to the grand canyon in arizona. we got there on a wednesday Morning. My brother, will, and I both wanted to go on the Helicopter tour first, but mom and dad said, "Later!"
>
> When we first walked to the Edge of the South Rim, our jaws dropped, and we exclaimed, "oh, wow!" at one time. Mom took a step back. "oh," She said, "I don't think I can hike this!"
>
> Some german Tourists, hearing our english voices, stopped by us at that moment to ask about the horseback tours. We helped them find the Camp office, and we spoke with kelly o'hara, the Park Ranger on duty. after giving us information about the Canyon and reassuring Mom about the bright angel Trail, Ranger o'hara asked if we were from the south. I guess our accents are more noticeable than i had thought.
>
> Since I know that you, as my english Professor, will be asking for this later, Maybe you could look over my Outline for the Annual "what I did this summer" paper.
>
> I. Memorial day pool Visit
>
>   A. sunburn
>
>   1. Second-degree burns
>
> sincerely yours,
>
> Leigh Harper

INTERNAL PUNCTUATION

Internal punctuation refers to the writing marks that are used within the structure of a sentence. They include **commas**, **colons**, **semicolons**, **apostrophes**, and **quotation marks**. The appropriate use of these marks adds clarity and logic to your writing.

COMMAS

The action of writing an essay has a certain flow and thought process in drafting and even in revising. This flow can create an engaging paper, but it can also lead to omissions of certain punctuation. Commas are often forgotten in the flow of writing. Proofreading for any missing commas is important for the clarity of your paper.

Commas can signal a contrast, set off extra information, or separate items in lists. There are other uses for commas as well. Consider what you know about using commas, and then begin the next exercise.

Practice 2: Commas

Read the student essay below carefully, looking for all missing commas. Insert commas where they are needed, and circle them.

Hint: There are twenty-five commas that are missing.

What's in a Car's Name?

In our college library I fingered the book's jacket in disbelief. The title had to be a joke or was it? The letters stood out lemon yellow on a cobalt blue background spelling out the words *How to Name Your Car*. I told my best friend Renata "Hey look at this!"

"Well yeah" she remarked in a bored tone. "I saw a book by T. S. Eliot kinda like that in my lit class about how to name your car. Crazy huh?" Still curious I headed to the nearest table to find out why this book was written and what it said.

When I began reading the book I realized that it detailed not only car names but also who would choose to name a car. Apparently Westerners who have not gone past the high school level in their education are more likely than other people to name their vehicles especially their mud-caked trucks and open-air jeeps. Sitting at that table I felt my past revealed. My parents with their two semesters of college between them had named our huge maroon station wagon—they had named her Battle Axe. It was a righteous and well-deserved title. My family also according to the book fell into the common-masses category by referring to this hulking machine with the pronoun *she*. In her glory days she plowed into several smaller cars—usually in the shopping center parking lot where my mother vainly tried to overcome the car's blind spot. Battle Axe always came away unscarred from the crashes but the other cars weren't so lucky.

After fourteen years we got our next car on May 17 2006. This new "she" had been pre-owned by my grandparents from Fort Collins Colorado. She was a pale yellow black-topped Chevelle with a sweet 350 engine—she could move out! What did we name her? We named her Cream Puff. She and her name lasted until the puff from her engine became a bluish-black oily cloud of smoke.

COLONS, SEMICOLONS, AND APOSTROPHES

The **colon** signals that there is a bit of information that the sentence needs. It most often sets off a list, a quotation, an appositive (which renames), an explanation, or an example. Colons are also used in number phrases like time notations or Biblical references. Two major rules about colons are as follows:

Rule 1.   <u>Never place it right after a verb (between the verb and its object).</u>

Rule 2.   <u>Never use it to separate two independent clauses with a coordinating conjunction between them.</u>

You may use a **semicolon** to separate two independent clauses which are closely related to one idea. (For more emphasis, you may also use a colon in this case, especially to emphasize the second clause.) Another common use of the semi colon is to separate items in a list when the item names contain commas.

Apostrophes do not separate words; they signal either possession or missing letters in contractions.

To improve your proofreading skill, consider the guidelines above, and consider how you normally use these punctuation marks. Then, complete the following exercise.

Practice 3:   Colons, Semicolons, and Apostrophes

First carefully read the story for content. Next, insert the missing punctuation marks and circle them.

Hint: There are twenty-four colons, semicolons, and apostrophes missing in the passage.

Rot a Good Book

An old warehouse in Detroit is the final resting place for tons of unused school supplies. Here's a partial list of the things piled in the warehouses mounds of filth toppled pallets of texts still wrapped in plastic, unopened chemicals for science class, cases of art supplies, calculators, scissors, rulers, globes, footballs, bookshelves, and desks. Fires sometimes spring up in the warehouse since nobody cares to put them out, they devour books until rain leaks through the roof to extinguish them.

How can this happen in a city that was once Americas pride? The public school systems administration is struggling yearly, they take in a billion tax dollars, but spend so little on supplies that students cant even study books at home. This happens because its cheaper to let books decompose than to deliver them to classes, maintain them, and replace them.

Still, there is beauty in the decay all is not lost. Like scenes from *I Am Legend*, mushrooms and flowers thrive in the waste. Artists and students make regular forages its almost like a tourist trap. Nearby homeless people claim they see dozens of visitors every day. Most dont take anything anything of value left long ago. But some people leave things. Graffiti, both the skilled and the pointless kinds, appears on columns, walls, and chalkboards. One colorful piece suggests at least one visitor to the dump has mustered up hope for the future. On the third floor, someone has painted a giant mural of a book rising from bright red flames, bringing to mind images of book burnings meant to destroy literature these attempts always seem to fall short. The book, with its pages spread like defiant wings, also alludes to the Greeks myth of the phoenix each time deadly flames consumed the phoenix, it would rise again. The flourishing trees nudging through the roof seem to be evidence of this hope in action.

Jack, one of the homeless men at the warehouse, a veteran of the Korean War who now sleeps on stacks of charred textbooks, wanted me to include this letter to you.

Dear Readers,

Im reading a lot so Im writing to tell you todays lesson. In the Physics book, I read that things doing something keep going unless something forces them to change thats hardly news, but we pondered it from about 130 to 230. Also, I read in World Literature that Noah was told in Genesis 9 1-17 that God would never again destroy everything, but it was up to Noah's family to protect their world for the sake of future generations. Thats a big responsibility, dont you think?

Take care,

Jack Gant

QUOTATION MARKS

Quotation marks are signals, framing words that belong to someone other than the author. When used in fiction, quotation marks help to keep the voices of different characters from becoming confused. There are two types of quotation marks.

Double quotation marks (" ") are used to signal direct quotes or some titles.

Single quotation marks (' ') are used to signal quotes within quotes.

Practice 4: Quotation Marks

Carefully read the story below, first for content. Then, look for missing quotation marks, and add the quotation marks where needed. Next, circle the ones you added.

Hint: There are eight pairs of double (" ") marks and one pair of single (' ') marks missing.

Summer Blight

Race you to that mimosa! challenged Sophie, pointing to a slender, pink-dotted tree.

You're on, dork, snorted Terrell and the loser has to bring everybody sodas.

We took off, with me dead last as usual. We ran to the tree and fell under its scant shade, panting and sweating from the summer's heat. I rolled onto my back to look up through the mimosa's fern-like leaves.

Did you know that these trees were all killed by a blight years back? I asked. My aunt Beryl always talks about climbing these trees as a kid, but they were huge then. Now the blight's over, and the mimosas are growing again, but they're all scrawny like this one here. Wonder when they'll be big enough to be good climbin' trees again…

Sophie sat up, frowning and fussing, Don't try to change the subject. You know it's you who has to get the sodas, and while you're at it, you might as well bring food too.

Terrell agreed with her (as usual) that, as the furtherest-back-of-all-time loser, I should bring anything they wanted. My speech had backfired—making them hungrier and thirstier than ever. I tried again.

With this drought going on, the worst in history even, I think we should forget the sodas. Just remember, I said raising a hand into the air, that old saying, Don't spit; you just might need it. And I think—

Sophie and Terrell threw dust, thistles, and rude names at me until I got up and trudged off, feeling as much a loser as Charlie Brown in the comic strip Peanuts. Then, as I got closer to our screened door, I started daydreaming about what would happen if I fell in a hole or was taken by aliens. Sophie and Terrell—well, I expect that they would just wither up and blow away like blighted mimosa shoots.

> Use appropriate internal punctuation within your sentences, including commas, colons, semicolons, apostrophes, and quotation marks.

GRAMMAR AND USAGE

Grammar and usage refers to the ways that writers put together words, phrases, sentences, and paragraphs. When you are proofreading, you want to make sure that you have followed the rules for Standard American English. Look for mistakes in your usage of nouns, articles, adjectives, adverbs, negative words, verbs, and subject-verb agreement.

NOUNS AND ARTICLES

Nouns are words that name people, places, things, ideas, and concepts. Common nouns name general examples of these. Proper nouns name specific people, places, things, ideas, and concepts and are capitalized. So, proper nouns are capitalized, and common nouns are not. There is a special group of nouns called collective nouns. Collective nouns name single units made up of many members. Two examples are a school of fish and a committee of delegates.

Nouns may be possessive, showing ownership or a relationship. There are several different ways to form the possessive of a noun. Two of the guidelines are as follows: for a singular noun, add an *'s*; if the noun is plural and ends in *s*, then add only an apostrophe after the letter (*s'*).

In English, **articles** like *the* or *a* are closely associated with nouns. These small words often give the reader essential information about the noun they accompany. There are three forms of articles:

- **definite**–*the*
- **indefinite**–*a/an*
- **zero**–*no article*

1. The first form, the **definite article**, is *the*. It can be used with any type of noun. *The* marks a thing that is known to readers either by general knowledge, the context of the rest of the writing, or by the information in the noun phrase.

    Example 1: <u>The</u> sun rises in the morning.

    Example 2: A wildfire blazed out of control in eastern Colorado. It was <u>the</u> worst fire seen in two hundred years.

    Example 3: <u>the</u> Great Basin Park

There are three instances where *the* is always needed:

- Before the word *same* (<u>the</u> same time zone)
- Generally before a written (ordinal) number (<u>the</u> first star I see)
- Before a superlative statement (<u>the</u> best music)

2. The second form, the **indefinite articles**, *a/an*, do not identify a certain thing. The writer may know of the particular noun item, but does not expect the reader to know it. The indefinite article *a/an* can only be used with singular nouns. The article *a* is used before a word that begins with a consonant letter or sound. The article *an* is used before words that begin with a vowel letter or sound.

   Example 1: I went to <u>a</u> concert.
   He worked on <u>a</u> railroad.

   Example 2: She had <u>an</u> egg for breakfast.
   They drove for <u>an</u> hour to get to the fair.

3. The third form, the **zero article**, means no article at all. No articles are used with plural or uncounted nouns. Often, vague generalizations are made with no article.

   Example 1: We will serve <u>hot tea</u> with lunch.

   Example 2: <u>Trees</u> give off oxygen, benefitting our atmosphere.

   Example 3: Religious texts are founded on <u>faith</u>.

Practice 5:   Nouns and Articles

A. In the first paragraph of this passage, look for nouns and articles. <u>Underline</u> all common nouns once. <u><u>Double-underline</u></u> all proper nouns. Finally, circle all the articles.

Hint: There are thirty-one common nouns, three proper nouns, and thirteen articles.

Not the Same Old Grind!

Have you been to the new recreational park? If not, you've got to go! It's so awesome! It's called Skateboard Survivor Park. The entire complex is arranged so skateboarders have the right-of-way. The park's property is a sprawling twenty-seven acres of convenient urban land. The park's compassionate leader is J. C. Powell, a lifelong educator. Mr. Powell's vision for the park was that it be a safe but challenging course for serious skateboarders. After only a few crises, construction was completed on schedule. The master-of-ceremonies' speech was made on a skateboard; an official showed off the park's unique features. There are grinding rails, half-pipes, ramps, multi-level shelves, and spirals for extreme speed and complicated maneuvers.

B. In the second paragraph, look for incorrectly written possessive and plural nouns and missing articles. Use proofreading notation to mark the mistakes. Above each error, neatly write in what should be there.

Hint: There are thirteen errors.

Previewing the park, I saw some skateboarderes shooting around like torpedos and others bailing out like dominois. A brand new skateboarding splash fountain has been put in for cooling off and jumping off. The huge food court, three storys high, can be reached by avenues that are marked "Skateboard Traffic Only." When has that been seen before? The walking crowd has its own pathwaies and food kiosks, which are set around the perimeter of park only. The best wayes to reach the park include city busis and the underground rail system. There is a small entrance fee that gives you run of the parks' grounds for as long as you can survive or until closing time. I don't know about you, but I'm going to grab my boards' and head over there right now!

PRONOUNS

Pronouns take the place of nouns in a sentence. A pronoun must agree in number and gender with the noun it replaces. Some examples of pronouns are *I, you, she, he, it, we, they, us, their, who, that, someone, whose, none,* and *nobody.* Some of these pronouns may act as adjectives when they are followed by a noun: for example, *that, those,* or *these.* Also, there are pronouns that may begin a question: for example, *what, who,* or *whose.*

Before beginning the next practice, you may want to consider how you use pronouns or review the use of pronouns in this book's companion text, American Book Company's *Basics Made Easy: Grammar & Usage Review.*

Practice 6:   Pronouns

Read the following passage. For each blank in the passage, choose the pronoun form that belongs there.

My mom is really great. She took my friends and (1)_____ to the mall for the Back-to-School Sale. Mom drove (2)_____ and helped (3)_____ find the stores we needed. My friend Kelly bought (4)_____ a giant cookie as a thank-you. When Mom ducked into a store, we all took a bite, even though it was (5)_____! Besides all the notebooks and pencils (6)_____ needed, (7)_____ also looked for a dress for my date with Chad. (8)_____ are going to a nice restaurant next weekend. When (9)_____ shopping bags were full, we headed home. Mom said she didn't mind my friends being along and that she really likes (10)_____. I'm glad to have such a cool mom.

1. A.   I   B.   me
2. A.   us   B.   we
3. A.   us   B.   we
4. A.   her   B.   she
5. A.   hers   B.   she's
6. A.   I   B.   me
7. A.   us   B.   we
8. A.   Him and I   C.   Him and me
    B.   Him and me   D.   He and I
9. A.   us's   C.   our
    B.   we's   D.   ours
10. A.   they   B.   them

ADJECTIVES, ADVERBS, AND NEGATIVE WORDS

Adjectives are words that modify, or describe, nouns and pronouns. Adjectives answer the questions *Which? How many?* or *What kind?* In contrast to many other languages, English almost always places adjectives BEFORE the word(s) that they modify. Pronouns and articles can also function as adjectives.

Adverbs are used to modify many different kinds of words. Adverbs can modify verbs, adjectives, or other adverbs. Frequently, adverbs end in *-ly*, but not always. All adverbs answer one of these questions: *Where? When? In what manner?* or *To what extent?*

Adjectives and adverbs are also used to compare or "weigh" differences. The comparative form of adjectives and adverbs (*-er*) is used to compare two things. The superlative form of adjectives and adverbs (*-est*) is used to compare three or more things.

Note: For words with one syllable, use the *-er* and *-est* endings. For words with two or more syllables, place *more, most, less,* or *least* in front of the comparing adjective or adverb. If the comparison is negative, use the words *worse* (two things) or *worst* (three or more things).

Two **negative words** cannot be used to express one negative idea. When they are, it is called a **double negative**. Unfortunately, it is one of the most common errors in English.

Example 1: I can't hardly wait for summer vacation.

There are many negative words including *nothing, not, nearly, never, hardly, neither,* and *no one.*

Practice 7: Adjectives, Adverbs, and Negative Words

Read the following story for content. Then, proofread the text for correct use of adjectives, adverbs, and negative words. When you find an error, neatly strike through the word, and clearly write the correct form above it.

Hint: There are twenty-nine errors.

The Emperor's Army

One warm morning in China, two brothers which had bought a small farm were scouting their fields, seeking a best place to dig a well. Ning chose a location, and they worked with them shovels as the sun rose. They began unearthing largest shards of pottery from the soil. At first, they didn't think nothing of it, but they began to pile the pieces together, thinking they may try to sell them to a wealth university. Finding none sign of water, they were about to quit when Chun struck a solid floor of clay at the bottom. Curious, Ning joined in. They smashed through, revealing a dim-lit cavern. Thinking they had just located an underground reservoir, they cheered very loud. Chun helped Ning climb down by rope. Ning clicked his flash light on and froze, his face turning palest.

"Do you see bury treasure?" Chun joked.

"I mean you no harm!" Ning shouted, shakingly.

"What are you talking about, crazied man?" Chun laughed.

"I will leave you peaceful! Chun, help me up!" Ning said, tugging frantic at the longer rope.

"You've gone insanity," Chun said as he lifted Ning from the pit.

"There's an army down there! A ghostly army!" cried Ning.

As Ning raced home to evacuate the farm, Chun chuckled and peered down. He gasped at the more incredible thing he'd never seen—hundreds of men arranged in rows that stretched as farther as his flash light shined. Ning was right; Chun hoped the soldiers had not noticed the intrusion. While scrambling to hurry home, Chun accidental kicked the pile of pottery. The shards of broke clay tumbled into the cavern, clattering and bursting, making a racket that sounded like a New Year's celebration.

Chun gulped down his fear. Knowing he was about to die, he looked into the cavern to watch the army rush to destroy him. Through the clouds of dust swirling from the avalanche of pottery, Chun was shocked to see the men standing still. He grabbed another shard and threw it forceful. It slid into a soldier's feet, but the army didn't move.

Chun quick returned home to convince Ning to enter the cave again. Ning insisted on taking gifts, but agreed. The two brothers entered and stood feet away from the army, asking for mercy. Creeping forward, Ning reached to touch the face of one of them. He was amazing to discover that the soldier was made of clay pottery.

In 209 BC, the body of the Emperor of the Chinese Qin Dynasty, the same man opposed by Jet Li's character in the 2002 film *Hero*, was buried with eight thousand life-size statues of her soldiers. The individually-carved statues and the enormous tomb took thousands of workers over a decade to construct. The Emperor had hoped the army would accompany him to the afterlife, extending his longest reign. The mightier army of the Qin Emperor had to wait two thousand years before being put to the test, but they did manage to scare poorer Ning pretty bad.

VERBS

A verb is a word or group of words which is a part of every complete sentence. A verb can describe action which the subject takes or receives. A verb can also link the subject to another word which describes it. Verbs must agree with the subject in a sentence in number and person, and verbs change tense to indicate the time of action.

Consider how you use verbs in sentences and in essays. Generally speaking, a verb tense should not change within an essay without a good, logical reason, but verbs do shift in number with the subject of the sentence. Think for a moment about how you use verbs, and then complete the following exercise.

Practice 6: Verbs

Read the following passage, first for content. Next, proofread for errors in verb form. Neatly strike through the errors, and then clearly write the correct verb above each error.

Hint: There are sixteen errors in the text.

Big Top: The Reign of Foopoo

Are you going to the movies? There's a great one at the Dollar Theater, and I seen it last night. It's about a clown who wanting to take over the circus, starring a guy who reminds me of Steve Carell. Foopoo the clown goes around making stupid bets. Like he betted the elephant trainer that he could feed the boss' cell phone to an elephant and then find it in the elephants' straw, still working. He loses that bet since the animal steps on the ringing phone before he can save it. Foopoo is tries other schemes: he sells real flamingoes as living lawn ornaments, he swim in the crocodile pool, he marries the bearded lady, and he tried to teach the donkeys to walk the tightrope. The donkeys, sadly, do not works out.

Foopoo then go to his boss, asking him to think of the most impossible stunt. His boss laughs, but does come up with one. He dares Foopoo to run for president. He sound serious, but he's joking. Foopoo, however, immediately agrees. Would you believe his stupidity unless you saw it? He actually wins the election and prevented a recount. I won't give the end away, but the whole thing is as ridiculous as a Will Ferrell movie. I was laughing about it right now. I thought about seeing it again, but the real election has been coming soon. If I want to saw clowns making crazy proposals, I can just watch that.

Practice 9: Forms of Verbs

Carefully read the following passage. Decide how each boldfaced verb should be changed, and then rewrite the words on the blanks provided.

Riding Part 2: Mounting a Horse for the First Time

Some horses are elegant and mild creatures; however, some **were**[1] rough and ill-tempered. The latter type of horse is an accident waiting to happen. **Did**[2] not let the accident happen to you. There are many ways to protect yourself while enjoying the ride. The first and best protection is education. A professional trainer **can taught**[3] you how to ride. Horses are intelligent, but that does not mean you **should have relied**[4] on their good sense. This basic horse care lesson **helped**[5] you stay in control. Riding is, above all, a lesson in the age-old communication between humans and horses. People **have rode**[6] horses successfully for eons.

Begin your approach to the horse slowly and quietly. **Spoke**[7] to the horse calmly as you are mounting, and always mount from the left side of the horse. Assuming that the horse is tacked up and held, first **have looped**[8] the reins in the palm of your left hand, and also hold the horn of the saddle with the fingers of your left hand. Second, lift your left foot and slide it through the stirrup; you **are needing**[9] to use your right hand to hold the stirrup steady. Next, reach with your right hand for the back rim (cantle) of the saddle while pushing off with your right foot. Continue that movement, and **swung**[10] your right leg over the saddle. You **are sat**[11] in the middle of the saddle. Be sure to put your right foot into the right stirrup, and **taken**[12] better hold of the reins with both hands. Take a look around before directing the horse to move.

1.	7.
2.	8.
3.	9.
4.	10.
5.	11.
6.	12.

Lie and Lay / Sit and Set

There are two sets of commonly confused irregular verbs. First, there is *lie* and *lay*. *Lie* is defined as "to recline," while *lay* is defined as "to place something." They are close in meaning, and in the past tense, *lie* is spelled *lay*. The other irregular verbs are *sit* and *set*, which have a similar problem: they are very close in meanings and spellings. See how these irregular verbs are used in the following sentences.

> **Example 1:** Raul sat in the café chair and set his cup on the table.

> **Example 2:** Marian said, "I am going to lay my book on the bed before I lie down."

In proofreading for errors involving the verbs *lie/lay* and *sit/set*, the first step is to remember the differences. Also, study the chart below which shows how these verbs are used in different tenses. If you are not clear about the appropriate use of these and other irregular verbs, refer to this book's companion text, American Book Company's *Basics Made Easy: Grammar & Usage Review* for lists of these verbs and for practice exercises.

Infinitive	Present Participle	Past	Past Participle
lie (to recline)	(is) lying	lay	(have) lain
lay (to put)	(is) laying	laid	(have) laid
sit (to rest)	(is) sitting	sat	(have) sat
set (to put)	(is) setting	set	(have) set

Practice 10: Lie and Lay / Sit and Set

Read the historical account below, first for content. Then, circle the correct verb form in the parentheses that completes the meaning of the sentence. There are eighteen pairs.

Casualty of War

During World War II, the United States Army kept many of its new recruits in training by (sitting / setting) up temporary camps in rural areas. One such area used by troops was the land (lying / laying) near Blackjack Mountain in Marietta, Georgia. Here, in the early 1900s, one could have seen soldiers (sitting / setting) on pine logs in between training sessions. Part of their training sessions involved learning how to fire weapons, including small cannons, which (set / sat) mini-bombs down upon faraway targets off the side of the mountain. These soldiers likely never guessed that, in the future, these pieces of ammunition would be found (lying / laying) on the ground, some still undetonated, and all kinds of people would collect them.

One of the more famous instances of this sort, at least in local lore, was that of a small boy whose father (set / sat) him up into a tree. Using a burlap sack, this father was harvesting pecans, which (lay / lie) under trees in the shadow of Blackjack Mountain. The child (sitting / setting) in the tree saw a hand-sized cannon shell, which had (lain / laid) in that tree for decades. The child broke off a limb and tried to pry the shell away from the tree. The father heard his small son's voice calling, "Look what I found!" The next sound he heard was an explosion that echoed off the rocks (set / sit) into the side of Blackjack Mountain.

Struggling back to his feet after having been (laid / lain) flat by the shock wave and the shock, the child's father saw pieces of shattered pecan limbs (lying / laying) over blasted clods of red clay. They say that the man first emptied the sack of pecans, placing them back where they had (lain / laid) before he came, and then he gathered up his child, wrapping him in the rough burlap material to carry him home.

The family and the community (laid / lain) the child to rest in a cemetery near Scufflegrit Road, the turn-off to visit Blackjack Mountain. No memorial was (sit / set) near the place where this young war casualty fell; neither teddy bears nor flowers ever marked the spot. The legend lives on, though, (sat / set) forever into the hearts and minds of a generation of Georgians who grew up (setting / sitting) on front porches listening to the call of whippoorwills and to the cautionary tale of the boy who (set / sat) in the wrong tree.

SUBJECT-VERB AGREEMENT

Subject-verb agreement means that both the subject and the
verb of a sentence or clause must be of the same number and
person. For example, a singular subject must be paired with a
singular verb, and a noun in the first person must be paired
with a verb in the first person. Consider first how you use
verbs to agree with subjects, and then complete the following
exercise.

Practice 11: Subject-Verb Agreement

**Read the following passage, first for content. Then, proofread for subject-verb agreement.
If the subject and verb do not agree, neatly strike through the error, and clearly write the
correct form above each part.**

Hint: There are fourteen errors to be found.

Been There?

Have you ever felt that life was stacked against you? Has your

sensed that there is a burden present that presses down unrelentingly? I

am experiencing that right now. It are a massive, quivering stack, con-

sisting of squished wood fibers in rectangular shapes, menacingly

growing before my face.

Yes! The "To Be Recyled" paper collect on my desk, daring me to

dislodge it with an ill-advised move. It silently dare me to reach for

paper clips or a white flag of surrender. The really bad news are that no

one listens to my pathetic wails drifting through the wall of paper.

Instead, the people in my office has impeccable timing. They

senses just when the stack has eroded to a manageable level. Then, they

marches by with all the righteous solemnity and shallow grief of failed

game show contestants, piling their orphaned projects and rejected

manuscripts onto my convenient desk. There go another group now. As

I fix a withering glare upon the back of the offenders (who can't be
bothered to take the stuff out to the bin), the slow march continue.

After wishing, vainly, that they suffer
some sort of disabling paper-cut on those
pointing fingers, calls for pizza. Moments
later, I watches with a smirk that would
leave the Grinch greener with envy as the
previously preoccupied staff scurry about.
Working feverishly, they all carts paper out-
side to the recycling bin to allow pizza boxes to be centrally deposited.

After the meal, who will recycle the boxes?

Subject-Verb Agreement with Collective Nouns

Collective nouns name single units made up of multiple members. Collective nouns have special rules regarding agreement with verbs. If the unit is truly acting as one, as in "A <u>swarm of bees</u> lives here," then the verb reflects the singular subject. However, if the unit's members act individually, as in "A <u>swarm of bees</u> perform their various jobs," then the verb reflects the plural nature of the subject.

Proofreading for collective noun errors concerns the verb form used with them. Think about the logic of using the singular and plural form with the action that is occurring: is it group or individual action? Then, complete the following exercise.

Practice 12: Subject-Verb Agreement with Collective Nouns

Read the passage below, noting the use of different collective nouns. Then go back, and decide if each collective noun is acting as a group or as individuals. Circle one verb in each pair to agree with the subject.

In Pursuit of Trivia

My senior class (know / knows) one thing for sure: we all love
trivia. We are putting on plays showcasing our knowledge of it as well
as the talents of other students.

The audience (clap / claps) when we act out animal behaviors
using obscure collective nouns for groups of animals. For example,
when in danger, a knot of toads (leap / leaps) into mud together; when

135

there is a regrettable roadkill incident, a murder of crows (take / takes) their favorite positions in the pecking order; and lastly, in a jungle river scene, a crash of rhinos (attack / attacks) a fishing canoe.

It is after this that the other student groups take their turns. First, the band (begin / begins) to play a thunderous medley of hits. Then, the skate club (demonstrate / demonstrates) their different special techniques, with trivial variations in moves. That is a very popular part of the show. Next, the debate team (argue / argues) about the relevancy of trivia. Lastly, the school choir (sing / sings) their favorite, though unheard-of, show tunes.

I believe that this trivia mania began when the student body (was / were) challenged to discover the origin of the school's name: Eagle Lake-Eight High School. Well, it was difficult, but our class found the secret. Apparently, the school board (has / have) some members who are avid fans of Andy Griffith (the Mayberry sheriff, you know). So they chose the name to honor him; in the '70s, he starred in a television show, *Adams of Eagle Lake*. It ran for only eight days before being canceled. Now that's trivia!

> Proofread your essay for proper usage of nouns, pronouns, articles, adjectives, adverbs, negative words, and verbs, as well as subject-verb agreement.

SPELLING

Spelling is the process of arranging letters to form words. This may seem simple, but spelling English words can be difficult. The English language has a history of taking words from other languages and trying to make their spellings fit into the rules of Standard American English. These rules are rather inconsistent in the first place, so it makes spelling twice as difficult. This chapter will provide you with hints and practice in finding **homonyms** and **incorrect spellings** while you proofread.

HOMONYMS

Homonyms are words that sound the same, even though they have different spellings and meanings. The best way to proofread for errors in the use of homonyms is to look first at the homonyms that you tend to misuse. You may also want to find a list of the most commonly misused homonyms. Study the list so you can recognize common errors.

ant   **aunt**

Practice 13: Homonyms

Read the following essay for content and word meaning. Then, circle which homonym in each pair is correct for the meaning of the sentence.

Hurdles

Having a birthday can be just (plane / plain) dangerous. You don't believe me? Well, then I'd like to (advise / advice) you better because you haven't had a birthday like mine. It's like this: I had the brilliant idea to take some of my friends to the Extreme Bike Course for my fifteenth birthday. Questioning the safety of this plan, my parents all but said no. They tried to give me wise (council / counsel) and good (advise / advice) instead. However, by promising to wear safety gear and do chores, I (won / one) the day and got the go-ahead.

My friends and I were hyped up for (to / two) weeks while planning this party. We could hardly (bear / bare) the wait. (Whose / Who's) to say that we should have been worried? My parents called the course to check out (it's / its) rules and party arrangements.

Finally, the day came, and my dad took us to (were / where) the course was located, over near Hoover Dam. I thought that we would just jump on our bikes and go. Not. (Writing / Righting) the check was the first hurdle that slowed us down, but Dad cleared that (won / one) just fine, filling in the dollar and (sense / cents) in the right places. Dad later described the next paper he had to sign as "(personnel / personal) information. You know, like the instructions on where to send your dead and broken body." He always exaggerates. It was just the usual disclaimer to relieve the bike course (personnel / personal) of any legal responsibility should I become, like, really hurt. I (blew / blue) this off by showing Dad my and my friends' safety gear; we were carrying full-body protection to (were / wear).

Outmaneuvered, Dad signed the release papers with his eyes shut. What a kidder! Well, after (hour / our) wait, you can imagine how bad we wanted to start. It was taking (two / too) long. So, we took off for the course looking cool in our backwards caps, bike shorts, and shirts with the arms cut out. Well, we wanted our biceps to be (bare / bear) didn't we? As the five of us mounted our bikes, we saw girls in the stands watching for guys; I mean they were trying to act smooth, but we could tell that we were having an (affect / effect) on them, and they were interested.

Interested! Really, they were fascinated. They told us later at the hospital, (were / where) they had followed us, that they had never seen human bodies contort that way while hurtling through the air like (plains / planes). I won't detail every crash, but you know, it looks easy to do those aerial moves that you see on TV. Lloyd lost a tooth—in his lip; Renaldo ripped his racing shirt and broke his wrist; Tito twisted and tore all the tendons in his knees; Cal careened into a corner and got a concussion; and I got injured just where I deserved it, (write / right) in the mouth. I needed stitches inside my cheeks and in my gums: fifteen of them in three places each, or forty-five to be exact.

Dad said it all when he observed that actually wearing the safety gear would have made more (cents / sense). If I make it to my next birthday, he suggested that we rent an extreme sports video. I was deeply (affected / effected) by his concern, but because of my swollen mouth I could not speak. So, I had to (right / write) my answer—"Sounds good."

INCORRECT SPELLING

Incorrect spelling can make your writing sloppy, confusing, or even incomprehensible. Proper spelling is an essential part of effective writing. Because so many words in English have irregular spellings, it is important to memorize commonly misspelled words. It is also helpful to follow a plan when proofreading for spelling errors.

First, consider the spelling errors that are typical for you, and look for those types of errors. Second, think about the basic structure of forming words, and correct any words that do not follow the structure. Last, use your sight memory—the memory that tells you when something just does not look right—and correct the word so it looks right. Using this plan, your proofreading for spelling should be successful.

Before you begin the practice, think about your own spelling patterns, and think about the rules for spelling that you know. In a notebook, make a list of words that you frequently misspell. Write them ten times each for practice. Be ready to use the proofreading plan (in the paragraph above) for your spelling errors.

Practice 14: Spelling

Read the following short essay carefully for meaning first. Then, proofread it for spelling errors. When you find a misspelled word, strike through it neatly, and then write the correct spelling clearly.

Hint: There are forty-one spelling errors in the essay.

NPR Today

Are you tring to find an intelligent, meaningful communications source? The easyest way to find what you are searching is to switch your radio dial to a National Public Radio station. The NPR station is a frist class educational resource, hepling schools in your city. Public radio stations rely on listeners, ordinery peple, for funding their bugdets. Becuase of that, thy can refuse to run commercials or to consider big buisness interests befor their audiances' interests.

In this way, public stations can offer viry differrant types of programming and can schedule the programming to meet their listeners' needs. Adults and children can unnite to support this resource. There are shows they can enjoiy together or individualy.

NPR stations broadcast an interesting vareity of shows about sience, history, cultural movements (includeing sports reviews), business trends, and film. This is just a bare sampeling of the varied broadcasts ofered to the public by public radio. The many station managers and jornalists, your freinds in radio, also formate the news programs to reelly explain issues and to take time over important events, instead of feeding their listeners sound bites from cheesy politicions' speaches.

Have you found a radio station that can offer all of this? KUNR, the public station in Renoe, for example, is one of the best. In Febuarary, this station will be having a fund drive for new fans to jion public radio memebership, allowing them to take control of their destinys. Tune your radio tommorow to your local public radio station and dicsover, all over again, how good radio can be.

> Spelling English words can be difficult, but studying regular and irregular words will bring you success.

SENTENCE FORMATION

Sentence formation is one of the key writing elements. To demonstrate skill in this area, you must use end punctuation appropriately, correct any sentence fragments or run-ons, correctly identify and punctuate phrases and clauses, and avoid misplaced and dangling modifiers.

END PUNCTUATION

End punctuation ends sentences. There are three ways to end a complete sentence.

- A **period** ends a complete statement.
- A **question mark** ends any question.
- An **exclamation point** ends a forceful or emotional statement.

These marks signal a definite end to one sentence and the beginning of the next sentence. End punctuation adds to the organization, variety, and tone of your writing.

Practice 15: End Punctuation

Read the following story carefully, and then add end punctuation as needed. Circle each added punctuation.

Hint: There are twenty-six end punctuation marks to add.

GREEN!

Has anyone out there noticed a government plot being carried out in dim grocery store aisles Yes, it's a top secret federal government plot that only certain foreign governments have paid to learn How do I know I read Stephen King novels, don't I But you, you need to look around you Look for GREEN, it's leaping out, screaming, grabbing at you everywhere you go

At one time, in years past, parents urged their children to eat green vegetables We are talking about naturally green things And just as naturally, the children turned away loudly exclaiming, "Yuck" These children are now the grownups driving SUVs Further study reveals an even deeper shame: these are the people who are voluntarily drinking—hold on—be prepared to be sickened They are drinking GREEN TEA Not only is this tea green, but it is flavored with other healthy things: peach, kumquat, lemon, and ginseng What's next, spinach-flavored green tea

Just to make sure that today's kids are not left out, the food industry has now funded research producing a truly grotesque, unnatural form of vegetable—GREEN KETCHUP The marketers using this research are based in Roswell, New Mexico They claim that kid experts chose this color over blue, yellow, and rainbow

But why toy with the artificially-enhanced natural red dye color at all Because as I said before, it is a government plot They are breaking down taboos—the natural order of the universe It is a law of nature: kids hate green food But if the government can break this taboo, breaching the limits of food color, think of all the other ways "Big Brother" can mold us Just watch for the acceptance of green eggs and ham Oh, no What am I saying It's too late

SENTENCE FRAGMENTS AND RUN-ONS

End punctuation errors may result in sentence fragments or run-ons. A **sentence fragment** is a phrase that is punctuated like a sentence, but it lacks a subject or verb. To correct one of these, simply add the missing element. A **run-on** occurs when two independent clauses are joined with no punctuation or connecting word between them. The combining of independent clauses requires either end punctuation, a semicolon, or a comma with a coordinating conjunction.

You have practiced using internal and end punctuation. Now, you can use commas with the following coordinating conjunctions to correct sentence fragments or run-ons: *for, and, nor, but, or, yet, so*. Remember these words by taking the first letter of each, spelling **F.A.N.B.O.Y.S.**

When writing for a test, you may stop a sentence too soon, or make one sentence blend into the next. As you proofread, make sure each sentence is complete and correctly punctuated.

Practice 16:   Sentence Fragments and Run-ons

Read the passage below. There are both run-ons and fragments in the story. Decide how to best correct each sentence error, and write your answer on the lines that follow. If there is no error, write the word *correct* **on the line.**

1.   Betsy was not the most graceful or athletic person in our class.

_____

2.   Seemed a little klutzy and a natural-born bookworm.

_____

3.   In our seventh grade year, however, a vast change.

_____

4.   Before, the basketball coach let everyone play he decided to hold team tryouts this year.

_____

5.   Appeared to be a challenge to Betsy.

_____

6.   She had never been interested in sports now Betsy stayed in the gym after school for weeks before the tryout.

_____

7.   Practiced dribbling, passing, and shooting the ball.

_____

8.   After school, bringing books on basketball strategy.

_____

9. Her hard work and single-mindedness got Betsy on the first-string as a guard.

_____

10. We elected Betsy to be the captain of the team she inspired us, on the court and off, in all our years in school.

_____

PHRASES AND CLAUSES

Phrases and clauses are both groups of words that help form the structure of sentences. A **phrase** is a group of words that acts as a single unit in a sentence, but it lacks either a subject or a predicate or both. Phrases can function as nouns, verbs, adjectives, or adverbs. A **clause** is a group of words that includes a subject and predicate. There are two kinds of clauses: dependent and independent.

An **independent clause** can stand alone as a sentence. If another independent clause is linked to it, the two clauses must be joined by a comma and a coordinating conjunction or a semicolon. A **dependent clause** relies on the controlling independent clause in a sentence. The independent clause and the dependent clause are linked together by a relative pronoun such as *which*, *that*, *whose*, or *those*, or by a subordinating conjunction like *while*, *because*, *since*, or *after*.

Being able to recognize these different sentence elements is the first step in learning how to use them in your writing. You may want to review phrases and clauses in American Book Company's *Basics Made Easy: Grammar & Usage Review* before starting this practice.

Practice 17: Phrases and Clauses

Read the following passage. In the numbered blanks on the next page, write whether the bolded group of words is a dependent clause, an independent clause, or a phrase. For extra credit, identify the type of phrase: prepositional, appositive, or participial.)

The State's Worst Swim Team

All swim teams have traditions **for celebrating**[1]. But our swim team celebrates the best, **especially after we swim for six-hour meets**[2]. However, we don't usually perform popular expressions of team spirit **like head-butting and chest-bumping**[3]. Instead, **there is cheering, eating, body art, and dunking**[4] on display.

Our coach writes our schedules of events on our wrists **with permanent markers**[5]. But later in the meet, we use these markers to create **an array of body art**[6]. During the closing hours, **we make our own statements**[7] on our bare skin, usually our arms, legs, and even backs. Coach tries to keep it to a minimum at the beginning, **since we still need to be able to read our race times**[8]. But when the other team begins to beat us, our body art becomes much sillier. Our swimmers try to outdo each other by inventing funny sayings **without getting thrown out of the pool area by judges**[9].

Coach stays alert for excessive rowdiness[10], but he also joins in cheering. Parents, grandparents, and other swimmers cheer loudly when their loved ones are **in the water**[11]. Also, **once the other team is winning by a gazillion points**[12], our coach orders pizza **before the last race has even been swum**[13].

The other big difference between our swim team and other teams **is the party afterward**[14]; instead of a meeting, we get to party!

1. _____   8. _____

2. _____   9. _____

3. _____   10. _____

4. _____   11. _____

5. _____   12. _____

6. _____   13. _____

7. _____   14. _____

MISPLACED AND DANGLING MODIFIERS

A **modifier** is a word, phrase, or clause that helps clarify the meaning of another word by describing it in more detail. However, if a modifier is positioned incorrectly in a sentence, it can confuse and frustrate the reader.

A **misplaced modifier** is positioned too far from what it is modifying in the sentence. This confuses the meaning, as in the following example.

Example 1: The painting had visible brush strokes that I was selling.

In Example 1, it is unclear whether the dependent clause, "that I was selling," describes the painting or the brush strokes. The clause "that I was selling" is a misplaced modifier. To correct this problem, place the modifying clause closer to the word that it describes, as in Example 2.

Example 2: The painting that I was selling had visible brush strokes.

Dangling modifiers are words that modify nothing in particular in the rest of the sentence.

They often seem to modify something that is suggested or implied but not actually present in the sentence. They dangle or hang loosely from the rest of the sentence. They frequently appear at the beginnings or ends of sentences. See Example 3.

Example 3: Dangling from a hook, our bird dove for the worm.

Does this sentence make sense to you? What is dangling: is it the bird or the worm? Obviously, the worm would be dangling from the hook, not the bird. "Dangling from a hook" is a dangling modifier because its position in the sentence makes it look like it is describing the subject, "our bird." However, it should be describing "the worm." Correctly wording this sentence would mean changing the position of the modifier, so it is closer to the object it is describing, the worm. Notice this correction in Example 4.

Example 4: Our bird dove for the worm dangling from a hook.

Your writing must be clear and logical. Using modifiers incorrectly will confuse your readers. Consider how to make your writing easily understood while using modifiers that add detail and color to your writing. Be aware of the position of modifiers when proofreading.

Practice 18: Misplaced and Dangling Modifiers

Read the following short passage carefully. Then, on the lined spaces below, rewrite the passage, correcting the modifiers that are misplaced or dangling.

Family Time?

1. We often lose track of each other, being such a large family on trips.

_____

2. So I knew what would happen before we went to the craft show.

_____

3. That's right; we lost someone after we arrived.

_____

4. The booths had a maze of walls where we were looking.

_____

5. Our parents forgot to meet us for lunch, running to see everything.

_____

6. Those of us who met for lunch ate hot dogs after looking and calling for them.

_____

7. After taking a boat ride across the lake, too late, our parents remembered the missed lunch.

_____

8. They ate stale chips and a pickle standing up.

_____

9. Sitting together on the fountain, we found them feeding some ducks.

_____

10. We suggested a new plan for our next trip, which will be flawless.

_____

11. Tuning us out, our parents formed their own plans for a no-kids-allowed date.

_____

12. Yelling loud approval, our fists pumped up and down, while insisting that we should have a kids-only party with our friends at the same time.

_____

13. Our plans have been left dangling; our hopes have been misplaced: we're stuck with family time.

_____

> To demonstrate skill in sentence formation, you must use end punctuation appropriately, correct any sentence fragments or run-ons, correctly identify and punctuate phrases and clauses, and avoid misplaced and dangling modifiers.

PUBLISHING

After you revise and proofread, your composition needs to be published. No, that does not mean your composition will go in a book. Publishing means that you will have a printed-out copy of your composition. Sometimes on tests, you'll handwrite your composition. For other class assignments, you can use a word processing program to publish your work.

CHAPTER 6 SUMMARY

The final step in the reading process is **proofreading**. In this step, you do a final check of your essay and correct any errors in the following:

- Capitalization
- Punctuation
- Spelling
- Missing words
- Grammar and usage
- Sentence formation
- Modifier placement

Make the corrections on your essay cleanly using **proofreading notations**.

CHAPTER 6 REVIEW: PROOFREADING THE ESSAY

A. Read the essay first for content. Then, read with an eye for internal punctuation, correct grammar usage, spelling, and sentence formation. When you find an error, use the proofreading marks from page 118. Neatly strike through the error, and clearly write the correct form above the error.

Odd Places to Get Married

Traditionaly churchs and chapels were the main places for young couples to get wed. In the past twenty years or so people have gone away from the traditional wedding's. To be married where you have meet is not that unusual or bizarre. Many couples have been getting more adventureous in their wedding locations; couples marry where they are happiest too. Weddings need to be meaningful to the people involved. Four popular places where they get married are underwater, on the beach, on a airplane, and sometimes in their schools.

Getting married underwater means that a scuba-diver lisence needs to be obtained for the bride and groom. Second, a good scuba-diving location needs to be found, for example, Key West and the red sea and the Barrier reef is considered the best diving in the world. Third, a pastor or priest with scuba diving experience need to be found. Those could be a difficult search. Underwater weddings cost the mostest money because of the extra variables.

Getting married on the beach is a odd, but romantic place to take wedding vows Standing in the sand with the waves roaring, and the sun setting can be romantic. Except for the danger of a jellyfish or stingray alert. Starting the honeymoon after a sting from one of these sea cretures could be unpleasant even with a romantic full moon and the smell of suntan oil. One advantage of beach weddings is that the wedding and honeymoon can be in the same city. The Virgin Islands, Cayman Islands, and Jamaica are good examples of places people pick for their beach weddings.

An airplane is a odd place for people too get married. Airplane weddings are small due to space. Some people like to parachute out of the plane after taking their wedding vows. Airplane weddings can be very expensive and difficult to plan. Because of having to rent a plane and the skydiving equipment and having to have good whether. There would also need to be a seperate place for the the reception or party afterwards. The things that must be considered are food (airplane food?), flowers (thrown to the winds?), and which hospital is closest (in case the wedding is no longer the main event cus of injury).

This last example of an odd wedding makes a school wedding seem quite common. To be married where you have met is very romantic and sweet. If two people can learn to love each other they also need to learn how to live together what better place symbolizes that intention than a school. Even if space may be cramped in the hallway, there is always a gym or cafeteria for lying out food and presents. Also most of the guests would be old friends and very familiar with the location; so fewer maps needed to be printed. All these people could help decorate with posters and streamers, and help mix the party punch. This is a win-win situation. The school is appreciated for it's community service, the new couple has a cheap but happy memory.

Getting married should be fun and a unforgettable memory. Underwater weddings and airplane weddings are more costly than beach and school weddings. People for some time have been looking for odd; yet meaningful places to get married. The most popular odd places to take wedding vows have been underwater on the beach or airplanes, and the old schoolhouse.

B. For the review in chapter 5: Revising the Essay, you revised several different essays that you wrote for the chapter 4 review. Return to those essays now. Proofread them based on the skills that you have practiced in this chapter. You may want to use the checklist below to help you.

- [ ] I checked for errors in capitalization.
- [ ] I corrected errors in internal punctuation including, commas, colons, semicolons, apostrophes, and quotation marks.
- [ ] I corrected any errors in grammar and usage, including nouns, pronouns, adjectives, adverbs, negative words, verbs, and subject-verb agreement.
- [ ] I made sure all words are spelled correctly.
- [ ] I looked for errors in sentence formation, including end punctuation, fragments, run-ons, and misplaced modifiers.
- [ ] I made my corrections neatly and clearly.

C. In chapter 5, practice 7: Revising (page 110), you revised several different essays. Based on what you have reviewed about proofreading, return to these essays and correct any errors you find. Use the checklist above to help you.

ADDITIONAL ACTIVITIES: PROOFREADING THE ESSAY

1. Make a list of your most common errors. Practice the skills you need to overcome these errors.

2. Select three of your essays from your portfolio. Practice proofreading these essays. Based on what you reviewed in this chapter, correct any errors.

3. Choose one essay from your portfolio, and exchange it with another student. Proofread each other's essay. Explain the errors you find in each other's essay. Then make the corrections, and rewrite your essays.

4. After you make your corrections and rewrite your essay, give it to your instructor to look for any errors you may have missed. Make special note of the errors you overlooked, so you don't overlook them on an essay you will be graded on.

5. Read several articles in your local newspaper. Look for proofreading errors that the newspaper editors may have missed. Even professional writers make mistakes!

6. With one other student, choose two Web sites from the list in Appendix B. You and your partner will each visit one of the Web sites. Try to find instruction and activities that will help you with proofreading. Report back to your partner, and compare the strengths and weaknesses of each Web site.

Basics Made Easy

Chapter 7
Persuasive Writing

This chapter covers the following McREL standard and benchmarks for Level III:	
Standard 1: Uses the general skills and strategies of the writing process	Benchmarks **5** and **10**

In **persuasive writing**, you try to convince readers to agree with your point of view. You can write a letter to persuade an employer to hire you. You can also send an e-mail to convince someone to go to the prom with you. Or, you may write a letter to the editor of a newspaper to express your opinion on a current issue.

In this chapter, you'll review more features of persuasive writing. These features are listed below.

- Purpose and Audience
- Using Persuasive Language
- Building an Argument
- Ethical Arguments
- Appealing to Emotion

PURPOSE AND AUDIENCE

Being aware of purpose and audience is particularly important with persuasive writing.

PURPOSE

With persuasive writing, your **purpose** is fairly clear: you want to convince readers to agree with you. However, the amount of convincing you need to do may depend on your topic. For example, convincing your dad to lend you one hundred dollars will be more difficult than convincing him to lend you ten dollars.

Copyright © American Book Company. DO NOT DUPLICATE. 1-888-264-5877.

151

AUDIENCE

Knowing your audience is especially helpful in persuasive writing. Then, you know what points of agreement or disagreement you may have with your readers. You also know which reasons your readers may accept and which reasons they may not. Your audience could be friends, parents, teachers, local citizens, or an employer to name a few. Before you write, carefully consider who your audience is and what you know about your audience.

Practice 1: Purpose and Audience

In the following practice exercise, decide on the audience and purpose for each topic. Keep in mind that you are trying to persuade your audience to agree with you. Then, compare your choices with those of other students.

1. Topic: Recycling   Audience: _____

Purpose: _____

2. Topic: Entertainer of the Year   Audience: _____

Purpose: _____

3. Topic: Safety Features on Cars   Audience: _____

Purpose: _____

4. Topic: Making Friends on the Internet   Audience: _____

Purpose: _____

5. Topic: Raising Money for the Homeless Audience: _____

Purpose: _____

USING PERSUASIVE LANGUAGE

When you are trying to persuade, you need to present information in a way that makes readers agree with your position. You must emphasize points of interest to the readers and describe them in appropriate language. For example, let's say you worked in a hardware store last year, and you are applying for a new job. When the manager asks what you did at your last job, you could answer with either of the explanations below.

Example 1: I worked for a while doing odd jobs.

Example 2: I mopped floors in the hardware store and then I took orders at the counter. After proving my abilities at these tasks, I was promoted to sales associate. I am very detail-oriented.

Both explanations provide the same truthful information. However, the second makes you sound like a responsible and hard-working employee, while the first isn't very impressive. If you want to impress a potential employer and convince the manager to hire you, the second explanation is a better choice.

Special Note: Paying attention to your audience does not mean telling people what you think they want to hear or giving false information. Make up your own mind, stay firm, and tell the truth. However, you want your audience to be able to understand and appreciate what you are saying. So, use language that will persuade your particular audience.

> Use words, phrases, and reasons that your audience will understand and appreciate.

Tips for Using Persuasive Language

1. **Use vivid description.** Notice how the writer in Example 2 uses phrases like "mopped floors" and "took orders at the counter." Persuasive language should include strong descriptive details. In Example 1, the phrase "I worked for a while" is vague and too general to convey a clear message.

2. **Use concrete language.** In Example 2, the phrase "promoted to sales associate" contains concrete and specific words. In Example 1, the phrase "odd jobs" does not provide a concrete picture of the work this person has done.

3. **Use figurative language when appropriate.** Figurative language does for words what spice does for food. It livens up your argument.

Practice 2: Persuasive Language

For each of the following situations, write two or three sentences that will influence or persuade the intended reader. The example provided is NOT persuasive.

1. Convince your mother to let your friend sleep over.

   Example 1: Mom, my friend wants to spend the night here.

2. Motivate your team to win.

   Example 1: It's halftime, and we're down by five points. We can win.

3. You took care of your sick brother last night, so you couldn't finish your homework. Persuade your teacher to give you an extension.

   Example 1: Is it OK if I turn in my homework tomorrow?

4. While mowing your neighbors' lawn, you ran over their flower bed. Convince them to give you another chance.

> **Example 1:** I think your flowers will grow back before I mow the lawn next time.

Practice 3: More Persuasive Language

A. Look through newspapers and magazines. Find three examples of persuasive language, and determine the authors' purposes. Then, find three examples in which the language is not persuasive, and rewrite them to persuade the reader to one side of the issue.

Hint: Advertisements and newspaper editorials often contain persuasive language.

B. Imagine that you are the salesperson at an electronics store. Write four to six sentences to persuade the man behind the desk that a laptop computer will make his work easier and more productive.

C. Imagine that you are running for president of your class. Write four to six sentences that would persuade your classmates to vote for you.

BUILDING AN ARGUMENT

Your ability to persuade depends not just on HOW you say something, but also on WHAT you have to say. You must be able to build a strong **argument**. In everyday speaking, an argument is a disagreement between family members, friends, or enemies who exchange heated words. However, in the context of persuasive writing, an argument is a carefully reasoned way of presenting a point of view. The three steps to building an argument are to **make a claim**, **support the claim**, and to **answer objections**. This process may be compared to building a pyramid.

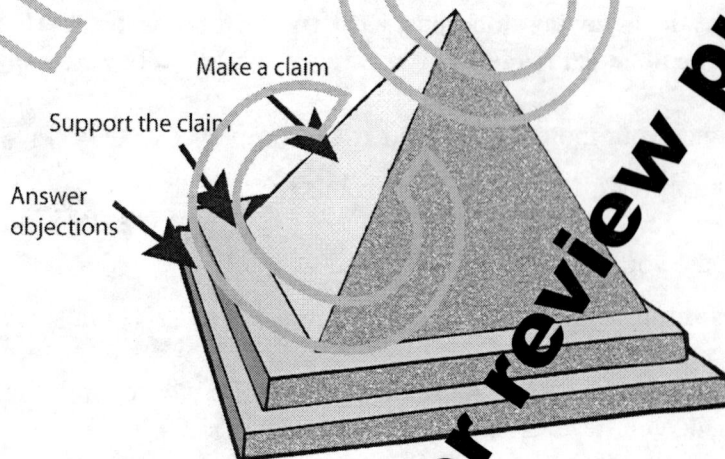

Make a claim

Support the claim

Answer objections

MAKE A CLAIM

The first step in building a good argument is to **make a claim**. A **claim** is the position you take on a particular issue. It can't be just a statement of fact. A **fact** stands alone and can be proved. A claim, however, argues for one side of a controversy. Someone may disagree with your claim, so you must support it, just like the pyramid builder needs to support the top of the pyramid.

The claim is the point you are trying to make, so keep it focused, like the pointed top of a pyramid.

Read the following six statements, and decide which claims provide a good starting point for an argument.

1. According to a 1999 Harris poll for the National Consumers League, a majority of Americans believe that water is our second-most-threatened resource, after air.

    – Sarah Milstein

2. Through personal choice, economic reform, and improved schools, we, the citizens of this great democracy, must stop the irreversible destruction of our most precious resources: air, water, and children.

3. We ought to be increasing programs that help the hungry children in our country rather than giving more money to an already well-financed program like the military.

4. Though the Cold War is over, the unpredictable nature of our present national threats demands that we maintain a strong military through increased funding.

5. The best, indeed the only, method of promoting individual and public health is to teach people the laws of nature and thus teach them how to preserve their health.

    – Dr. Herbert Shelton

6. Over the past three decades, there has been increasing public interest in personal self-help books, including the maintenance of health through self-regulated programs of exercise and diet.

Statements 1 and 6 present information in a factual, non-persuasive way. The information presented could be used to support a claim, but neither statement encourages one belief over another. Statements 2, 3, 4, and 5 urge the reader to take a certain action or have a certain belief. In other words, they make a claim. These statements use words like *must*, *should*, *ought*, *demand*, *only*, and *best*. These key words often indicate that the author is taking a position and encouraging the reader to do the same. You may also notice that the persuasive statements sometimes use the subject *we* in an attempt to involve the reader in the position or idea.

Statement 2 requires a special note. It makes a claim that requires support, but the claim is not focused. Air, water, and children are, indeed, precious resources. However, protecting the environment and improving schools are two topics that would be better addressed by two separate arguments. Try to pick ONE side of ONE issue, and take a stand. Make sure your pyramid has a focused point.

Practice 4: Making A Claim

For each topic, write a statement of fact and a claim statement. Make it clear that they are different types of statements. The first one is done for you.

1. Topic: foreign language instruction

Fact: <u>People disagree about whether it is vital for students to learn a foreign language in school.</u>

Claim: <u>Schools should encourage learning another language because it improves overall academics and prepares students for the real world.</u>

2. Topic: limiting the number of cars on the roads

Fact: _____

Claim: _____

3. Topic: mix of negative and positive news in the media

Fact: _____

Claim: _____

4. Topic: our increasing need for computers

Fact: _____

Claim: _____

5. Topic: wealthy nations assisting poor nations

Fact: _____

Claim: _____

SUPPORT THE CLAIM

The entire structure of a pyramid comes to a focused point at the top. Each block of the pyramid supports this point. In a similar way, you want each and every sentence of your argument to support your claim. You also want to support your argument with solid blocks so it will stand. A **strong argument** is supported by good logic, solid evidence, and appropriate reasons or examples. A **weak argument** suffers from poor logic, weak evidence, and **fallacies** (faulty reasons or examples). Like a pyramid, a strong argument will stand the test of time.

Read the following two passages about weight loss, and decide whether the arguments are strong or weak.

Rapidly Burn Off Pounds and Inches
with SUPER DIET PILL!

You can lose 10, 20, 50, even 60 pounds!

This is it! This is the diet pill researchers around the world have hailed for its powerful, quick-working ingredients that help people shed stubborn fat—fast!

This super diet pill satisfies the need for fast action without strenuous dieting.

So fast-working, you can see a dramatic difference in just two days, without complicated calorie-counting or suffering from biting hunger pains. Even people with long-time weight problems find they can burn off up to a pound of fat and fluid every five hours.

Fifty percent fat loss in 14 to 21 days.

The longer you use the super diet pill, the more weight you lose. You don't have to stop until you reach the weight that *you* want. Without making major sacrifices or drastic changes, you can shed as much as 50 percent of your fat in just two or three weeks.

Increased Metabolism Means Weight Loss

One-half of the women and one-fourth of the men in the United States are trying to lose weight and become fit. The sad truth is that most of us will regain our original weight in a year or less. What's the real secret for losing weight and keeping it off?

The answer is developing and maintaining a healthy metabolism. Metabolism refers to how the body burns energy. A person with a high metabolism burns more calories than a person with a low metabolism. Consequently, the person who burns more calories has an easier time losing weight. Here are some tips for improving your metabolism and melting away that extra fat:

1. **Drink plenty of water.** Filling up on water decreases the appetite.

2. **Don't skip meals, especially breakfast.** Eat small meals every two to three hours. In this way, carbohydrates and protein will not be converted to fat.

3. **Eat fat-burning foods.** Raw vegetables, whole grains, fruits, and legumes are your best choices. Consume fruits between meals for extra energy. This healthy snack won't be converted to fat.

4. **Exercise regularly.** Aerobic exercises like swimming, running, and walking are best. Also try lifting weights—a good muscle builder and fat burner. Exercise before you eat. It will decrease your appetite and increase your metabolism.

Each passage strongly suggests a way to lose weight and provides reasons to support its method of weight reduction. Which one is based on valid reasons, and which one is based on fallacies?

There are two big clues that the diet pill advertisement is based on **fallacies**:

- 1) It sounds too good to be true.
- 2) It doesn't offern any proof.

Examination of the evidence shows that the diet pill ad offers very limited information about the diet pill. Little proof is presented to support its dramatic claims. The ad never mentions the names of the diet pill researchers, the people who lost weight, nor where or when the testing was done.

The description of metabolism, however, bases its argument on biological principles that are common knowledge to most people who have taken a biology class. From this basis, it provides logical explanations of how to increase your body's metabolism. The author is not selling anything and is not offering an easy "quick fix." A decision to follow the suggestions for changes in diet would be based on much better information than a choice to try the diet pill.

Tips to Build a Strong Argument

1. **Show cause-effect connections** between your position and the reasons you use to support it. Use clear logic and valid facts. Avoid fallacies, and use commonly known, easily proven facts.

2. **Illustrate your point of view with a personal story.** Although each person's experience is different, your reader can understand or empathize with events from your life that illustrate your point of view.

3. **Contrast your choice or position with another.** One way to show the strength of your choice is to show the weakness of another choice.

Practice 5: Analyzing an Argument

Read the following argument for CFLs (compact fluorescent lamps). What is the claim? Is the argument strong or weak? Cite examples from the passage to support your viewpoint.

Light Up Your Life!

The best improvement to our house this year has been the addition of compact fluorescent lamps (CFLs). This, no doubt, sounds like an incredibly boring change. However, if you consider the environmental and economic impact of these little gadgets, it can be quite "enlightening." For example, nearly 99 percent of the energy used by a regular incandescent bulb is turned into heat. I don't know about you, but I don't think light bulbs are a very efficient way to heat a house. I want light bulbs to give off light. That's what fluorescent lamps use 90 percent of their energy to do.

Another great thing about compact fluorescent lamps is that you hardly ever have to change them. Unlike traditional light bulbs that may only last a few months, CFLs last from five to seven years. Yes, that's years, not months! Of course, these long-lasting bulbs are more expensive to buy than the old bulbs. However, when you add up the money that you save in using less electricity, a CFL pays for itself three times over the course of five years. So as you can see, a simple change in your life can have a big impact.

_____

_____

_____

_____

_____

_____

ANSWER OBJECTIONS

Knowing your audience not only helps you choose an appropriate language and tone, but it also helps you anticipate objections to your position that your audience may have. Answering these possible objections is like building a wall around your pyramid to protect it from anyone who may want to tear it down.

Let's say that you wanted to go out dancing on Saturday night until 1:00 a.m. Your parents want you home by eleven. You would have to answer their objection to staying out until 1:00 a.m. Since your audience is your parents, you would have to decide how you could convince them to let you dance longer. Think of three ways you would respond to their objection. Would you use impassioned pleas, logical reasoning, or an objective third person's opinion? What type of language and tone works best with your audience? This is a good question to ask yourself before you begin any persuasive writing.

Read the following passage about conservation. Decide which objections the author is trying to answer.

One Person Can Help Save the Earth

Pollution threatens animals and human health. Energy supplies are dwindling. Nature is being jeopardized every day. Sometimes it seems that the problems we dump on our earth are overwhelming. How can one person do anything to turn the tide?

The fact is that each of us can have impact. The simple things that every person can do really help. Dozens of Web sites offer hundreds of simple ways to improve the environment—just Google them. Walk, bicycle, or take public transportation when you can. When you do have to drive, group your errands to conserve fuel and limit pollution. Carry reusable bags with you to use for those shopping trips. Next time your home needs a new appliance, choose one that is truly efficient. Turn off the lights when you leave a room. Switch to compact fluorescent light bulbs (CFLs).

Do you doubt that these small changes make a difference? They do, and they can also save you time and money. As an example, the US Environment Protection Agency reports that in 2007 Americans saved about $1.5 billion by replacing old light bulbs with CFLs. This switch saves so much energy that it could light a city the size of Washington, DC, for thirty years! It reduces the same amount of greenhouse gases as planting 2.85 million trees or taking 2 million cars off the road. Now that's impact, and it all comes from something that is very simple to do. If every person begins to do his or her part, we can improve the environment more than we think.

The author of this passage wants to convince people that one person can make a difference in the effort to improve the environment. In doing so, the author addresses these common reasons people use to disagree that one person can make a difference:

- The problems are overwhelming, so individuals can't do anything about them.
- Changes that one person could make are too complicated.
- It is difficult to find out what an individual can do.
- Small changes made by individuals really do not have great impact.
- It costs too much for the individual to make changes that help the environment.

> The three steps to building an argument are to make a claim, to support the claim, and to answer objections.

Practice 6: Answering Objections

Return to practice 4: Making a Claim. For each topic you chose, list three possible objections to your claim.

Example: Foreign language classes take time away from core studies like math and science.

1.

_____

2.

_____

3.

_____

Practice 7: Writing Persuasive Paragraphs

Write a persuasive paragraph for each of the topics you have been working with in practices 4 and 6. Here's an example:

> Parents should not rely on record companies to decide what music their children should or should not buy. Each parent has different standards for what kind of music is appropriate for his or her children. Some people say that parental advisory labels will weed out the really rude music. However, couldn't this also lull parents into a false sense of security, tempting them to rely only on the record companies? When parents listen to what their children are hearing, they can then discuss the music with their children. If parents don't think they have time for this, then they should reexamine their priorities. Parents have the responsibility to raise their own children. They can't let record companies do it.

ETHICAL ARGUMENTS

Ethical arguments deal with issues regarding what is right or wrong. Some people consider ethical positions to be matters of opinion rather than true arguments. However, in the last section, you read an example of an ethical argument for CFLs. The author supported the argument with statistics, authoritative information, and common sense. It was more than a matter of opinion that CFLs save energy.

It is true that an ethical argument is based on certain **assumptions** (ideas, facts, or principles that the author believes are true). However, every argument is based on certain assumptions. Every argument makes a claim, and a claim is a position that the author believes is right. It must be explained and supported with evidence. It is not a self-evident truth or fact. Therefore, you can use the same skills you practiced in the last section to build a strong ethical argument.

Read the following two arguments regarding abortion, and write down what you think are the assumptions of the authors. Then, compare your responses with the answers that follow each argument.

Abortion is Child Abuse

> The cruelty of abortion must be stopped. America has many laws against child abuse. In fact, state governments have the legal power to take children away from their parents if a social worker shows that they are being mistreated. Yet, in this same country, the same governments have passed laws that allow parents to kill their children before they are born. The law does not protect children from abuse in their first home: the mother's womb.
>
> There is terrible inconsistency in how our laws treat children before and after they leave the womb. What if a mother, father, or doctor smothered a child the day after he or she was born? The adults involved would be arrested, sent to jail and perhaps face execution.

161

What about before the child is born? Then, it's called abortion and everything is legal. Please write to your representatives and demand that they pass laws to protect innocent children.

Author's Claim

_____

Author's Assumptions

_____

Protect Women's Rights

The United States government has an obligation to protect a woman's right to make choices about her own body. What could be a deeper violation of democratic ideals than for the government to control a woman's reproductive decisions? In no fair and just area of law is there a question about a person's right to make decisions about his or her own body. Lack of control over one's own body is a throwback to the days of slavery.

Today, medical procedures are decided between the patient and the doctor. The government has no place in these decisions. This is true of decisions for men, and it should be the same for women. Our country claims to provide "liberty and justice for all." Women have as much of a right to liberty and justice as men. The Supreme Court has ruled that women have the right to make their own reproductive choices. Please make sure that your representatives know that you want to keep it that way.

Author's Claim

_____

Author's Assumptions

_____

You may have written that the author of "Abortion is Child Abuse" approves of government interference in the lives of its citizens, while the author of "Protect Women's Rights" opposes government interference. This is what appears to be the difference on the surface. However, there is an assumption that lies under these two opposing views. The first author assumes that a developing human fetus is a child even before it is born. The author of the second passage assumes that the developing fetus is part of the woman's body. These two authors will continue to talk past each other until they address their underlying assumptions, which are basic to both of their arguments.

Practice 8: Ethical Arguments

Take a position on two ethical problems. Write a paragraph in which you defend your opinion. Then, list your underlying assumptions. The topics below are suggestions.

animal experimentation   cheating on tests in school

euthanasia   genetically modified food

sending economic aid to devastated countries   sex before marriage

---

SAMPLE TOPIC AND ASSUMPTIONS

End Animal Torture

Even though medical experimentation on animals may sometimes produce health benefits for humans, it also brings into question our own humanity. The word *humane* means to be concerned about the welfare of other humans, but doesn't this also extend to animals?

Build strong ethical arguments in the same way you would other arguments.

APPEALING TO EMOTIONS

The arguments discussed so far have appealed to readers' logical reasoning and their ethics. However, **appealing to the emotions** of your readers can be a powerful force for persuasion.

When you buy new sports shoes, do your parents point out that some generic brands are half the cost of a brand name and that they are just as good? They are appealing to your rational side, which is concerned with quality and price. However, when you go to school, your friends may laugh at a generic brand of shoes while a name brand may impress them. Your friends will appeal to your emotions, which are concerned with whether you are "cool" or not. Advertising often appeals to emotion more than to logical reasons, as in the following phrases:

- Mega-white toothpaste will give you that knock-out smile.
- Twinkling facial cream gets rid of unsightly wrinkles and makes you look young all over again.
- US Motor Company's new Safari sports vehicle gives you the excitement you deserve.
- The new Super Wave speakers from Totalsound let you enjoy theater-like sound without leaving the comfort of your own home.

These advertising claims boast of higher quality, a better value, or an unconditional guarantee. They simply claim that their product will make you feel better. Appeals to emotion may not be based on good reasons, but they can be very convincing.

Emotions are very strong, and, at times they are stronger than reason. So an appeal to emotion may win out over an appeal to reason. For example, Adolf Hitler stirred up Germans' feelings of fear and insecurity during the 1930s. He used these strong emotions to convince his audience that Jewish people and other minorities should be killed. This is one example of how emotions can be a powerful persuasive force.

Adolf Hitler

There are many times, however, when an appeal to emotion is practical, effective, and innocent. Consider the following example.

> Sophomores, get ready to show your school spirit at Friday's pep rally. Our school is preparing for the biggest sports event of the year: the homecoming game. In past years, sophomores have not played much of a role, but this year is different. This year, the team's star player is a sophomore! That's right. Without us, the team would not be in contention for the district championship. Let's show the other classes that we deserve respect. Bring your voices, bring your whistles and noise-makers, and make sure you wear the school colors. So, when it's time to show your school spirit, scream as if your life depended on it.

The author of this passage is appealing to the pride of the sophomore class. The author gives an example of why the sophomores should be proud and encourages them to gain even greater respect in the school by showing great school spirit during the pep rally.

Practice 9:   Emotional or Rational Arguments

Write "E" next to the claims that appeal to emotion and "R" next to the claims that appeal to reason.

1. _____ The school policy clearly states that students may carry only clear plastic or mesh backpacks.

2. _____ The backpack rule is a stupid and useless invasion of our privacy.

3. _____ Standardized tests are a valuable tool to assess student progress in learning.

4. _____ After your first time riding the cyclone, the thrill will keep you coming back again and again.

5. _____ Don't get left behind; stay in touch; sign up for a Communicom cell phone today!

6. _____ The Computech 6500 is rated the fastest, most reliable computer by the three leading computer magazines.

CHAPTER 7 SUMMARY

In **persuasive writing**, you try to convince readers to agree with your point of view. To do this well, you need to address these areas.

- Be aware of **purpose** and **audience**.
- Use appropriate **persuasive language**.
- **Build an argument** by **making a claim**, **supporting the claim**, and **answering objections**. Consider whether your topic can use an **ethical argument**, and learn to **appeal to emotions** as a **rational argument**

CHAPTER 7 REVIEW: PERSUASIVE WRITING

Read the following two reports. Then answer the questions below using complete sentences.

Report 1

The county government meeting broke up after a long debate. Bill Smith's supporters claim that he is the duly elected representative of the people and should be allowed to take his seat on the council. His opponents disputed this, saying that his previous protests of council activities disqualify him from holding public office.

Report 2

We elected Bill Smith, and he's our man. His enemies are just jealous. They think they can throw some mud around and make it stick to Bill. No way! He's squeaky clean. There ain't nothin' they can do to make him look bad. He stood up for us before, makin' sure the council listened to us. Now those jokers say that's a bad thing. Stick by Bill. He stuck by us!

1. What is the author's purpose in each report?

2. Compare and contrast the persuasive language of these two reports. Which report appeals more to emotion? Explain your answer.

Read the following excerpt, and complete the writing exercise that follows.

From *Shams* by John S. Draper

I stand as firm as the rock of Gibraltar on the right that women have to shape the thoughts, socially and politically, of the world. They can make our country better and purer, just as they appreciate their own rights. I am in favor of women's rights—in their rights to rise up in the majesty of the nature their Creator gave them and emancipate themselves from the foolish fashions and sentiments of the age. When they do rise, they will be more respected by all mankind than all the rulers of the earth from Adam down to the present day.

3. Write one paragraph in which you evaluate the language and tone of this excerpt. What are some strengths of the author's choices in language and tone, and what are some weaknesses? How do these affect the persuasiveness of the writing?

Read the following excerpt, and complete the writing exercise.

There is still a great deal of controversy about the future of the space program. While some people believe it is a waste of much-needed funds, others point to the great scientific and technological advances that have resulted from the exploration of space. Supporters of the program cite the wide uses of microprocessors as one of the major contributions to space-related research. Opponents believe the billions of dollars dedicated to the space program would be better spent on the needs of education, health care, and job training for the disadvantaged.

4. Pick one side of the controversy described in this passage about the space program, and write a paragraph to persuade other students of your point of view. Share your paragraph with your classmates. Ask for feedback that would strengthen your argument, and incorporate it into your paragraph. Then, write a letter to the President of the United States expressing your opinion. Show the letter to your teacher. Then, mail the letter to President (Full Name), The White House, 1600 Pennsylvania Avenue, Washington, DC, 20500.

Read the following two letters that nominate Mr. Jimenez for Teacher of the Year. Then, complete the writing exercise that follows.

Dear Fellow Students,

I am nominating Mr. Jimenez for Teacher of the Year, and you should too. Whether you've been in this school for one or four years, you know he's got a reputation for being tough. But, he's also known for spending hours after school with kids who need help. (And most of us need help to pass his class.)

You also know how much work he put into the school fair last fall. What a blast that was! Remember how shocked we all were to find out HE was the clown?! This is only one way he has shown his love for this school and its students.

Think of how great it would be to hear the announcement that the Teacher of the Year is from Eastside. People across the state would see what a great school we are. So, when the nominating paper comes around, sign it, and show Mr. Jimenez your support.

Thanks,

Bill Johnson

Bill Johnson

Dear Members of the School Board,

I am writing to nominate Mr. Victor P. Jimenez for Teacher of the Year. As the chair of the Biology Department at Eastside High School, he has challenged his students with a rigorous curriculum and demanding standards of excellence. At the same time, he has shown true devotion as an educator by helping students meet those standards through after school tutoring.

Mr. Jimenez is not only dedicated to academic excellence but also to the development of the school community. Just one example of this is the after school hours he spent in organizing our school's fall fair. During this successful event, Mr. Jimenez showed his sense of humor and surprised us all by dressing up like a clown.

The Teacher of the Year award will honor not only Mr. Jimenez and Eastside High School, but it will also honor the State School Board by showing the high educational standards set by this state. Mr. Jimenez provides an example of academic rigor coupled with school spirit that has been an inspiration to our school. He well deserves the title of Teacher of the Year.

Sincerely,

William H. Johnson

William H. Johnson

5. The same student wrote the above letters about the same topic for the same purpose. However, each letter is addressed to a different audience. Write a paragraph which describes how these two letters differ because of audience. Be sure to discuss language and tone as well as how the letters appeal to emotion and reasoning.

Read the following two letters about trash pick-up, and answer the questions that follow.

To the Editor:

This is America! Some people want to decide for me who's going to take my trash away. They say there are too many trash trucks in this neighborhood. Well, my son owns a trash company that services this neighborhood, and he says there is only a few other companies that he competes with, and he should know.

Each resident in this city has the right and the responsibility to choose the trash company that he or she wants. Whichever company provides the best service for the needs of its customers should get the most business. Only in a communist state could it be legal for groups of citizens to band together and limit free choices of consumers and businesses alike. Where would the limitation end? Maybe the different churches shouldn't have their services on the same day because it causes too many cars to drive through the neighborhood.

I wholeheartedly oppose any attempt by the neighborhood association to regulate which company can pick up my family's trash and on what day they can do it. I've been living in this neighborhood for forty-five years, and I've never heard of such a ridiculous idea. And, if the neighborhood association tries to pull off such an unfounded scheme, they will find themselves in court!

Your Fellow Citizen,

Joan Zemsy

Joan Zemsy

To the Editor:

Lately, our neighborhood has seemed like a cross between Grand Central Station and the city dump. In the process of gathering information to present to the neighborhood association, I sat by my window and counted the number of garbage trucks that passed in one week: eleven! Is that an incredible number? I surveyed twenty residents in our neighborhood and found that, in fact, they contract with twelve different trash companies.

I am certainly in support of free enterprise; I believe that freedom of commerce is one of the things that make America great. However, I also believe in peace and quiet, proper sanitation, and the safety of my children.

I guess I'm lucky that only eleven trucks pass by my house instead of the twelve that could possibly rumble past my door, shaking my windows and rattling my teeth. A trash truck is a huge vehicle that makes a lot of noise when the massive hydraulic compactor goes into action. Once per week this inconvenience may be tolerable, but not two or three times per day.

These trucks also spit out a lot of foul smells and black smoke into the neighborhood. And what about the safety of our children? Should they have to dodge piles of garbage that line our sidewalks every day of the week? And when they ride their bikes to a friend's house, should they fear that from around each corner could come a thundering garbage truck?

Simple common sense demands that all residents of our neighborhood band together to hire one trash company to come once per week to take away our trash.

Sincerely,

James Waterford

James Waterford

6. How do the language and appeals differ in the two letters? What are the ethical assumptions behind each argument?

7. Which letter is more persuasive? Why? Explain your answer.

ADDITIONAL ACTIVITIES: PERSUASIVE WRITING

1. In Practice 7 of this chapter, you wrote three different paragraphs on three different topics. Now, write three more paragraphs on the same topics, but each for a different audience. You will want to vary your language and tone, answer different possible objections, and use different support. Return to practices 4, 6, 7, and 8 to help you develop your paragraphs.

The paragraph below is an example of writing to other students about Parental Advisory labels. Compare this paragraph with the one on page 161.

> Record companies should not place Parental Advisory labels on music. The record industry wants us to believe it's helping unknowing consumers. As young consumers, we know what is on an album before we buy it. We hear songs on the radio, talk to friends, watch MTV, and decide what music we want to purchase. If a song has controversial lyrics we know it, and we know what our parents will not allow. All the music industry is doing is creating controversy and hype over bad music. Some people say the labels help parents. Well, all parents are different, and they need to listen to the music themselves. Parental Advisory lables create more sales because of publicity. However, they are not much help to parents and should be removed.

2. Develop three persuasive letters on the same topic but for three different audiences, such as high school students, teachers, your principal, parents, members of the local school board, readers of the local newspaper, or the programming director of a television station. Here are some possible topics with which you can agree or disagree.

   raising the driving age to eighteen   voting on the Internet
   using cell phones while driving   no-homework policy for high school students
   banning offensive bumper stickers   strict airport security
   praying in school   prejudice against non-English speakers

3. Make a list of three or four movies you have seen recently. Choose one of them, and write a composition in which you persuade your readers why they should or should not see the movie.

4. A new student is attending the first day of class in your school. In an essay of four to five paragraphs, advise him or her on how to enjoy and succeed in your school.

5. Several girls in your high school want to play on the football team. In an essay of four to five paragraphs, convince the coach, the principal, or the school board why these girls should or should not play on the football team.

6. While you were washing your hands in the rest room of the locker room, you saw your best friend sneak into the locker room and steal money from the pants pockets of students who were out in gym class. In a four to five paragraph essay, persuade your friend to confess the crime and accept the consequences.

Basics Made Easy

Chapter 8
Expository Writing

This chapter covers the following McREL standard and benchmark for Level III:	
Standard 1: Uses the general skills and strategies of the writing process	Benchmark **5**

The purpose of **expository writing** is to explain a topic. Essays of this type can include such topics as "Learning on the Internet," "How to Sink a Free Throw Every Time," "Why Skateboarding is Popular," and "What to Look for in a Good Movie." From these examples, you can see that expository writing provides information. It helps us learn more about the world around us.

The word *expository* is related to the word *expose* which means "to show" and the word *explain* which means "to make clear." In expository writing, you can explain how something works or why something happened. You may want to present general information by answering questions like *who, what, when, where, why,* and *how* about a subject. These key questions are sometimes called the **five Ws and H.** Pointing out similarities and differences between two subjects or ideas is also expository.

You can find expository writing in newspapers, magazines, and on the Internet. Cookbooks, instructional manuals, and schoolbooks include expository writing. Menus, food labels, prescriptions for medicines, billboards, and museum brochures contain expository writing too.

You will need to learn how to write various types of expository essays. You may also be asked to write expository essays as part of your activities in middle or high school English classes.

In this chapter, you will learn and practice writing the following types of expository essays. They are listed below:

• Basic Expository Essay	• Cause-Effect Essay
• Process Essay	• Comparison/Contrast Essay

BASIC EXPOSITORY ESSAY

In chapter 3 of this book, you read about the basic structure of an essay. This structure consists of three main parts: an introduction, a body, and a conclusion. A **basic expository essay** also contains these three parts. Its purpose is to inform or to explain a particular topic.

Let's say that a student named Emmi has a writing assignment. She must write an essay about a particular animal. Since she is being asked to explain or inform her audience about this animal, she is writing a basic expository essay.

Based on chapter 3, the first step for writing her essay would be to **brainstorm** about the topic. Emmi's brainstorming list looks like this:

Animals I Could Write About	
dog	*squirrel*
cat	*parrot*
hamster	*lizard*
rabbit	*monkey*

The second step for her essay is to choose the animal that she will discuss. Emmi chose her dog, a purebred Labrador retriever. Once she chose to write about her dog, Emmi moved to step three, developing the thesis or controlling statement for her essay. Here is what she wrote for her thesis:

> The Labrador retriever is an interesting breed of dog. Learning about this dog can help anyone who wants a Lab for a pet.

EMMI'S OUTLINE

Creating a rough outline, Emmi used the **five Ws and H** to develop the body of her basic expository essay. Here is what she wrote for the outline:

The Labrador Retriever	
Who?	Labrador retriever, a type of dog
What?	Size, weight, colors, personality, life span
When?	Feeding times, play time
Where?	Origins
Why?	Benefits of owning a Lab
How?	Treating diseases, puppy care

EMMI'S ROUGH DRAFT

Now that Emmi has decided on a specific topic, a thesis, and a rough outline, she is ready to write a rough draft of her basic expository essay. As she writes, she will incorporate information from her own experiences with her pet Lab. Read her draft for content, organization, and English language conventions:

The Labrador Retriever

There are many kinds of dogs. Some are big. Some small. They come in many colors too. The Labrador retriever I know best because I own one. The Labrador retriever is an interesting breed of dog. Learning about this dog can help anyone who wants a Lab for a pet. My veternarian, Dorothy Howe, says these dogs came from Newfoundland in Canada. The Labrador retriever stands about two feet tall. It weighs sixty pounds sometimes seventy-five. Puppies weigh less of course. Howe says a dog should match your personality. So observe a dog before picking one out. So both of you get along. You can also expect Labs to live eight to twelve years or longer. depending on keeping up with shots and illnesses.

Care of the Labrador retriever involves regualr feeding. Usually two cups of food each day with plenty of fresh water. A high qwuality dog food should be bought. Snacks are ok, but not too many. Labs will overeat if allowed. So don't overfeed them. labs also love to play fetch. So keep a frisbee or rubber bone handy. A Lab are also a very strong. They'll pull *you, train it to walk with you and not chase other dogs.*

I also know that these dogs can get diseases like dihrea, blindess, worms, especially heartworm, distemper, and hip disease so they need regulr checkups. A Lab can also get skin infecsin. So be careful. Puppies can die quick if its too cold. So keep it warm. Pups are nice too because they play a lot. He knows you right from birth.

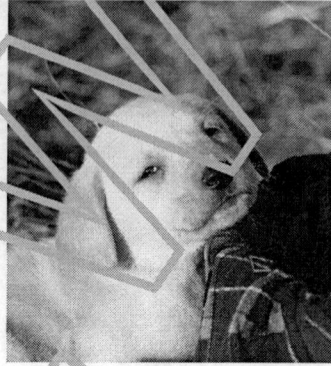

Lab retrievers are an animal that eevery one likes. They're playful, loyal, and good hunting dogs too. I look into my dog's eyes and see smart and loving eyes. That's what I know about Labs.

Practice 1: Evaluating a Draft of a Basic Expository Essay

Read Emmi's rough draft on the Labrador retriever. Then, answer the following questions.

1. What makes Emmi's essay expository? Cite examples from her rough draft.

2. On your own or in a group, evaluate the content and organization of Emmi's essay on the Labrador retriever. List the strengths of this essay. Suggest ways that Emmi could improve the content and organization of her essay.

3. Review Emmi's essay for sentence variety. Does she vary the types of sentences she uses in her essay? Or are the sentences similar? Would you change her sentences? How?

4. Read Emmi's essay for correct use of English language conventions. What changes would you make in grammar, spelling, and punctuation?

Emmi's Revision

After feedback from other students and her teacher, Emmi wrote the following revision of her basic expository essay on the Labrador retriever:

The Labrador Retriever

Dogs come in many sizes, shapes, and colors. Some dogs are large while others are small. I own a Labrador retriever, which is an interesting breed of dog. Learning about this dog can help anyone who wants a Lab for a pet.

My veterinarian, Dorothy Howe, says Labrador retrievers originally came from Canada. These dogs stand about two feet tall and weigh between sixty and seventy-five pounds. They come in either black, yellow, or chocolate, and they are sometimes used for bird hunting. Howe says the personality of a Lab should match that of the dog's owner, so, before choosing a Lab, a person should oserve its personality and behavior. Labrador retrievers can live eight to twelve years or longer depending on their health.

Care of the Labrador retriever involves regular feeding, usually two cups of food each day with plenty of fresh water. Dog experts recommend a high quality dog food with a few nutritious snacks now and then. Labs should never be allowed to overeat. Labrador retrievers love to play fetch, so always keep a frisbee or rubber bone handy. Labs are also very strong dogs who will drag you along on their leash unless they are trained to walk with you. They also must learn not to chase other dogs or cars.

I learned that Labrador retrievers can get diarrhea, worms, especially heartworm, and distemper. They also can become blind, get hip disease, or a skin infection. They need checkups and shots on a regular basis. As puppies, Labs can die quickly if they become too cold. Both puppies and adult Labs are fun-loving, affectionate, and protective of their owners.

Most people enjoy Labrador retrievers. They're playful, loyal, and good hunting dogs too. When I look into my Lab's eyes, I see a smart and lovable dog. That's what makes him interesting to me.

Practice 2: Evaluating a Revision of a Basic Expository Essay

Reread Emmi's revision of her expository essay on the Labrador retriever. Then, answer the following questions.

1. Compare Emmi's revision of her essay with her rough draft. What improvements did she make in her revision?

2. Based on your answers to practice 1, did Emmi make changes in content, sentences, and English language conventions? Explain.

> When writing a basic expository essay, you can use the five Ws and H to guide you in explaining a particular topic.

Practice 3: Writing Basic Expository Essays

To build your writing proficiency, write two or three basic expository essays. Organize each essay into four to five paragraphs. Use Emmi's revised essay on the Labrador retriever as a model. Follow the writing steps of choosing your topic, brainstorming, developing your thesis, creating a rough outline, writing a rough draft, making corrections, and revising your essay. Decide on your own topics, or select some of the following topics:

an animal	a sport
an athlete	an entertainer
a book	a movie
a restaurant	a car
a hobby	a store
a place	a fad
a food	a planet

If you wish, use the following questions based on the five Ws and H as a guide for writing your basic expository essay.

What is the title of your essay?
State your thesis
What will you explain about your topic?
When or where did you learn about your topic?
Why are you writing about this particular topic?
How will you explain your topic?
Express your concluding statement.

After you complete each essay, share it with your teacher or with other students for feedback. Then, revise each essay as needed.

Copyright © American Book Company. DO NOT DUPLICATE. 1-888-264-5877.

PROCESS ESSAY

Have you ever followed a recipe while preparing a meal or a dessert? Or perhaps you have taken lessons to learn the steps for a new dance. You may even have taught someone else a game or how to administer first aid. For each of these activities, you followed a process, a step-by-step procedure. These steps also occur in a time sequence.

The purpose of a **process essay** is to explain how to do something or how to make something. A process essay can also include an explanation of how something works, such as how the heart pumps blood through the body or how a tiny computer chip processes many bits of information.

Like the basic expository essay, a process essay consists of an introduction, body, and conclusion. It includes a thesis in the introduction and two to three body paragraphs. Sentence variety is also important.

In addition, a process essay contains the following key features:

- focused step-by-step instruction
- a clear and logical sequence
- frequent transitional words that lead the reader from one step to the next step

Now, let's begin by looking at a simple paragraph example that explains how to cut grocery bills.

You can follow several easy steps to cut the cost of groceries. First, purchase generic or store brands of groceries instead of the popular brands advertised on television. Cereal, peanut butter, and canned vegetables with store brand labels are usually of the same quality as widely advertised national brands. Next, clip money-saving coupons from newspapers and magazines to save on your grocery bill. Thirdly, buy groceries in bulk sizes to cut per-item expenses. Furthermore, shop for fresh fruits and vegetables when they are in season to reduce your grocery bill. Finally, bring a shopping list with you to the supermarket, and stick to it. In this way, you will avoid buying something on impulse, which can raise your grocery bill.

Notice how, even in this simple example, this student presents each step clearly and logically. The topic sentence, the first sentence of the paragraph, alerts the reader that steps for cutting the grocery bill will be the focus of the paragraph. In addition, the student uses several **transitional words** to guide the reader easily from one step in the process to the next step. Words like *first*, *next*, *third*, *furthermore*, and *finally* help the reader see the progression of steps.

In chapter 4 of this book, you saw how transitional words help the reader understand the relationship between the writer's ideas. Here are some transitional words that you can use to explain a process:

first, second, third, etc.	next	also
in addition	then	furthermore
finally	later	after that

> Explaining a process involves clear steps in a logical sequence with transitional words for each step.

Practice 4:   Analyzing a Process

Complete the following activities to improve your understanding of the process essay.

Introduce the topic that matches the sentences below. Then, put these steps in a logical sequence with transitional words.

Do the same for the other slice using jelly.

Open the jar of peanut butter.

Put two slices of bread on a plate.

Take a bite, and enjoy.

Put the slices together so the peanut butter and jelly are completely touching.

With a knife, spread the peanut butter on one side of one slice of bread.

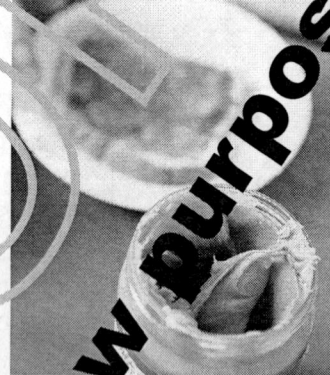

2. In the following exercise, practice writing steps in a process. Use the suggested topics shown below, or choose your own topics. Keep your explanations to one paragraph for each topic.

how to wash your hands properly   how to program a VCR to record

how to make a milkshake or a smoothie   how to play a game

how to wash a car   how a hair dryer works

how to fly a kite   how to do a dance (choose one)

how to catch a fish   how to choose the right skateboard

how to get an autograph of a musician   how to live a healthier lifestyle

3. Read the process essay below on shooting free throws. Then, answer the questions that follow on your own paper.

How to Sink a Free Throw

The sure fire way to sink a free throw every time is to practice, practice, practice. A basketball free throw is just what it sounds like: an opportunity to toss the ball through the hoop while you are free from other players trying to guard you. You just stand at the free throw line (fifteen feet from the basket), with no other players defending you, and take a shot. It should be easy, but many players miss because they don't practice the essential elements of free-throw shooting. The first thing to do is to relax. When you practice your shot, set your feet shoulder-width apart, with your shooting foot slightly forward of the other foot. In other words, if you shoot with your right hand, put your right foot slightly forward. Then, you should look at the hoop to let your eyes register the distance. This lets your brain know where you want the ball to go.

After you bounce the ball a few times to relax your shooting muscles, hold the ball gently but with confidence. Make sure your shooting hand is directly under the ball and your elbow is pointing down at your knee. Then, look again at the hoop, take a deep relaxing breath, bend your knees, and take your shot. After you release the ball, remember to follow through with your fingers pointing toward the hoop, and watch the ball swish through the net.

Finally, repeat these steps, establish a routine that works for you, and practice it regularly. Stand in the same place on the free throw line. Bounce the ball the same number of times. Take your breath at the same time. Keep your routine the same. this way, every time you

179

step up to the free throw line, you don't have to think. Your body goes on automatic pilot, and you sink the free throw every time!

A. What is the topic for the paragraph above?

B. List all the steps. Then, put them in order by writing the numbers next to each step.

C. Write any key terms that the author uses and explains.

D. What transitional words does the author use?

Practice 5: Writing Process Essays

For practice, write two or three process essays. Organize each essay into four to five paragraphs. For a model, use the essay "How to Sink a Free Throw Every Time." Choose your topic, brainstorm, develop a thesis, create a rough outline, write a rough draft, make corrections, and then revise each essay. Decide on your own topics, or choose some of the following topics.

how parents and teenagers can communicate better	how to care for a pet
how to solve school conflicts based on race or culture	how to prevent tardiness
how to celebrate a birthday	how to pack for a rafting trip
how teachers and students can communicate better	how to waste time
how to make someone laugh	how to reduce stress
how to conduct a lab experiment in science class	how to fix a flat tire

If you wish, use the following guide for developing your process essay. Combine one or more steps into paragraphs as needed.

Title of Essay	Next Step/Third Step/Fourth Step, etc.
Thesis	Final Step
First Step	Concluding Statement
Second Step	

After you finish each process essay, seek feedback from your teacher or from other students. Revise it as needed.

CAUSE-EFFECT ESSAYS

Using **cause and effect** is another way to explain a topic. Both cause and effect involve ways of showing relationships between one event or idea and another event or idea. Let's say that one morning you notice that a classmate is extremely cheerful, singing and telling jokes on the way to school. You are curious about this unusual behavior. You wonder why this person is acting so cheerfully. As a result of this experience, you soon find that you are feeling happy too. Later that morning, you learn that your classmate entered a contest and won a free computer. In this example, you can see how cause and effect work. You were curious about why your classmate was acting so cheerfully. You were trying to determine the cause of her happiness. Later, you found out the cause—winning a free computer. The effect or result of this good news was that you felt happy too.

> **The cause is the reason for an event, and the effect is the result of the event.**

The purpose for writing a cause-effect essay is to explain relationships between issues, ideas, or events. These cause-effect relationships impact us, our friends, our community, and our world. For example, forgetting to put out the trash on time (cause) can affect you and others. The importance of graduating from high school requires that you understand the reasons and advantages (causes) of completing high school and the negative results (effects) of dropping out of high school. To reduce drug addiction, researchers must study the causes and effects of this health problem. To stop terrorism, countries must investigate why terrorism occurs (causes) and its impact (effects) on humanity.

PROBLEM-SOLUTION

In fact, **problem-solution** is closely related to cause-effect relationships. You need to determine the cause of the problem and identify its effects in order to suggest an effective solution. Business leaders use this format when writing proposals to offer solutions to problems. Editorials frequently identify a problem and suggest a solution.

Problem: The company is not making a profit

Cause: Company officials are spending more than they are making.

Solution: 1. Increase the cost of the product **or** 2. Cut expenses.

181

BRAINSTORMING CAUSES AND EFFECTS

In the following diagram, notice how one cause can lead to an effect which itself becomes the cause for another effect, and so on. This is caused a cause-effect chain.

cause	→	effect (cause)	→	effect (cause)	→	effect

Now, study the cause-effect chain that Kurt created to show the causes and effects of his not putting out the trash on time. Notice how the main event (forgetting to put out the trash) has both causes and effects. As you read Kurt's chain, think of other reasons (causes) and results (effects) of his actions.

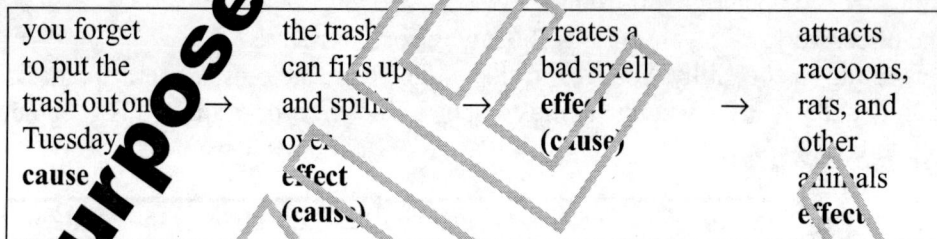

you forget to put the trash out on Tuesday, **cause**	→	the trash can fills up and spills over **effect (cause)**	→	creates a bad smell **effect (cause)**	→	attracts raccoons, rats, and other animals **effect**

Practice 8: Brainstorming Causes and Effects

A. Using Kurt's cause-effect chain as a model, brainstorm about causes and effects for three or more of the topics below. Or choose some of your own topics. Next, discuss your diagrams with a partner or with a group of other students. See if they can add any more causes or effects to your diagram. Then, share your findings with the class or your teacher.

exercise	dirty laundry
surfing	poverty
earthquakes	volunteering
overspending	stress
family harmony	family conflict
new hairstyles	tattoos
messy room	good grades
success	gossip

B. The essay describes four general causes for one specific effect. Write these on the lines below the essay.

Why Are Some People Late?

There are many different reasons why people are late getting to places. The first thing that makes people late is incorrectly estimating how long it takes to do something. For example, if you think it will only take you fifteen minutes to ride your bike to school, and it really takes you thirty minutes, then you will be late to school. Another thing that prevents people from being on time is getting distracted from the task at hand. If you stop to talk to someone while you are riding your bike to school, you may lose track of time and end up being late for school. Getting distracted happens much more easily if you don't have a watch on. Not having a watch or a clock nearby prevents people from knowing what time it is and can lead to tardiness.

The last thing that can make people late is something called "unforeseen circumstances." An example of an unforeseen circumstance is a flat tire. If you get a flat tire on your way to school, you probably won't have a repair kit with you, which means you will have to walk to school. Walking takes a lot longer than riding a bike, so guess what? You're going to be late.

As you can see, even if you do everything right to be on time, including planning enough time for travel, not getting distracted, and keeping an eye on your watch, your plans for being on time can still be undermined by the dreaded unforeseen circumstances. Even if you make every attempt to be on time, there are events that you just can't plan on. Everyone is late once in a while, so estimate time correctly, don't get distracted, and keep an eye on the clock. With this plan, your chances for being on time will improve.

Effect _____

Cause _____

Cause _____

Cause _____

Cause _____

Practice 7: Writing Cause-Effect Essays

For practice, write two or three cause-effect essays. Each essay can focus on causes or on effects. Organize each essay into four to five paragraphs.

For a model essay that presents causes, review the essay "Why Are Some People Late?" For a model essay that explains effects, read the essay on the next page entitled "Consequences of Pursuing a Rich Lifestyle." Use the topics you developed in practice 6, or create some new ones of interest to you.

Brainstorm, develop a thesis, create a rough outline, write a rough draft, make corrections, and then revise each essay. Whenever possible, use key words to signal the purpose of your discussion. If you wish, use the following outlines as a guide for writing your cause or your effect essay.

Essay About Causes	Essay About Effects
Title	Title
Thesis	Thesis
First Cause	First Effect
Second Cause	Second Effect
Third Cause	Third Effect
Concluding Statement	Concluding Statement

After you complete each cause or effect essay, seek feedback from your teacher or from other students. Revise each essay as needed.

SAMPLE EFFECTS ESSAY

Consequences of Pursuing a Rich Lifestyle

A majority of people in the world dream of being rich, but only a few of them will realize their dream. The reason why most people struggle financially is because they want to look rich, even if they are not. This behavior can be very dangerous, indeed, people are willing to do anything to achieve their goal. However, there are consequences to pursuing a rich lifestyle.

One of the most common consequences of pursuing a rich lifestyle is the financial struggle. I remember one of my father's friends who used to change his car every three months. Even though he didn't have enough money to finance this kind of expense, he continued doing so until he ended up selling his house to pay off the debts he had. Even after that, he got so used to spending incredible amounts of money that he couldn't handle the fact that he had no money left.

The second possible consequence of pursuing a rich lifestyle is related to stealing. I had a friend in Morocco whose parents "lived well," were not rich, but had enough money to send their son to a good school and enough extra to go on holiday to Paris every summer. My friend used to come with us to a nightclub every Saturday. He was used to stealing money from his parents just to feel rich and buy us some dinners. Even today, he still steals money from his father to go out on Saturday nights. That is, in my opinion, the worse thing that a child can do to his parent. And once again, he did that only because he wanted to feel rich.

The last consequence of pursuing a rich lifestyle is that some people lose their personality. Indeed, they are so possessed by money that they will do anything just to have some of it. A friend of mine told me one day about a guy who used to study in France. This guy used to work every day and every night at two different places, so that he could save some money in order to go to clubs when he returned home and to buy fancy clothes that cost more than a hundred dollars. These kinds of people are not themselves anymore because they don't live to impress themselves. They live to impress people; they live to prove to other people that they can afford some "stupid" expenses like the ones I talked about.

People react differently to different situations and behaviors, but pursuing a rich lifestyle can affect people in a negative way. The main problem still is that these people don't have a strong personality to affirm themselves as they are. They try to act rich, and the consequences are that they hurt themselves and others.

A COMPARISON/CONTRAST ESSAY

The words *comparison/contrast* sound complicated, but you compare and contrast things more often than you think. For example, when stopping for fast food, you may compare taste, quantity, or price before deciding on which menu item you will buy. Comparing style, comfort, and mileage can help you select one car over another car. You probably choose the friends you hang out with based on how similar all of you are in the hobbies you share, the music you enjoy, or the places you like to go.

The purpose of a **comparison/contrast** essay is to explain the similarities and differences between two things or ideas. Therefore, it is another type of expository essay because you are trying to inform or explain a topic to your audience. You are presenting a new view of things, people, or ideas by **comparing** (showing how they are alike) and **contrasting** (showing how they are different) from each other. This type of expository writing can also provide more understanding or new insights about a topic.

While you can just compare or contrast two things, it is more common to link the two together in an essay. In addition, when you compare or contrast two things, they must have something in common. A cat and a bowl of spaghetti share little in common other than that the cat might decide to eat the spaghetti when you aren't looking. However, a cat and a rabbit do share some common characteristics. They are both animals, they have fur, and they are kept as pets. Therefore, finding something in common (compare) or not in common (contrast) is an important starting point for comparing and or contrasting two persons, things, or ideas.

> When you compare and contrast, you show similarities and differences between two persons, things, places, or ideas.

BRAINSTORMING TO COMPARE AND CONTRAST

Let's say that your assignment is to compare and contrast cats and rabbits. A good way to begin would be to try **brainstorming** about your topic. One way to brainstorm would be to create three columns. In the first column, you would list what cats and rabbits share in common. In the second column, you would list what is different about cats, and in the third column, you would list what is different about rabbits. Here is an example:

Cats and Rabbits		
Share in Common	Cats Only	Rabbits Only
animals	cat family	rodent family
fur	coarse fur	soft fur
ears	short, pointed ears	long, narrow ears
eyes	small, narrow eyes	large, round eyes
tail	long, narrow tail	round, stubby tail
movement	running, leaping	crawling, hopping
eating	eats cat food	eats plants
kept for pets	family pets	pets and food
hunt for food	climb trees	can't climb trees

Another way to brainstorm about cats and rabbits would be to use a **Venn diagram**. A Venn diagram can help you organize ideas that are similar and different. You simply draw two ovals that overlap. In each oval, you list the details that are different for each subject you are comparing. Where the ovals overlap, include the details that both subjects share in common. To understand this type of brainstorming, study the following Venn diagram that again compares and contrasts cats and rabbits:

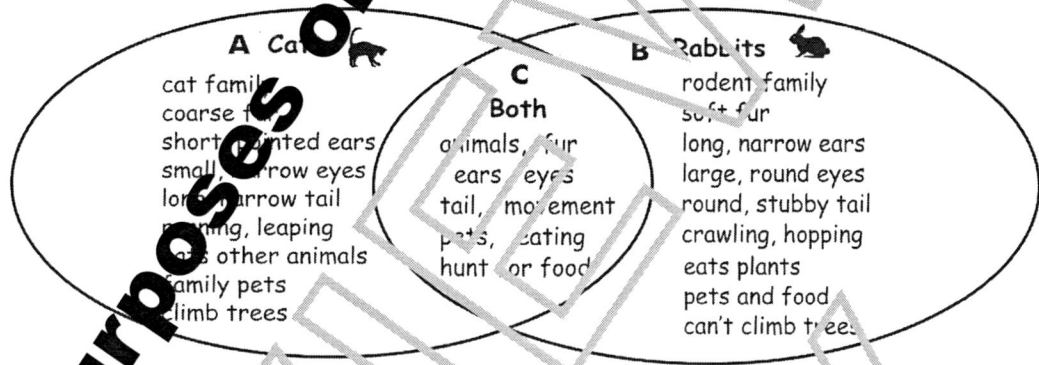

A Cats
cat family
coarse fur
short, pointed ears
small, narrow eyes
long, narrow tail
running, leaping
eats other animals
family pets
climb trees

C Both
animals, fur
ears, eyes
tail, movement
pets, eating
hunt for food

B Rabbits
rodent family
soft fur
long, narrow ears
large, round eyes
round, stubby tail
crawling, hopping
eats plants
pets and food
can't climb trees

You can also create an **H-map** to brainstorm about the similarities and differences about two topics. An H-map is a simple diagram shaped like the letter H. In the bridge of the H, you list the similarities. In each column of the H, you list the differences. Make sure you label each column with the key concept you are comparing and contrasting.

Below is a completed H-map. It shows the similarities and differences between skateboarding and ice climbing.

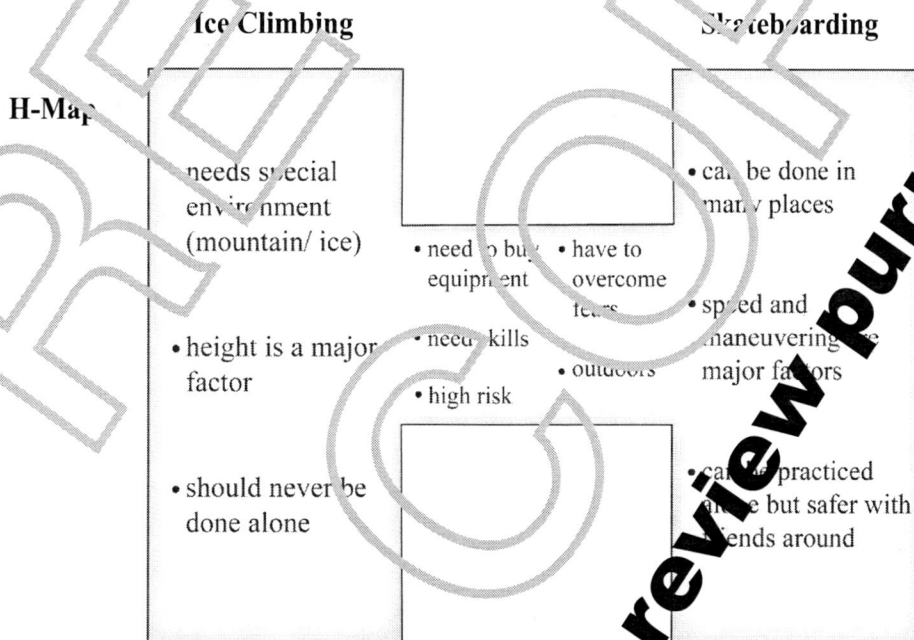

Ice Climbing

Skateboarding

H-Map

needs special
environment
(mountain/ ice)

• height is a major
factor

• should never be
done alone

• need to buy
equipment

• need skills

• outdoors

• have to
overcome
fears

• high risk

• can be done in
many places

• speed and
maneuvering are
major factors

• can be practiced
alone but safer with
friends around

187

Practice 8: Brainstorming Compare and Contrast

Brainstorm about similarities and differences for three or more of the following topics, or think of some of your own topics. Brainstorm about these topics using any or all of the following approaches: three columns, Venn diagram, or H-map. Share your brainstorming with a partner or group. See if they can add any similarities or differences to your topics. Then, share your work with the class or with your teacher.

a city and a small town	an apple and an orange
an apartment and a house	a car and a motorcycle
you and a cousin	you and a friend
a car and an airplane	football and soccer
a shake and an ice cream cone	a book and a movie
two types of cars	two theme parks
two holidays	two summer jobs
two types of music	two schools
two movies	two entertainers

WRITING A FINAL DRAFT

To better understand what a comparison/contrast essay is, read the following sample essay in which the author explains how he and his brother are both similar and different:

Two Family Members

My brother Thomas and I are very similar but very different in many ways. Thomas and I grew up together in the same household and shared the same bedroom. Eventually, Thomas got a bedroom of his own after my older brother moved out. But, through the years, he and I have grown very close and have begun sharing goals and hobbies. Also, Thomas and I have developed our own personalities and habits.

I feel Thomas and I are very similar. For example, Thomas and I really enjoy playing sports; both of us played high school football and basketball. He and I have spent many evenings playing basketball together at the gym. In off-seasons, Thomas and I have spent a lot of time working out in the weight room. He and I also like staying up late at night and looking at car magazines, and we often talk about having fast cars. On the weekend, we enjoy going to the mall and purchasing nice clothes. Also we both enjoy spending time with our dog. For example, we both like to take the dog for walks or wash him. Every Sunday, Thomas and I go to church. We both feel church is very important. I feel the biggest goal in our life is to succeed in school, and we both work very hard in school.

I feel Thomas and I also have some differences. First of all, Thomas is just starting high school, and I am a junior. I have better communication skills than Thomas. For example, Thomas is quiet around people, and I like to talk to people. Thomas is going to be the richest man in the world. He saves more money than any man I know. However, I can not save money. I spend more money than I make. Also, I would have to say that Thomas is a pig. His room is messy while I could not have a messy room. My room has to be clean. Thomas's personality is different from my personality because he is laid back, and I am very active and outgoing.

Since Thomas and I grew up sharing a room, he and I have grown very close. I feel we have more similarities than differences. For example, he and I will always work hard and enjoy sports. I will never forget all the good times spent with my brother.

Notice how the author establishes a clear introduction and a thesis: "…he and I have grown very close and have begun sharing common goals and hobbies. Also, Thomas and I have developed our own personalities and habits." From this thesis, we learn that the author is going to compare their common "goals and hobbies" and contrast their personalities.

In the second paragraph, the author writes about Thomas and his own common interests in sports, cars, clothes, the dog, church, and school. In the third paragraph, the author writes about the differences between him and Thomas in their personality and habits. Thomas is shy while the author is outgoing. The author also keeps a neat, clean room while Thomas's room is messy.

In the final paragraph, the author restates his thesis while expressing that he and his brother are more alike than they are different. In addition, the author has revised and edited his essay, paying attention to correct use of English language conventions in grammar, punctuation, and spelling. He also includes a variety of sentences in his essay.

USE OF TRANSITIONAL WORDS

In "Two Family Members," you should be aware of the **transitional words** used. These transitional words are often used to compare and contrast ideas. They help to signal the similarities and differences between the author and his brother. These words also help the audience read the essay more easily.

How many transitional words did you find in this essay? When you write a comparison/contrast essay, learn to use some of the following transitional words:

Comparison	Contrast
similar	different
and	but
both	while
alike	unlike
in the same way	however
in addition	in contrast
the same	instead of
also	whereas

Practice 9: Understanding a Comparison/Contrast Essay

For practice in understanding comparison/contrast essays, read the essay entitled "My Sister and Me." Then on your own paper, answer the questions that follow.

My Sister and Me

My parents' friends think that it is strange that two children can come from the same parents and be so different. We had the same family, shared the same hobbies, and even shared the same room. When we were little, we looked identical, but as we grow older we don't even look the same. Our personalities are like summer and winter. Even though we are different, we are still sisters and love each other no matter what we look like or how we think.

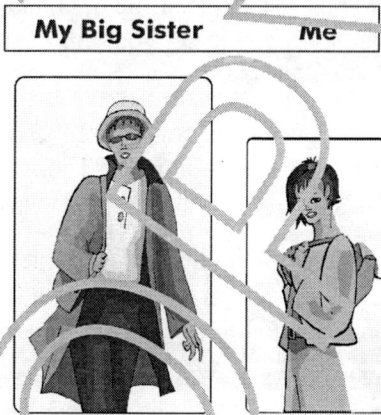

My sister is five years older than I am. She has always been my big sister. We both have dark hair and brown eyes, but she is almost six feet tall and I am barely 5'5". She stands a whole head and a half taller than I do. That never made much difference except that she could reach things on the top shelf for me. Since she was older, she usually got to do things before I was allowed. She went to high school before I did, but that was nice since she told me what to expect. She got to take horseback riding lessons before I could. That made me jealous, but my time came.

Even more than our physical features, our personalities are different. I was always good in school, while my sister was always good with horses. I would bring home straight A's on my report card from school, unlike my sister who would bring home championship ribbons from horse shows. I am outgoing and social whereas my sister is an introvert. She would much rather spend time with the horses instead of being with another person.

Even though my sister and I are very different, we are from the same family. Rather than be jealous of each other, we try to share our strengths. She is tall, so she helps me get things I can't reach. I am good in school, so I help her write her papers. She is good with horses, so she gives me riding lessons. Math comes naturally to me, so I help her figure out how much she can save in a store sales event. I guess what's most important is that we will always be there for each other.

1. What is the thesis of this essay? Is the author's focus on comparing or contrasting herself and her sister?

2. List three or four examples of comparison or contrast in this essay.

3. Does the concluding paragraph summarize the key points of the essay?

4. List four transitional words that the author uses to connect her ideas together.

5. Has the author paid attention to English language conventions (grammar, punctuation, spelling) and sentence variety? Cite examples.

6. Rate this essay on a scale of 1 to 6, with six being the highest and one being the lowest. Use the material in this chapter to develop reasons for the rating you chose to give the essay.

Practice 10:   Writing Comparison/Contrast Essays

For practice, write two or three comparison and/or contrast essays. Each essay can focus on similarities, differences, or both. For models, review the essays "Two Family Members" and "My Sister and Me." Use the topics you brainstormed about in Practice 8, or you may also create new topics to write about.

Brainstorm, develop a thesis, create a rough outline, write a rough draft, make corrections, and then revise each essay. Use some transitional words to connect your ideas.

After you complete each comparison/contrast essay, seek feedback from your teacher or from fellow students. Revise each essay as needed.

CHAPTER 8 SUMMARY

Expository writing explains something. Different types of expository essays include the following:

- Basic expository essay
- Process essay
- Cause-effect essay (including problem-solution essay)
- Comparison-contrast essay

There are specific ways to plan and organize each essay. Each type also uses different types of **transitional words** to signal the organization.

Good **brainstorming** tools include **Venn diagrams** and **H-maps**.

CHAPTER 8 REVIEW: EXPOSITORY WRITING

To improve your understanding of expository writing, complete the following activities.

1. Find three or four examples of expository essays in newspapers, magazines, textbooks, or on the Internet. Try to find essays that are 400–1000 words. Decide whether each of these essays is primarily a basic expository essay, a process essay, a cause-effect essay, or a comparison/contrast essay. Form a group and make copies of these essays for each member of the group. The group will exchange these essays among its members, and each will respond to the following questions.

   A. Which essay did you enjoy the most? Why?

   B. Which essay did you enjoy the least? Why?

   C. How would you classify each expository essay? Is it a basic expository essay, a process essay, a cause-effect essay, or a comparison-contrast essay? Offer three or four examples from the essay to support your answer.

   D. Evaluate each essay by responding to the following questions:
   - Is the thesis clear and concise?

   - Does the author support the thesis well? Cite three or four examples or reasons from the body paragraphs of the essay.

   - What transitional words does the author use to connect the ideas? List three or four examples.

   - Is the essay organized around an introduction, body, and conclusion?

   - Point out examples of each of these parts in the essay.

   - Are there any pictures, charts, or diagrams in the essays? Do they help or hinder the understanding of key ideas and facts? Explain.

   - Is the diction (use of words) vivid, concrete, and clear?

- Does the author include a variety of sentence lengths to maintain interest in the essays?

- Who is the primary audience for the essay? Is there evidence in the essay to support your answer?

- Does the author use the English language conventions such as correct grammar, punctuation, and spelling? What might account for any errors you find?

If possible, ask your teacher to model this assignment for you with a sample essay before you begin this assignment in your groups.

2. Write a process essay that gives directions to a particular place. Include specific turns, landmarks, and a map for a visual aid. Share your essay with the class, with a small group, or with your teacher. If the place is within walking distance, have members of your group follow your directions to see if they can find the place.

3. Lorri wrote a cause-effect essay for her English class. Her topic was the following: If you could change some things in your life, what would they be? Why would you change them?
Read and evaluate this essay. Rate the essay on a scale of one to six, with one being the lowest rating and six being the highest. Use the material in this chapter to develop reasons for the rating that you choose.
If corrections are needed, revise the essay. Then, share the revision with your teacher or with the class.

Oh, Grow Up!

I wish I were older so that I could drive and have money for things I want. But since I can't change time, I'll have to figure out how to get the government to change the driving age and the working age.

I want to change the driving age so that I can go places. I live far away from any kind of civilization. Any time I want to go to the mall with my friends, I have to ask my older brother or my parents. My parents are always busy working on something. My brother doesn't want to be seen anywhere with his little sister. He says it would kill his social life. If I could drive myself, I wouldn't have to bother any of them when I wanted to go somewhere. I could go where I want and do what I want. I could even get a job to buy a car and pay for the gas.

If the working age were changed, then I could work to earn money for the things I want. I could buy my own clothes and wouldn't have to wear the things my mom buys for me. I could even buy some things for my family. My dad needs a new briefcase. My mom could use a new cell phone. My brother could use a new attitude, but I can't buy that. He'll have to settle for new headphones.

If I were to try to change the ages for driving and working, I would start a campaign. First, I would talk to my friends and tell them my ideas. Then, I would ask them to tell their friends and have their friends tell their friends. Finally, I would get everyone to write letters to their local and state representatives to lower the driving and working ages because kids shouldn't have to wait.

4. Chad's assignment was to write a comparison/contrast essay about himself and another member of his family. He decided to write about himself and his father. Read and evaluate Chad's essay. Rate the essay on a scale of one to six, with one being the lowest rating and six being the highest. Use the material in this chapter to develop reasons for the rating that you choose.

If any changes are needed, make them. Then share your results with the class or with your teacher.

Like Father, Like Son

My father and I are very close. He has always been the one to teach me the importance of life, and what it has to offer. My dad knows a great deal about life, and for that reason he is the best teacher a son could ever have. My father and I are much alike, but our most comparable attributes are friendliness and honesty.

My father and I share many of the same characteristics, but the most notable one is that of being friendly. Dad has always been the one who starts a conversation. I have tried to followed in his footsteps, and often find myself making the first attempt to start a conversation with all those around me. Telling light jokes is a trait my father has mastered. I find myself coming to school and telling the same jokes, and being the same "class clown" that my father is. He has always taught me to treat everyone the same, this teaching has become a motto for me. I find myself helping those who are less fortunate. Helping others is a trait my father is famous for, and I hope I can carry on this tradition. Being friendly is a notable characteristic that my father and I both share, and so is that of being honest.

Being honest is a very important attribute in life, and it is one that my father and I both have. My father has spent many hours trying to teach our family about the importance of being honest. Ever since I was a small child my father has taught me to tell the truth. Telling the truth has now become a habit to me. My father would not lie to anyone. He is the most honest man I knew. His honesty has effected me greatly. I now find it hard not to tell the truth. I dislike very much when people lie to me, and I feel that this is a peeve that my father and I both share. I recall when I was a child I accidently broke a lamp. I lied to my father, and did not tell him the real reason why I had done it. He knew that I was lying, and took the opportunity to teach me. From that day on I knew not to tell lies. I am glad that my father has taught me to be honest. I know that being honest is a great attribute that my father and I both posses.

I try to be friendly and honest like my father. I know that by his example he has taught me a great deal. I hope that one day I can be even more like my father. I pray that one day I can be as good to my future children as he has been to our family.

Basics Made Easy

Chapter 9
Descriptive Writing

This chapter covers the following McREL standard and benchmark for Level III:	
Standard 1: Uses the general skills and strategies of the writing process	Benchmark **5**
Standard 2: Uses the stylistic and rhetorical aspects of writing	Benchmark **1**

Descriptive writing is important to use when you are writing a narrative (telling a story) or writing a description. It is one way for you to share your own experience or knowledge with your audience. The goal of descriptive writing is to put readers in your shoes for a while. Through the words you write on the page, you want the readers to see what you see, hear what you hear, and experience every detail of the person, place, or thing you are describing. In this way, you keep the readers interested in the story you're telling.

The word *description* often refers to how something or someone looks. However, we observe not just with our eyes, but with all five of our senses: **sight**, **sound**, **touch**, **smell**, and **taste**. When you describe a person, place, thing, or event, try to use words that will appeal to several of the reader's five senses. Do not limit yourself (or the reader) to sight words only. For example, if you write about a walk in the woods, you might describe the following:

what you see: the sunlight streaming through the lush foliage above, and any furry woodland creatures that scamper across your path

what you hear: the chorus of high-pitched bird calls

what you smell: the freshness of early summer growth mixed with the stale odor of decaying leaves

what you feel: twigs snapping under your feet and a cool breeze tickling the back of your neck

what you taste: the juicy, tart berry you picked from a bush and popped into your mouth.

By including words that relate to several of the five senses, you will give the reader a full sensory experience. In this chapter you will develop your descriptive writing skills by using the following tools:

• sight words	• taste words
• smell words	• touch words
• sound words	

SIGHT WORDS

Sight is perhaps our most precious sense, and we rely on it more heavily than the other senses. Therefore, you should make your descriptions appeal to the mind's eye. There is a saying that "a picture is worth a thousand words." This means that a picture can relate an image very quickly. However, it also implies that words can describe the picture just as well. With some practice, you will become a skilled "painter" with words. You can use sight words to describe size, shape, color, surface appearance, or action.

SIZE

You can describe size as *big* or *small*, but this won't tell readers much because these terms are relative, that is, they depend on the situation. For example, an amusement park may seem very big to a five-year-old, while a teenager might consider it small. Therefore, use specifics as much as you can, such as *a forty-foot tall spruce tree* or *a hummingbird that couldn't be more than two inches long.* Also, consider using some of the size words listed below.

Size Words				
broad	enlarged	spacious	bulky	enormous
hulking	gigantic	colossal	towering	soaring
unfathomable	bottomless	bloated	expanded	wide
extended	swollen	inflated	miniature	infinitesimal
petite	shallow	tiny	minute	shrunk
contracted	cramped	flat	compressed	condensed
abbreviated	deflated	shriveled	wizened	minuscule

SHAPE WORDS

Many **shapes** are familiar, such as *oval*, *triangular*, *circular*, or *rectangular*. You can describe unfamiliar shapes by using the names of familiar shapes. For example, to describe a pyramid with a trapezoidal base, you can write, "The huge structure was trapezoidal on the bottom, triangular on four sides, and came to a point at the top." You can also compare the shape of an unknown object to the shape of a known object, as in *pear-shaped*, *heart-shaped*, *kidney-shaped*, or *bell-shaped*. Also use the shape words listed below:

Shape Words				
symmetrical	unsymmetrical	crumpled	bowed	crooked
lopsided	twisted	slanted	deformed	straight
linear	vertical	horizontal	angular	bent
triangular	rectangular	square	arched	semicircular
curved	perpendicular	serpentine	diamond-shaped	

COLOR

Red, *orange*, *yellow*, *green*, *blue*, *indigo*, and *violet* are the basic **colors** of the rainbow. These colors, however, come in an almost infinite number of shades. Although a large box of crayons could give you names for hundreds of colors, these names are probably not familiar to readers. Instead of using a specific color name, you can combine two familiar color names. For example, instead of writing *rouge*, write *reddish orange*. You can also name colors by comparing them to familiar objects, such as *sky-blue* or *navy-blue*, *rust-red* or *fire-engine-red*, *forest-green* or *olive-green*, *canary-yellow* or *lemon-yellow*. Also consider the color words listed below:

Color Words					
bright	vivid	brilliant	rich	loud	screaming
glaring	flashy	blinding	gaudy	harsh	clashing
pale	washed-out	flat	faded	colorless	soft-colored
discolored	dim	weak	faint	pastel	pasty

SURFACE APPEARANCE

"Beauty is only skin deep," but one way to get below the surface of something is to describe its surface. Someone's or something's **surface appearance** can often tell you what's going on inside. *Clenched* teeth and a *sweaty* brow indicate a person's fear or anxiety, while *twinkling* eyes and *rosy* cheeks reveal a feeling of joy. If you describe the earth as *arid* and *parched*, the reader will know that it has not rained for some time. However, a description of *wet, muddy* soil gives the impression that the rain has only recently stopped, or it is still falling. Of course, *dry* and *soft* are sensations of touch that you can also learn through sight. Use the words below to help you describe surface appearance.

Surface Appearance Words					
wet	slick	rough	dry	parched	studded
covered	encrusted	veiled	wrapped	coated	enveloped
bumpy	smooth	moistened	rigid	sandy	rocky

ACTION

On your walk through the woods described in the beginning of this section, you may see small creatures move quickly or slowly. You can create a vivid picture by describing **action**. There are some animals that *scamper, scurry, scoot, dash, dart, sprint, leap,* or *bound,* and other creatures that *creep, crawl, plod, trudge, dawdle,* or *meander.* The words listed below are just a few examples of the different ways to describe simple activities like walking, talking, and eating.

Action Words					
Walk		**Talk**		**Eat**	
amble	stroll	speak	chatter	consume	ingest
saunter	strut	converse	state	gobble up	devour
shuffle	hobble	discuss	gossip	dine	forage
stride	stagger	declare	remark	gulp down	wolf down
pace	march	comment	recite	graze	chew
slide	swagger	gab	divulge	nibble	munch

Practice 1: Sight Words

A. Choose one photograph or poster in your bedroom or home and describe it in one paragraph. Use the list below to help you. Try using words listed in the boxes in this chapter.

- How big is it?
- Does it have an unusual shape?
- What people and/or objects are in the picture?
- What kind of frame is it in?
- What colors are in the picture?
- What action is taking place in the picture?

- What is the surface appearance of the objects in the picture?

B. **Choose your favorite place. It may be a regular hangout, your room, the beach, a vacation spot, a friend's house, or some other place. Whatever your favorite place is, think about the last time you were there. Write one paragraph to describe what you saw. Be sure to include specific words that describe size, shape, color, surface appearance, and action.**

TOUCH WORDS

Through the sense of **touch** you can learn the following about an object: texture, temperature, shape, weight, and density. If you close your eyes and reach into a bag of various types of marbles, you can choose one marble and describe its various aspects. For example, the texture is probably smooth, its temperature may be warm if you had the bag in your pocket, its shape is spherical, and its weight may be light or relatively heavy. If the marble is relatively heavy, though quite small, then it has a high density.

TEXTURE

By running your fingers over an object, you can feel its **texture**. The object may feel *smooth*, *rough*, *lumpy*, *sharp*, or *scratchy*. You will probably need more than one word to describe the texture of an object. For example, silk, glass, metal, and paper are all *smooth*, but they each feel different. Also, a touch on a person's face may be described as a *gentle stroke* or a *hard slap*.

Texture Words

rough	coarse	granular	nappy	fuzzy	shaggy	nubby
studded	knobbed	pitted	smooth	downy	fluffy	velvety
satiny	silky	grainy	soft	delicate	woven	rubbery

TEMPERATURE

If you touch a hot stove or get your finger stuck on a piece of ice, you know pretty quickly what the temperature of these objects is. Describing the **temperature** of a particular scene is a great way to enhance your writing. For example, a winter evening may be *frigid* and *blustery*, while a summer evening may be *sweltering* or *sultry*.

Temperature Words

cold	blustery	chilly	invigorating	brisk
nippy	boiling	icy	frosty	tepid
warm	toasty	temperate	tropical	lukewarm
summery	hot	roasting	bitter	sizzling
sweltering	scalding	scorching	frigid	cool

WEIGHT

You can't tell the **weight** of something just by looking at it. You need to pick it up, or at least try to push it. After that, you may determine that the object is *heavy* or *light*. Those words, however, are relative. You may think an object is very heavy, while the weightlifter pictured to the left may think it is light. Try to use specific descriptive words like *fifty pounds* or comparisons like *as light as a feather*. Also use the weight words listed below.

Weight Words

massive	immovable	airy	feathery	wispy	bulky	unwieldy
heavy	stationary	light	weighty	loaded	hefty	tonnage

DENSITY

Density refers to the amount of stuff (or people) in a particular space. For example, a chocolate cake may be *light* and *fluffy*, or it may be *heavy* and *dense*. There might be *a dense crowd gathered around the ticket office* right before concert tickets go on sale. Also, to say that *there is a low population density in the Mojave desert* means that few people live there. Remember that density is different from weight. Try using the words listed below to describe density.

Density Words

solid	thick	crowded	condensed	congested
dense	firmness	compact	hardness	impermeable
closeness	viscosity	jammed	clustered	impenetrable

Practice 2:   Touch Words

A. Find an object in your backpack, locker, or home. Pair up with another student. With your partner's eyes closed, place the object in his or her hand. Your partner will then feel the object (with eyes still closed). Then, take the object back, hide it, and your partner can open his or her eyes. Now do the same thing, except YOU close your eyes and your partner gives you an object. Finally, each of you will write a paragraph describing how the object feels.

B. Consider your favorite place again. Think about the way different parts of that place feel. How hot or cool is it? What do you sit on in this place? Write one paragraph describing the texture, temperature, shape, weight, density of this place and/or objects in the place.

SOUND WORDS

Sound can be a difficult sense to describe. One helpful way to describe sounds is to use other sense words. For example, one bird's song may sound like a soft trilling, while another bird's song may sound like a raspy wheezing. Or, a person's voice may be gravelly or smooth, or it may have a warmth or coolness to it. Another helpful way to write about sound is to describe how the sound was made. For example, a crying person may wail, bawl, sob, whimper, or moan. Also, a dog may bark, yip, growl, howl, huff, or grunt.

Take three minutes right now to write down on your own paper as many sound words as you can think of.

You can also describe sounds by volume, pitch, or quality.

VOLUME

Volume describes the intensity of a sound. The most common descriptive words are *loud* and *soft*. Your writing will be richer, however, if you describe someone as speaking in *hushed tones* or *a booming voice*. Here are some other words that can describe the volume of a sound:

Volume Words				
thundering	scream	booming	whisper	murmur
rumble	droning	buzzing	whizzing	muted
softened	dampened	shout	clamor	din
outcry	racket	deafening	tumult	faint
rattling	roar	thunder	peal	blare
blast	shriek	earth-shattering		

PITCH

Pitch refers to how low or high a sound is. For example, a foghorn blasts at a very low pitch, while birds chirp at a relatively high pitch. The following are some other words that describe pitch:

Pitch Words				
guttural	shrill	piercing	bass	tenor
alto	shrieking	baritone	soprano	nasal
tonal	flat	sharp	whiney	deep

SOUND QUALITY

The **quality** of a sound is what distinguishes it from other sounds of the same pitch and volume. For example, a note played on a guitar may sound *soft* and *sweet*, while the same note played on a trumpet may sound *clear* and *bright*. Keys may *rattle*, *tinkle*, *jangle*, or *jingle*. Water in a brook or stream may *babble*, *gurgle*, *lap*, *splash*, or *swish*. The list below provides just some of the words you can use to describe sounds.

Sound Quality Words						
clatter	roar	chirp	buzz	barked	click	cluck
croak	sing	huff	grunt	plink	clink	hum
bang	rattle	whirring	purring	sigh	whine	murmur
mutter	clatter	clap	jangle	honk	beep	bray
ring	hiss	fizz	whiz	zip	wheeze	clatter
sniffle	sniff	squawk	squeak	howl	hush	growl
snarl	grumble	groan	clunk	clang	clangor	pop

Practice 3: Sound Words

A. At some point in your day, whether it's in the middle of the lunchroom or lying in bed before you go to sleep, close your eyes and listen. Listen to all the sounds you can hear. Think about how to describe them in regard to volume, pitch, and sound quality. Then, write a paragraph that describes all the sounds you heard. Exchange papers with another student. See if each of you can guess when and where the other person heard the sounds that are described in the paragraph.

B. Think again about your favorite place. What did you hear the last time you were there? What about these sounds draws you to this place?

SMELL WORDS

The average nose can recognize over two thousand different odors, but often we have trouble choosing a word to describe a particular **smell**. You may use *stale* to refer to the smell of an attic, or *musty* to describe the odor of a basement. Some substances produce such a unique odor that naming the substance gives the reader all the necessary information. Examples of these substances are *gasoline*, *ammonia*, *bleach*, *vinegar*, *jasmine*, *vanilla*, *cinnamon*, and *mint*. Study the list of words below to help you describe various odors.

Smell Words					
smoky	burnt	flowery	fresh	sweet	lemony
fishy	fragrant	acrid	rank	musty	earthy
stale	scented	dusty	pungent	rotten	sweet-smelling

Practice 4: Smell Words

Take a fifteen-minute walk around your school. Pay attention to the various smells in different parts of the school. Obviously, the cafeteria is going to smell different from the locker room in the gym. Write a paragraph that describes these smells and compares them to one another.

B. Think again about your favorite place. What did you smell the last time you were there? What about these smells makes this place attractive to you?

TASTE WORDS

Unlike the nose, the tongue can detect only four **tastes**: sweet, sour, salty, and bitter. Of course, you can describe far more tastes. Temperature, texture, and smell contribute greatly to your sense of taste. This is primarily why freshly brewed coffee tastes so much better than coffee that is left to stand for a little while. The aroma of the brewing process and the warmth of the coffee enhance the taste experience of the drinker. Therefore, you can use a variety of specific words, such as those listed below, to give the reader a good sense of what something tastes like.

Taste Words					
light	dry	warm	salty	juicy	tender
flaky	crisp	syrupy	tangy	refreshing	robust
acidic	spicy	sour	crunchy	metallic	rich
heavy	flavorful	tasty	delicious	succulent	scrumptious
hot	tart	spoiled	overripe	inedible	mild
sharp	zesty	appetizing	bitter	chocolatey	mouth-watering

Practice 5: Taste Words

A. As a homework assignment, eat your favorite food. As you eat it, close your eyes, and pay attention to the flavors you taste. Remember that texture, temperature, and smell play an important role in your sense of taste. Take notes on the tastes you experience. Then, write a paragraph that describes the flavors of your favorite food and why you enjoy them. Use specific words so that the reader will want to run out and try your favorite food.

B. You have already described four sensory aspects of your favorite place. The last one is taste. Think of some way you experience taste in your favorite place. Maybe you eat your favorite food there. In this case, your paragraph is already written. Otherwise, write a paragraph that describes your experience of taste in your favorite place.

Chapter 9 Summary

Descriptive writing is important to use when you are writing a narrative (telling a story) or writing a description.

When you describe a person, place, thing, or event, try to use words that will appeal to the reader's five senses: **sight**, **sound**, **touch**, **smell**, and **taste**.

- You can use sight words to describe **size**, **shape**, **color**, **surface appearance**, or **action**.

- Through the sense of touch you can learn the following about an object: **texture**, **temperature**, **shape**, **weight**, and **density**.

- You can also describe sounds by **volume**, **pitch**, or **quality**.

- The average nose can recognize over two thousand different odors, but often we have trouble choosing a word to describe a particular **smell**.

- Unlike the nose, the tongue can detect only four tastes—**sweet**, **sour**, **salty**, and **bitter**—but there are many ways to describe them.

CHAPTER 9 REVIEW: DESCRIPTIVE WRITING

A. Read the responses to the following two writing prompts. Then, underline any sight, smell, touch, sound, and taste words. Which sense is dominant in each description?

> Describe one person you have met or known. Include details such as this person's appearance and mannerisms.

1. When I first met my grandfather, I noticed his wide smile and how he made me feel special. His eyes sparkled with a youthful intensity that seemed to clash with the white hair and beard he had. His skin was wrinkly, and his ears had long, whitish hair growing on them about the length of match sticks.

   His hands were large and calloused from all the hard work he was accustomed to doing. His shoulders and neck were massive. He definitely looked as if he had been the football captain when he was a teenager. His voice was low and gravelly, but every word he spoke was kind. He reminded me of a cross between Santa Claus and a gentle giant. There was a sense of enthusiasm for meeting people that they immediately understood from the large bear hugs he gave everyone who entered the home.

   His shirts were usually cotton or wool plaid. His shirts smelled of a combination of sawdust and the musty cologne he wore. His hands were usually hidden by the old, leathery work gloves he wore. He mostly wore blue jeans for pants and enjoyed riding loud and fast motorcycles when he was not making some new piece of furniture in his shop for us, his grandchildren.

   You knew when he was coming or leaving a room. His large boots plodded in and out with the confidence of a man who has a purpose to every daily movement. His shoes were worn thin, but he wore them as if they were part of his feet. Mostly, I remember the way he made me feel every time I came over—safe and loved.

2. My friend, Brittany, is one of the most interesting people I have ever met. Her long, flowing skirt swishes through the halls at school. People always stop and stare at her, but she does not care. She wears these multicolored clothes. Between the skirt and the loose-fitting, ruffled blouses she wears, she looks like a gypsy.

   She wears her hair long and curly, and it falls down her shoulders thickly like dark vines, and her earrings are very large, usually with vibrant images of delicious-looking fruit on them. Her makeup is very striking. Swirls of purple eye shadow and pink blush cover the upper part of the face, followed by a deep crimson lipstick and lip liner.

When she walks, she seems to sail effortlessly across the floor. Her pointed shoes sparkle in the sunshine of the skylight hall. People usually hear the rustle of her skirt before they see her. Everyone always turns around to notice what new accessory she's purchased for her outfits.

She wears a perfume that reminds me of almonds, and her skin is the color of cinnamon. She said she was born here, but her exotic appearance reminds me of another time and another place. Some people make fun of her, saying the fabric she wears in one outfit could easily make three dresses, but she does not care.

> Describe your favorite food. Include all aspects of the food which make it delicious to you.

3. My favorite food would have to be the lasagna that my mother makes for me. The lasagna is memorable for its taste, feel, and smells.

    The mozzarella cheese on the top of the lasagna has a gooey and juicy feel to it. As I bite into the noodles, my teeth easily slice through the moist noodles.

    The inner layers of ricotta cheese are also very satisfying. The ricotta cheese has a grainy texture. Of course, the lasagna in the center areas is very hot. You can see steam rising more quickly out of the lasagna as your fork punctures the central layers. The round pieces of chopped Italian sausage and spiced hamburger meat make a delectable addition to the central layers.

    Towards the bottom, the red tomato sauce mixes together with bits of the ricotta and the meats. The sauce tastes fresh because it comes from freshly diced tomatoes. You can almost smell the earth the tomatoes grew in, along with the aromas of sun-dried oregano and basil, as you bring the last juicy bites of the lasagna to your mouth.

    All in all, the robust flavors and aromas of the lasagna, combined with its texture, make it a rich, savory dining opportunity worth repeating and a great addition to my list of favorite foods.

B. **Think about someone you admire. This person can be real or imaginary. In four or five paragraphs, describe this person using several senses to create a detailed portrait of this individual.**

C. **In four or five paragraphs, create a scene of a real or imaginary place. Include specific details using several of the five senses.**

Chapter 10
Narrative Writing

This chapter covers the following McREL standard and benchmarks for Level III:

Standard 1: Uses the general skills and strategies of the writing process	Benchmarks **5** and **7**

Narrative writing tells a story. It may be a real story, or it could be one you make up. To do this, you must become a storyteller. There are different kinds of narratives you could write. Now, read about two specific types.

A **biographical narrative** presents a brief sketch of a literary or historical character. It focuses on a series of events or actions in the life of that character and points out the importance or significance of these events. You could also include background information or a physical description of this person. You may even compare and contrast this person to others. An example would be a composition about why the life of your favorite athlete is important to you.

Be sure not to confuse biographical narrative with **autobiographical narrative**. An autobiographical narrative is a story about yourself. You could write about a specific event in your life and the personal significance of it. Or, you could reveal your attitude about an incident. An example would be an essay about your first day at a new school.

These are several steps to writing any kind of narrative. This chapter will go into more detail about how to write a narrative essay.

WRITING A NARRATIVE

Writing a narrative involves learning the key steps for this type of writing. Applying and practicing what you learn in this chapter will help you improve your ability to write a successful narrative.

KEY STEPS FOR WRITING A NARRATIVE

When writing a narrative, follow these simple steps:

- Step 1: Analyze the Writing Topic.
- Step 2: Organize Your Narrative.
- Step 3: Write a Rough Draft of Your Narrative.
- Step 4: Edit and Proofread the Draft of Your Narrative.
- Step 5: Write a Final Copy of the Narrative.

By studying these steps, you can gain a better understanding of how to write a narrative. They can also guide you in the writing process. In this way, you should be more prepared for your writing tests, and you should feel more confident about your ability to write a narrative.

In this chapter, you will review the steps for writing a narrative. Study these steps carefully, and practice the activities as you complete each section.

STEP 1: ANALYZE THE WRITING TOPIC

Analyzing the writing topic is the first step in learning how to write a narrative. The **writing topic** helps you think about what you will write. It establishes a focus for your writing. You should read and reread the writing topic carefully. In this way, you will respond only to the stated topic without straying from it.

Now read the following writing topic that would require a narrative response:

> Tell a story about a first-time experience such as driving a car, riding a horse, a skateboard, a roller coaster, and so on.
> Develop your story with specific details about the experience.

IDENTIFY YOUR AUDIENCE

Once you understand your writing topic, you should **identify your audience**. You will want to use words that most readers would understand, so you should avoid slang or foul language as well as words that are too simple or too difficult.

To illustrate the importance of audience, look at the three sentences below. All of them are about the same topic, but only one of them would appeal to educated adults. Which one is it?

A. When we were persons between the ages of thirteen and nineteen, we would avail ourselves of the contingency of the piscatorial sport at an acquaintance's water-filled cavity in the ground.

B. When we wuz dudes, we'd chill out at our bro's crib and ketch some fish in his mud hole.

C. When we were teenagers, we would go fishing in our neighbor's pond.

If you chose sentence C, you are correct. This sentence captures the reader's interest, and the words are easily understood. Sentence B contains slang and improper English, and the words in sentence A are long-winded and too difficult to understand.

DEVELOP IDEAS FOR THE TOPIC

Notice that this writing topic requires you to think about a first-time experience. A good way to prepare for this writing topic is to **brainstorm** (see chapter 3) about some of your first-time experiences.

Here is how a student named Ben brainstormed for this writing topic:

First-Time Experiences I Could Write About	
When I played first basketball game	My first date
Time I had to go to the hospital	My wild horseback ride
First fast food job	My first driving lesson

As you can see, Ben has started to brainstorm about some of his first-time experiences. Eventually, he decided to write about one of these experiences for his narrative essay. He felt he could write a good narrative about his wild horseback ride.

Practice 1:   Brainstorming about First-Time Experiences

On your own or in a group, think about some of your favorite first-time experiences. If you cannot recall any, think about such things as foods, clothes, trips, sports, school, jobs, books, movies, or other topics that will trigger ideas. On a separate sheet of paper, make a list similar to Ben's. List experiences you could share with others. Discuss your lists with your group or with your teacher. Identify your audience. Then, choose the best topic for your narrative essay.

ESTABLISH A POINT OF VIEW

When you write a narrative, you should choose a **point of view** or perspective from which the story is told. A point of view is the position or outlook from which a character tells the story. Establishing a clear and consistent point of view in your narrative helps your reader to follow the events and characters in your story more easily.

The typical points of view to select would be either a **first-person point of view** or a **third-person point of view**. When you tell a story about a personal experience or an autobiographical sketch, you would write from a first-person point of view using words such as *I, me,* and *my*. When you write as an observer rather than a participant, like a biographical sketch, then you would use words such as *he, she, her, him, his, they, their,* and so on.

Now, let's look at two passages on the same subject. The first passage conveys a first-person point of view, and the second passage is told from the third-person point of view. As you read, notice the differences between these two points of view.

209

FIRST-PERSON POINT OF VIEW

School was over, and my dream vacation was about to begin. I took off my shoes, so I could run in the soft, wet sand. An endless stretch of beach welcomed me into a world of rolling waves, soaring sea gulls, and serene solitude. The soft salt spray tickled my face as I turned on my iPod. I ran into the breakers ahead of me. Then I felt something large, rough, and scaly rubbing my ankles.

THIRD-PERSON POINT OF VIEW

School was over, and his dream vacation was about to begin. He took off his shoes, so he could run in the soft, wet sand. An endless stretch of beach welcomed him into a world of rolling waves, soaring sea gulls, and serene solitude. The soft salt spray tickled his face as he turned on his iPod. He ran into the breakers ahead of him. Then he felt something large, rough, and scaly rubbing his ankles.

As you can see, the words *I* and *my* are used to represent the first-person point of view in the first passage. The writer tells the story as a participant in the actions. It is a natural way to tell a person's experience. It gives a story a feeling of immediacy, and the readers can put themselves in the place of the narrator, seeing through the narrator's eyes.

In the second passage, however, the writer does not take part in the story. Instead, the writer becomes an observer, describing the thoughts and actions of another character. This can give credibility to a story and a more complete picture of the characters since the inner thoughts of many characters can be described, not just the narrator's.

Ben needed to decide on a point of view for his narrative about the wild horse ride. Since he personally experienced the wild horse ride, Ben chose the first-person point of view for his narrative. He felt that the story would have a greater impact on the reader with the use of the first-person point of view.

Practice 2: Establishing a Point of View

Like Ben, you should now have chosen a topic for your narrative essay. The next step is to decide on a point of view. Choose either a first-person point of view or a third-person point of view. Provide one or two reasons for your choice. Then, discuss your choice with your group or with your teacher.

STEP 2: ORGANIZE YOUR NARRATIVE

Ben was not sure about how he should organize his narrative. However, he took careful notes in Mrs. Connor's English class and learned how to organize a narrative. She said that a story should begin by establishing a **setting**. A setting is the time, place, and general background for a narrative. Ben chose his setting to be near Yellowstone Park in the summer of his fifteenth birthday. He would describe the mountains, valleys, the lodge, and the stables where he picked his horse to ride on the trail.

Mrs. Connor also explained that a narrative needs one or more **characters** (persons in the story). Ben decided that he and his family would be the characters. In addition, a story must contain a **plot**, a series of related events including **conflict** (struggle between different forces in a story) and leading to a **climax** (turning point in a story). A writer should also use **suspense**, so readers look forward to the next event in the narrative. Therefore, a narrative essay should have a setting, one or more characters, a clear plot with a beginning, a middle, an end, and suspense.

Mrs. Connor, then, stressed that most narratives follow a **chronological order**, which is one event following another event in the order of time. The reader can then experience each event as it happens in a logical time sequence. She recommended that her students create a **plot diagram** before they write their narrative essay. In this way, students would have a basic outline to follow as they list the main events in their story. Here is Ben's plot diagram for his wild horseback ride. Notice how he labeled the events that show setting, suspense, conflict, climax, and so on

Plot Diagram for Wild Horseback Ride in Chronological Order		
1. day of horseback ride at Yellowstone Park (setting)	2. woke up and ate breakfast at lodge (plot)	3. drove to stables; saw a bald eagle (setting)
4. family and I picked out our horses (characters)	5. started riding up the ridge to higher trails (setting)	6. goal was to reach top of mountain (plot)
7. my horse got hungry and left the trail (suspense + conflict)	8. horse neighs loudly; we see mountain lion (suspense + conflict)	9. lion tries to attack; horse rears up (climax + suspense)
10. horse races down mountain with me hanging on (suspense)	11. safe return to stables; family follows later (plot)	12. helicopter ride; I refuse to ride a horse again (plot)

After Ben showed Mrs. Connor his plot diagram, she praised him for following a chronological order and including setting, characters, conflict, suspense, and a climax.

Mrs. Connor also suggested another strategy Ben could use to organize his narrative. He could create an outline for a narrative using the five Ws (*who, where, when, what happened,* and *why*). She stated that the five Ws would still include the main parts of a story such as setting, character, plot, and chronological order. Here is how Ben used this outline to organize his narrative essay:

My Wild Horseback Ride	
Who?	*Ben, Jess, Mom, and Dad (Characters)*
Where?	*Near Yellowstone Park (Setting)*
When?	*Summer when I was 15 (Setting)*
What Happened?	*Woke up, ate breakfast at lodge, drove to stables, saw an eagle, picked out horses, rode the ridge, climbed the tougher trails, my horse leaves the trail, my encounter with a mountain lion, my horse rears up and races down the mountain, safe return to stables, helicopter ride, I won't ride a horse again (Plot)*
Why?	*To reach the top of the mountain to see the view (Purpose)*

Mrs. Connor mentioned that students could decide whether they wanted to use a plot diagram or outlining to organize their narratives. Now that Ben has practiced these two strategies, he is ready to write his rough draft.

Practice 3: Organizing Your Narrative

Review Ben's plot diagram and outlining for his narrative essay. Using his examples as guides, create either a plot diagram or outline about the topic you chose for your narrative essay. Then, seek feedback by sharing the results with your class or with your teacher.

STEP 3: WRITE A ROUGH DRAFT OF YOUR NARRATIVE

In class, Mrs. Connor told her students that they should write a **narrative essay** of **four to five paragraphs**. In the first paragraph, the writer introduces the story by describing the setting and by stating the purpose of the narrative. In paragraphs two through four, the writer tells the main parts of the story. In the last paragraph, the writer ends the narrative. This ending is sometimes called the **resolution** because it wraps up the loose ends of the story so the writer can conclude the plot.

Based on Mrs. Connor's guidelines, Ben plans the paragraphs of his essay. He also decides to change the title for his narrative.

My First (and Last) Horseback Ride
Introductory Paragraph
Introduces the characters and the setting
Narrator and family go horseback riding in Yellowstone Park.

↓

Paragraphs 2-4
Narrator tells main events of the story, leading to the climactic action
Narrator describes hair-raising ride on Hyper, the horse.

↓

Paragraph 5
Narrator explains the resolution
Narrator reunites with the family and gives up horseback riding.

Mrs. Connor further explained that the rough draft will contain errors and will probably need some changes, but the reader should be able to read the entire narrative from beginning to end. In addition, the rough draft contains sentences and paragraphs and, therefore, is a big step toward the completion of a narrative essay.

Later that evening, Ben starts to write a rough draft of his narrative essay. He gives the narrative a title and follows the format for an essay of four to five paragraphs. Using his plot diagram and outline as guides, he chooses a first-person narrative point of view. In addition, he adds more details to the plot and tries to connect the events together in chronological order. Now read and evaluate Ben's rough draft of his narrative essay.

My First (and Last) Horseback Ride

The sunrise over the skies of Yellowstone National Park. The mountains in the morning. Barely fifteen years old I was on a two week vacation out West with my family. We were spending our last day horseback riding in the mountains and valleys. The night before I dreamed, my horse was riding along the ridges and mountain tops. That took us into the clouds and back to earth again. Little did I realize. What an day was I about to have.

213

Early that morning my older brother Jes and I got out of bed, dressed, and ate breakfast in the lodges dining room. we had to drive to the stables, so Mom and Dad hurried along for the short drive their. we arrived at the horse stables, I noticed a bald eagle flaping overhead, his screeches sounded an alarm throughout the valley. we reached the stables, we picked out our horses. I chose a horse that I nicknamed Hyper. Jes rode a stalion named Snowball, Mom and Dad settled for two horses called Dolly and Sam.

We were starting to climb the path along the ridge above the stables. Ahead of us was another ridge that led us on to the trails above. we would be able to reach the top of the mountain we could view the entire valley and the surrounding mountains. we climbed higher, I was feeling dizzy. Hyper ahead, suddenly turning and galuping far off the trail to reach the wild grasses that grew along a gully.

With my family out of sight, Hyper started neying, I could sense something was wrong. and it was. Ahead of us on a rock ledge was a loud mountain lion with a menacing look in his eyes. Suddenly, Hyper got up on her hind legs I hung on her back with all my might. Eying those dangerus hoofs, the mountain lion sqweealed out backed away from an attack. At that moment, Hyper quickly twisted and headed down the mountain. Scared and angry. I continued to hang on the falling rocks and clouds of dust from our quick dip. Hyper was amazing as she bounced over rocks, leept over gullies, tore through the plants. I could tell that her idea was to get back to those stables and then, we were almost there.

Practice 4:   Evaluating Ben's Rough Draft for Content and Organization

Reread the rough draft of Ben's narrative essay "My First (and Last) Horseback Ride." Then critique the content and organization of his essay by analyzing its strengths and areas for improvement. As a guide, respond to the following questions.

1.   What is the purpose of Ben's narrative? Where in the narrative does Ben state his purpose?

2.   Does Ben describe the setting well? Cite some examples.

3.   List the key events in the narrative. Is the story chronological?

4.   Briefly describe each character in the narrative, including the main animal characters.

5.   Identify the main conflict(s) in the narrative.

214

6. List two examples of suspense in the story.

7. State the climax of the narrative.

8. Is there a clear resolution when the story ends? Explain.

Analysis of Content and Organization of Ben's Rough Draft

Ben states the purpose of "My First (and Last) Horseback Ride" in the first paragraph of his rough draft: "Little did I realize. What an day I was about to have." As Mrs. Connor advised, he states the purpose of the story in the introduction. However, she has told him to strengthen how he stated his purpose.

In several places in the narrative, Ben describes the story's setting: the mountains and valleys around Yellowstone Park, the ridges and trails on the mountain, and his age at the time of his vacation. However, his description of the setting needs to include more specific words.

The narrative follows chronological order although, based on Ben's outline, there seem to be some gaps in the action at the end. Otherwise, Ben tries to follow his plot diagram and includes those key events in his narrative. Ben adopts the first-person point of view for his main character, while the minor characters are his brother, Jes, his mother, and his father. Ben's horse, Hyper, becomes a character because of her independence and courage. The mountain lion's menacing character contrasts vividly with the horse's bravery.

Ben does a good job of creating conflicts between the human characters, the rugged mountain terrain, the horse, and the mountain lion. The writer includes suspense several times in the narrative, particularly when Hyper leaves the trail and when Ben and Hyper confront the mountain lion. The climax of the narrative occurs when Hyper threatens the mountain lion by rearing up on her hind legs, and the mountain lion backs away. This action allows horse and rider just enough time to escape the danger.

In Ben's rough draft, Mrs. Connor indicated that the resolution of the narrative is not clear. In his rush to finish his rough draft, Ben forgot to include the final events of the story. When Ben and his teacher reviewed his plot diagram and outline, they found the events that Ben had omitted. Mrs. Connor suggested that he create a **dialogue** (conversation between characters) in the last paragraph. Readers like to hear people talking, and dialogue can be an engaging way to wrap up a narrative.

Practice 5:   Evaluating Your Rough Draft for Content and Organization

Based on what you have reviewed in this section, write a rough draft of your narrative essay. Use your plot diagram or outline from Practice 3 to guide your writing. Then, critique the content and organization of your essay by analyzing its strengths and areas for improvement. Use Ben's questions from Practice 4 to help you evaluate your work. Also seek feedback from your teacher or peer group.

STEP 4:   EDIT AND PROOFREAD YOUR NARRATIVE'S DRAFT

The next step in writing a narrative essay is to edit and proofread the rough draft.

After completing a rough draft of his narrative essay, Ben started to reread what he had written. His English teacher, Mrs. Connor, also offered feedback on Ben's use of language, sentence variety, and writing conventions (spelling, punctuation, and grammar and usage). She recommended that he review previous chapters on drafting, revising, and proofreading an essay.

Practice 6:   Editing and Proofreading Ben's Rough Draft

Reread the rough draft of Ben's narrative essay, "My First (and Last) Horseback Ride." Based on editing and proofreading strategies he learned in previous chapters, what corrections should Ben make in his rough draft? As a guide, respond to the following questions about language and writing conventions. Discuss the findings with the class or with your teacher.

1.   Are there clear transitional words in Ben's narrative that show the relationship between the various events in the story? List them.

2.   Could Ben strengthen his choice of words to improve the narrative? How?

3.   Does the narrative include a variety of sentences? Explain.

4.   What changes in spelling, punctuation, and grammar should Ben make in his narrative essay?

ANALYSIS OF LANGUAGE AND WRITING CONVENTIONS

To strengthen the chronological order in his narrative, Ben needs to add transitional words as he writes the story. These words clarify the time relationships between the events. They also help the narrative to flow smoothly. Here are some transitional words and phrases Ben could use to improve his narrative essay:

Transitional Words and Phrases		
after	before	as
then	second	third
finally	at that moment	during
meanwhile	eventually	when
next	now	soon
while	early	in a short time
last	later	first

Working with Mrs. Connor, Ben found out that he needs to strengthen his choice of words. Specific and concrete words are more effective than general or vague words. For example, Ben changed the phrase, "I chose a horse" to "I chose a lively brown mare." Instead of the general phrase "loud mountain lion," he used the more vivid expression "snarling mountain lion." Ben should start adding more vivid and specific adjectives, adverbs, nouns, and verbs wherever possible.

Mrs. Connor also pointed out that Ben's sentences needed more variety. His rough draft contains mostly simple sentences, so she suggested that he review the section on "Developing Sentence Variety" in chapter 5 of this book (pages 108–109). Ben began to combine his simple sentences. He also worked on starting his sentences with something other than a subject.

For example, in his rough draft, Ben wrote the following three simple sentences in a row: "we arrived at the horse stables. I noticed a bald eagle flaping overhead, his screaches sound an alarm throughout the valley." To vary his sentences and words in this example, Ben combined these three simple sentences, introducing them with a dependent clause. Notice how Ben's revision of these sentences creates a smoother flow of ideas and spurs the reader's interest in the events to come. "Before we arrived at the horse stables. I noticed a majestic bald eagle overhead, his screaches sounding an alarm throughout the valley." As he rewrote the final draft of his story, Ben continued combining his sentences and varying the pace of his narrative.

After reviewing errors in writing conventions with Mrs. Connor and with his peer partners, Ben also found that he needed to improve his capitalization, spelling, punctuation, and grammar in the narrative. For example, in the second paragraph, he misspelled *flaping*, *screaches*, and *reeched*. In addition, each paragraph contains punctuation errors that result in either fragments and/or run-on sentences, missing commas, or other types of punctuation errors.

For example, in the third paragraph, Ben saw these two run-on sentences: "we would be able to reach the top of the mountain we could view the entire valley and the surrounding mountains." He corrected them by adding and capitalizing the transitional word eventually followed by a comma and then adding the conjunction where: "Eventually, we would be able to reach the top of the mountain where we could view the entire valley and the surrounding mountains."

Finally, Ben's errors in grammar are minimal. He consistently maintains the past tense throughout the narrative, and his subject-verb agreements are generally correct. He also uses the nouns, pronouns, adjectives, and adverbs correctly. However, in the first paragraph, he noticed an error in his use of indefinite articles. He changed "What an day" to "What a day."

Practice 7: Editing and Proofreading Your Rough Draft

Reread the rough draft of your narrative essay. Based on editing and proofreading strategies you learned from Ben's experiences, what corrections should you make in your rough draft? As a guide, respond to the questions about language and writing conventions from practice 6. Discuss your findings with your peer group or with your teacher.

STEP 5: WRITE A FINAL COPY OF THE NARRATIVE

This is the fifth and last step of the writing process. After thoroughly revising his essay, Ben has written the final draft of his narrative. He added a fifth paragraph that concludes the story with some dialogue and a fuller resolution of the plot. Now his narrative contains a setting, plot, characters, and suspense, with a clear beginning, middle, and end.

Ben has also included appropriate transitional words so the reader can follow the events in the narrative more easily. By using more vivid and concrete words and expressions, he has strengthened the narrative. In addition, he has worked on varying his sentences, and he has corrected most of his errors in capitalization, spelling, punctuation, and grammar.

Now, read and evaluate Ben's final copy of his narrative.

My First (and Last) Horseback Ride

The sun rose brightly over the clear blue skies of Yellowstone National Park. The surrounding mountains reflected the glow of a new morning. Barely fifteen years old, I was on a two-week vacation out West with my family. We were spending our last day horseback riding in the mountains and valleys near this magnificent park. The night before, I dreamed that my horse was almost flying along the ridges and mountain tops in huge leaps that took us into the clouds and back to earth again. Little did I realize what an incredible day I was about to experience.

Early that morning my older brother Jes and I jumped out of bed, dressed, and ate breakfast in the huge lodge's dining room. First, we had to drive to the stables, so Mom and Dad hurried us along for the short drive there. Before we arrived at the horse stables, I noticed a majestic bald eagle gliding overhead, his screeches sounding an alarm throughout the valley. After we reached the stables, we picked out our horses. I chose a lively, brown mare that I nicknamed Hyper. Jes rode a big white stallion named Snowball, and Mom and Dad settled for two gentle older horses called Dolly and Sam.

In a matter of minutes, we were starting to climb the well-worn path along the ridge above the stables. Ahead of us was another, higher ridge that led us on to the steeper, more challenging trails above. Eventually, we would be able to reach the top of the mountain where we could view the entire valley and the surrounding mountains.

As we climbed higher, I felt light headed and dizzy. Meanwhile, Hyper forged ahead, suddenly turning and galloping far off the trail to reach the wild grasses that grew along a gully.

With my family out of sight, Hyper started neighing loudly. I could sense something was wrong, and it was. Ahead of us on a rock ledge was a snarling mountain lion with a menacing look in his eyes. Suddenly, Hyper reared on her hind legs as I hung on her back with all my might. Eyeing those dangerous hooves, the mountain lion howled and screamed but backed away from an attack. At that moment, Hyper quickly pivoted and headed straight down the mountain. Scared and angry, I continued to hang on despite the falling rocks and clouds of dust caused by our quick descent. Hyper was amazing as she bounded over rocks, leapt over gullies, and tore through the underbrush. I could tell that her intent was to get back to those stables, and in a short time, we were there. Then, I thought about my dream the night before and how different my ride turned out to be.

About an hour later, Mom, Dad, and Jes returned to the stables. "I guess you took the short cut," said Jes. Shaking my head, I told them about the mountain lion.

"We're glad you're safe," Mom said, relieved.

"Well, we went looking for you, Ben, and never got to the top of the mountain," remarked Dad. "Would you like to try again?"

"No, thanks, Dad," I stated firmly. "How about a helicopter ride instead?"

So on that last day, we finally saw the top of that mountain and many other mountains besides and valleys too and, from now on, I'll stick to horseback riding in my dreams.

Practice 8: Comparing the Rough Draft and Final Copy of Ben's Narrative

In a group or on your own, reread the rough draft and the final copy of Ben's narrative, "My First and (Last) Horseback Ride." Using the following questions as a guide, compare the two versions. Record your responses, and then discuss them with your class or with your teacher.

1. Explain the resolution in the final draft of Ben's story. Compared to the rough draft, does it improve the narrative? Why or why not?

2. Foreshadowing is a hint of events to come. Although it is not essential to a story, foreshadowing can add suspense and interest to a narrative. Cite an example of foreshadowing in Ben's final copy. Does it improve the narrative? Explain.

3. Compare Ben's dream about riding a horse in the beginning of the story with his actual horseback riding experience in the story. How is his dream different from the real experience? Then look up the word *irony* in a dictionary or literature book. Does Ben's final copy of his narrative contain irony? Explain.

4. Find four examples of transitional words in Ben's final copy. How do they improve the narrative?

5. Circle four examples of vivid, concrete words in Ben's final copy. How do they improve the rough draft? Explain.

6. Compare Ben's sentences in his rough draft and in his final copy. Cite two or three examples of improvements in sentence variety in his final copy.

7. In Ben's rough draft, find four or five examples of each of these errors: punctuation, spelling, and capitalization. How did Ben correct them in the final copy of his story?

8. A flashback is a scene or event that happened earlier in the story or in a character's life. In some stories, a character may experience a flashback. A flashback can be in the form of a story retold, a dream shared, or a promise remembered. Point out an example of flashback in Ben's final copy. What is the purpose of the flashback in Ben's story?

Practice 9: Writing the Final Copy of Your Narrative

Based on the corrections in your rough draft, write a final copy of your narrative. Then, share your final copy with your teacher or peer group. Have them rate your rough draft compared with your final copy. Evaluate your strengths and challenges in narrative writing.

Practice 10:   Model Stories or Narratives

The final copy of "My First and (Last) Horseback Ride" is an example of a well-written story. To find other model narratives, ask your teacher for examples. You can also work with a partner or group and search through newspapers, magazines, textbooks, or the Internet. Locate stories that contain 400–1000 words, in which the author uses first-person or third-person point of view. Make copies of these narratives and share them with your partner or group. Then evaluate them for content, organization, language, and writing conventions. Choose the best ones, and keep them as models for your own narrative writing. Make copies of these to discuss what makes them model narratives.

CHAPTER 10 SUMMARY

Narrative writing tells a story.

A **biographical narrative** presents a brief sketch of a literary or historical character.

An **autobiographical narrative** is a story about yourself.

The best way to write a narrative is to follow these steps:

- Analyze the Writing Topic
- Organize Your Narrative
- Write a Rough Draft of Your Narrative
- Edit and Proofread the Draft of Your Narrative
- Write a Final Copy of the Narrative

The **writing topic** helps you think about what you will write.

Your **audience** consists of the people reading your story.

A **first-person point of view** uses words such as *I*, *me*, and *my*.

A **third-person point of view** uses words such as *he*, *she*, *they*, and so on..

A **setting** is the time, place, and general background for a narrative

Characters are the persons in the story.

A story must contain a **plot**, a series of related events including **conflict** (struggle between different forces in a story) and leading to a **climax** (turning point in story). The ending is sometimes called the **resolution** because it wraps up the loose ends of the story.

A writer should also use **suspense**, so readers look forward to the next event in the narrative

Most narratives follow a **chronological order**, which is one event following another event in the order of time.

To help organize ideas for a narrative, use a **plot diagram** or an **outline** of the five Ws (*who*, *where*, *when*, *what happened*, and *why*).

CHAPTER 10 REVIEW: NARRATIVE WRITING

To improve your proficiency in writing a story or narrative, complete the following activities.

1. Using the five steps for writing a narrative, write two or three more stories. Organize each story into several paragraphs. For models, review Ben's final story about his horseback ride. Or reread the model narratives you found in practice 10. After you complete each narrative, share it with your teacher or with your class for feedback.

Choose some narrative topics from Appendix A or select some of the following topics:

- Tell a story about a time you were really afraid. What made your experience so frightening? How did you feel when it was over? Develop your story with details.
- Write an imaginary story about meeting an alien from another planet for the first time. Tell the reader about the experience. Develop your story with details.
- Write about a dream you have had. If you cannot recall a dream, make up a dream. Tell what happened in the dream. Develop your narrative with details.
- Tell a story about a friend or family member who made everyone laugh. Write a narrative about the experience. Develop your story with details.
- Write about an experience you had that taught you a valuable lesson about life. Tell about the main events of that experience. Develop your story with details.
- Tell about an experience that made you happy, sad, or upset. Write a story about that experience. Develop your story with details.
- Skim through a photo album, a magazine, or a book and find an interesting picture. Write a story about the person(s) in the picture. Include details in your story.

2. A student wrote a story on the following topic:

> Write a story about an unusual vacation experience. Tell what happened. Develop your story with details.

On your own or in a group, review the story, and decide whether it needs to be revised or not. List the reasons for your decision. If the story needs revision, suggest ways that the student could improve the narrative.

My Trip

I went to the Virgin Islands last year. My sister Shonda and my mom went also. The water so blue, cabs were everywhere. we took a cab first to our hotel. The winding road up the mountain. Then we ate seafodd and watch the sun set on the beech. What a site.

Next day we take a cab to downtown but cab very high price. We see many ship people leaving ship to shop every where. Donkees on streets make me laugh with thare funny hats and faces. Downtown is full of many color, sizes, and shape. So many people, so much to buy. But we get tird and spent a lot of money.

Next day we rent a car. That was wild. Shonda said I shoud drive. Then I see you drive on left side of street. Not the right side. Mom and Shonda screemd at me a lot. Your gonna kill us, they say. I didn't know. I turn left and go to rite side of street but I must go to left side of street. Many drivers beap at me and yell I was nervus.

Then we went under the sea to watch fish, sharks, and tirtels. Then a lady snuk in ore car at the grocery store, she ate ore leftover food. Then she wanted a ride to a hotel cuz she was broke. We took her and left the next day flew back to Cleavland.

3.   Alex's assignment was to write a story about someone else. His topic was:

> Tell a story about your favorite or least favorite student at school. Create a real or imagined narrative about this person. Develop your story with details.

Read and evaluate Alex's story, which continues on the next page. On your own or in a group, review the story, and decide whether it needs to be revised or not. List the reasons for your decision. If the story needs revision, suggest ways that Alex could improve his narrative. If changes are needed, revise the story. Then, share the revision with your class or with your teacher.

Jason

My least favorite student in school is Jason. He's a show off. One day in math class he started humming real loud, Mr. Logan was writing on the board, and turned around but Jason stopped. Jason hummed again when Mr. Logan's back was turned. Mr. Logan said to the class to stop that. Then Jason stopped, but a few minutes latter, Mr. Logan was writing more math problems on the board. Jason motioned to the class to be quiet. Then he stood up and started doing the moves for that dance the macarena. Some students broke out in a laugh. Then before Mr. Logan turned around, Jason sat down.

Nobody would tell on him Jason's a show off and also keeps us from learning. Mr. Logan knows about Jason. But he ignores what Jason does. Couldn't he say, stop acting dumb, Jason or I'm teaching a lesson, so behave, dude. In the lunch room Jason calls some of us nerds. Some of us want to finish school and go to college. Where will Jason be in a few years? Jason can learn but does he want to.

4. Read and evaluate the following student stories. The topic for these stories was as follows:

> We all experience times when nothing seems to go right with our lives. Tell about a time when nothing seemed to go right. Develop your story with details.

On your own or in a group, review each story, and decide whether it needs to be revised or not. Next, list the reasons for your decision. If a story needs revision, suggest ways that these students could improve their narratives. Then, when changes are needed, revise each story on your own or in your group. Finally, share the revision with your class or with your teacher.

Wings & Strings

Fran and her college roommate, Philena, enjoyed listening to bluegrass music. Sounds of guitars and fiddles could be heard coming from their dorm room every night. Fran's father belonged to a band, so she was raised listening to the lively music.

One fall, Fran's parents asked the girls if they wanted to go to the Wings and Strings festival, a bluegrass festival. The festival was held on the grounds of an old airfield, and many vintage airplanes were parked there; that's how the festival got its name. The event was several hours away in Polk City, Florida, so it would be a nice weekend getaway with Fran's family and friends. Several members of her father's band were going to be there. Philena liked Fran's family and wanted to go, but being poor college students, neither of them could afford a hotel room for the weekend. They decided to pitch a tent and make it a camping trip.

After packing up the cars, the vacationers left Miami for Polk City. Four hours later they arrived at the airfield where the festival was taking place. Fran and Philena immediately began to set up their tent. They got everything out of the back of Philena's truck only to find that they had the tent but left the tent poles behind. They couldn't sleep out in the open; they'd freeze. It was November and cold for the warm-blooded teenagers from Miami. Fortunately, they had an air mattress, and the truck had a cap. They could safely sleep in the back of the truck. With that crisis averted, they began to dig around for the pump to the air mattress.

It didn't take them long to discover the poorly repaired hole in the air pump. After one compression, the adhesive gave way on the duct tape and a gust of air blew back in Philena's face. Being industrious college students accustomed to thinking outside the box, they figured out a way to hold the hole in the pump closed enough to get a little air into the mattress. It would be slow going, but it was better than trying to blow it up the old-fashioned way. Two hours and several hand cramps later, the girls had filled the air mattress to their liking.

Just as they were finishing up, a man, who had been sitting in a camp chair watching the process for most of the time, yelled out to them that he had an electric air pump that would have filled the mattress in ten or fifteen minutes. But, he added that he admired the perseverance they showed. They smiled politely and groaned in frustration. They had missed most of the day's activities but were ready to forget their troubles and dance the night away.

Finally free from their preparations, the girls headed for the stage where they found Fran's parents and friends. Fran's father asked Philena to dance and taught her to Louisiana two-step. By midnight, they were danced out and tired. They headed back to the truck and a hard-earned night's rest on their old adversary, the air mattress.

Gettin' Thru the Blues

I always wore that blue dress when I went out, even if I were just goin' to store to pick up some onions for a stew. My mama always said that you should look your best in public, 'specially when you might run into your future husband. It wasn't really blue, but navy blue, almost black and made of gauzy nylon that lets the cool breeze through. It has short gathered sleeves. Some of the threads that pucker the fabric have pulled loose from me reaching too far in front of myself. That's another thing mama always told me not to do. "Don't go reaching too far ahead of yourself. You'll only be disappointed when you can't get hold of what you want." That's a piece of advice I never heeded, as you can see by those danglin' threads on my dress. It's a good thing I listened to those first bits of wisdom, 'cause just last month, I was in the store tryin' to get a gumball out of the machine, and I met my husband-to-be. I was wearin' the blue dress, and when I bent forward to collect my gumball, I heard those last few stitches give way. I was so embarrassed and sad. This was my only dress. Now, I couldn't come to town in my overalls. I could just hear mama, "Just wouldn't be right for a young lady, traipsin' around town in work clothes." I just may never get to come into town again. With that thought, all the muscles in my face started to tremble, and I started to cry. Just then, I felt a large hand on my shoulder and saw the other one holding a handkerchief in front of me. He asked me not to cry, sayin' if I kept up with the tears, he'd have a cry right along with me. And it doesn't look good when a man cries standin' next to a gumball machine. Well, that made me laugh so hard I almost finished off the dress right there. He introduced himself as Harry. When I went to shake his hand, I noticed the gumball I'd been clutchin' melted and left my palm a bright blue. I felt like such a child, but he just handed me the handkerchief again and got me a new gumball a yellow one. The next week, a delivery boy from the store came to our door with a package all wrapped up in paper. There was a note attached that said, "So you can continue your visits." Inside there was a new blue dress, just like the one I'd torn.

Basics Made Easy

Chapter 11
Writing about Literature

This chapter covers the following McREL standard and benchmarks for Level III:	
Standard 1: Uses the general skills and strategies of the writing process	Benchmarks **5** and **12**

Sometimes, you will be asked to write about literature. In this section, you can prepare to write such responses for classroom work or standardized tests by learning more about writing a response to literature. You may choose your own literature selection, or you may be assigned what to read. Your first step for an effective response to literature is to read the selection carefully. Be sure to identify different **literary elements and devices** the author is using such as description, characterization, conflict, personification, simile, irony, and so on. Also be sure to identify the tone, point of view, and theme.

You may be asked to write an **essay response to literature** for class or for exams. Like the other types of writing in this book, an essay response to literature requires practice so that you can become proficient and confident in writing this kind of composition. Although this type of writing may be challenging, you can prepare yourself for that possibility by learning more about writing a response to literature.

SAMPLE TOPICS

Here are some sample questions that would require you to write a response to literature:

- Describe a piece of literature you have read. Explain why you liked or disliked it. Use specific examples from this work of literature

- What character in literature, TV, or movies most resembles you and why?

- Books, movies, and television can offer opportunities to learn valuable lessons. Write about a lesson you learned from a book, movie, or television show that proved to be of value to you.

FORMS OF LITERATURE

To write a response to any of the sample topics, you would need to decide on a piece of literature, a TV show, or a movie that you like. In addition, you would need to remember enough about what you read or saw to develop a satisfactory response to the topic.

Hint: One way to prepare yourself to write a response to literature is to jot down, before the deadline, the titles of a favorite story, poem, novel, TV show, and movie. Then, brainstorm about the characters, events, or details relating to these types of entertainment. Before starting your essay, review and memorize the titles and as much of your brainstorming as you can to write an effective essay about literature.

WRITING AN ESSAY ABOUT A POEM

Robert heard from his teacher that his class would be writing an essay response to literature next week. To prepare the class for this assignment, Robert's teacher, Ms. Angeli, required her students to write an essay on the following topic.

> Choose a favorite piece of literature. Explain what it means to you in your life.

Robert's favorite piece of literature is a poem by Emily Dickinson. Prior to the assignment, he read this poem several times:

This World Is Not Conclusion
by Emily Dickinson

This world is not conclusion;

 A sequel stands beyond.

Invisible, as music,

 But positive, as sound.

It beckons and it baffles,

 Philosophies don't know,

And through a riddle, at the last,

 Sagacity must go.

To guess it puzzles scholars;

 To gain it men have shown

Contempt of generations,

 And crucifixion known.

Ms. Angeli then told her students to brainstorm and jot down details and thoughts about the piece of literature. Here is what Robert wrote about the poem:

Copyright © American Book Company. DO NOT DUPLICATE. 1-888-264-5877.

This writer says there is life after we die, our life on earth continuing into the next life. It's like music. We can't see eternity. It's very real like the sound of music. People talk about the life after death. It's really a mystery, hard to explain. Some people live like there is nothing beyond this life. Others would rather die than give up their belief in eternal life.

I can relate to this poem. My friend, Todd, died in a car accident. It really affected me. He was one of my best friends in school. I really miss him. We all do. I believe he's not really dead. He's moved on to a better life in the beyond. Todd and I went to the same church, we were in youth group together. He had a strong faith and stood up for his beliefs in eternal life. So I feel better, knowing that Todd isn't gone, he's in God's house now.

After her class took notes on their favorite piece of literature, Ms. Angeli gave them time to review what they had written. Then she directed them to discard their notes and respond to the topic in an essay of 400–500 words. Here is what Robert wrote about the Emily Dickinson poem:

Life After Death

My friend, Todd, died in a terrible car accident two months ago. Witnesses said he hit a guard rail and then rolled over several times before hitting the side of a mountain. He was dead before the rescue team got to him. This news devastated me because Todd and I grew up together and went to the same school and church. He was one of my best friends, and I miss him. I was very depressed and even thought about death a lot. My counselor helped me and told me to read a poem by Emily Dickinson called "This World Is Not Conclusion." This poem has become my favorite piece of literature because it helped me deal with the loss of my friend, Todd.

One of the reasons I like this poem is because the poet says, "This world is not conclusion." Todd and I were in the same church and youth group together. Sometimes we would talk about death and he would say, "Robert, God promises eternal life. We don't have to worry. Just love God and your neighbor." When I read this poem, I hear Todd telling me not to lose hope. There is a life after death.

Another reason I like this poem is because, without faith, philosophers are always trying to figure out how there can be a life after death. Such a belief doesn't make sense knowing what happens to the body after we die. How can you prove we live forever? The answer is that our knowledge is not enough. We have to trust and believe that the soul goes on. This poem expresses this belief and helps me accept Todd's death better.

Finally, the poet mentions that sometimes people have to die because of what they believe. This may sound strange. In the United States, we are free to say and practice what we believe. However, not everyone has had this freedom. Some people would rather die than give up their beliefs in God and a life after death. Christ, for example, was crucified for what he believed. I could also imagine Todd dying for his faith. He would never give up his beliefs. So I feel better knowing that Todd died with a strong faith in God and life eternal.

I'm glad my counselor recommended that I read "This World Is Not Conclusion" by Emily Dickinson. This poem helped me recover from the loss of my friend, Todd. The thoughts and beliefs expressed in this poem helped pull me out of my depression. Now, I can move on with my life.

After reading Robert's response to what this poem meant to him, Ms. Angeli wrote the following comments about Robert's essay:

Robert, you would definitely receive a passing grade on this essay. You respond clearly to the topic and you explain in detail why this poem helped you recover from the loss of your friend. You include examples and reasons that support your main point. You also organize and connect your sentences effectively. In addition, your grammar, usage, and spelling are very good.

WRITING AN ESSAY ABOUT A STORY

Carefully read and study the literary selection below based on the folk story, "The Crane's Reward." Then, read both the sample writing task and the sample response that follows.

The Crane's Reward

Before the humans came and frightened away many of the animals, the lion was the king of Kisii. Sometimes the elephant thought that an elephant should be the king of Kisii, but then the lion would roar about what a tasty king the elephant would be. The elephant would agree quickly that lions were better at being king.

A great and fearsome lion went out hunting. It was not long before he caught and killed a zebra that was big enough for his lionesses and cubs to eat their fill, with plenty left over for himself. When he and his family were eating, a small bone got caught in the great lion's throat.

He could barely squeak to his lionesses that a bone was caught in his throat.

One lioness tried to get the bone out with her paw, but she could not get her great paw far enough into the lion's mouth. The cubs could get to his throat with their little paws, but they were too clumsy to get the bone out. The lionesses tried to ask other animals to help, but they were all afraid of being eaten and ran away.

Soon the lion saw a crane sitting on a high branch watching him. "Crane," squeaked the lion. "Help your king. Your neck is long and thin, and so is your beak. You can take this bone from my throat."

The crane was in no hurry. "Why would I do that? One bite and the bone and I will both be in your stomach."

"I shall reward you," said the lion. "I do not want you both stuck in my throat. Then who would help me?"

The greedy crane could not resist the promise of a reward. He flew down to the lion and ordered, "Open your mouth as wide as you can." With the lionesses and cubs watching, the lion opened his mouth widely. The crane stuck its bill down the lion's throat until its whole head and part of its neck were in the lion's mouth. The bone was easily plucked out and dropped at the lion's feet.

"I'll have that reward now," said the crane.

"You already have it," said the lion. "Now you can tell the other animals that you gave an order to your king, and he obeyed. You can boast that you put your head into a lion's mouth and lived to tell of it."

The crane started to argue, but even the mighty elephant knew better than to argue with a group of lions. Amid the roars all around him, he stretched his wings and flew away to tell his story, as far from any lions as possible.

– Courtesy of the *Afro-American Almanac*

Sample Writing Task

In the folk story "The Crane's Reward," the author is conveying a life lesson or theme through the actions of the crafty lion and the greedy crane.

Write an essay in which you discuss how the author communicates this theme. Include examples of the author's use of plot, character, and personification to convey this theme. Explain how the writer's use of literary devices adds meaning to the story and illustrates the lesson or theme.

SAMPLE ESSAY RESPONSE

In the folktale, "The Crane's Reward," the author is able to convey a lesson or theme on how personal vices such as greed can be used against a greedy person. Those who are wise learn how to use these vices to their advantage. The author uses two animals of Africa, the lion and the crane, to illustrate this life lesson. The characters of the folktale seem all the more relatable through the author's use of actions, character development, and personification.

The lion is described in the story as king of Kisii. He is the most powerful animal in the area, and all other animals are afraid of him. The lion even intimidates the mighty elephant. However, the lion soon finds himself in a vulnerable position when he gets a bone stuck in his throat. He is choking, and none of his family can get the bone out. The lion calls out to the animals to help, but they are too afraid of being eaten—all except the crane.

The crane in this story is the only animal who has a beak long enough to pull the bone out of the lion's throat. He is also frightened about being eaten by the lion, but when the lion promises him a reward, he cannot resist. After taking out the bone, the crane immediately demands, "I'll have my reward now," exposing his true reason for helping the lion. The lion's crafty response about giving the lion orders, entering his mouth, and living to tell about it as a reward stumps the crane, and he flies away without the reward he was expecting.

This folktale draws on the personification of animals to make the characters' personalities more exaggerated. People keenly understand the power of the lion and the wisdom the lion possesses. The crane, on the other hand, is always flying around looking for an opportunity to score a quick meal. The storyteller draws on this personal knowledge to portray the lion as smart and the crane as greedy. At the same time, the folktale is an allegory describing a lesson for all humanity—a lesson of the folly of greed.

234

Notice that this student states the life lesson or theme in the first paragraph of the essay. Each of the other paragraphs explains how the actions and personalities of the lion and the crane convey the story's theme. This student also writes clearly and accurately about the story with minimal errors in grammar and usage.

Practice 1: Writing about Literature

Make a list of your favorite story, poem, novel, TV show, and movie. Review Robert's brainstorming and notes on his favorite poem. Then brainstorm and jot down details and thoughts about each of your favorites. Choose one of these favorite works of literature, and write an essay of 400-500 words on why it is your favorite piece of literature. Use Robert's essay as a model.

Practice 2: More Writing about Literature

Nora's favorite movie is *The Wizard of Oz*. She jotted down thoughts and details about the movie. Then she was going to review her notes as much as she could in preparation for writing a response about a lesson she learned from a movie.

Now review Nora's notes. What suggestions would you make to help her improve her notes about this topic?

Then write your own notes about *The Wizard of Oz* or another favorite movie from which you learned a lesson. Share your notes in a group or with your instructor so you can get some feedback on your work. Then, on your own, or in a group, write an essay and explain the lesson or theme the movie taught you. Use examples from the movie to support your views.

I like the Wizard of Oz. It's a grate movie, lots of action. This girl gets cute in a hurricane. Then her house blows away and she's in it. Her dog goes too and they wind up in Oz, a colorful land. She meets a scary crow and a tin man and a lion man. They have many adventures, dance and sing, and a which scars them sometimes. Then they meet the mean old wizard. He's a fake and a fraid. The girl cries to go home so ifairee wich wavs her wond and the girl end up back home with a big hedach but happy to be home.

I like this movie. Lots of ecsitmnt. Lots of lafs a whole lot of fun. See it agin And agin. I lerned a lot about the land of Oz and how to live a happy life.

Practice 3:   Writing an Essay about a Poem

Read and analyze one of the following poems. Brainstorm about it, make notes, and review them carefully. Put aside your notes, and then write a response of 400–500 words to this poem, explaining how it relates to your own life. Use Robert's essay about the Emily Dickinson poem as a guide.

The Sick Rose
by William Blake

O Rose, thou art sick!

The invisible worm

That flies in the night,

In the howling storm,

Has found out thy bed

Of crimson joy:

And his dark secret love

Does thy life destroy

Loss and Gain
by Henry Wadsworth Longfellow

When I compare

What I have lost with what I have gained,

What I have missed with what attained,

Little room do I find for pride.

I am aware

How many days have been idly spent;

How like an arrow the good intent

Has fallen short or been turned aside.

But who shall dare

To measure loss and gain in this wise?

Defeat may be victory in disguise;

The lowest ebb is the turn of the tide.

CHAPTER 11 SUMMARY

You may be asked to write an **essay response to literature** for class or for exams. You may choose your own literature selection, or you may be assigned what to read. Be sure to **identify literary elements** and **devices** the author uses. Also identify the tone, point of view, and theme.

CHAPTER 11 REVIEW: WRITING ABOUT LITERATURE

1. To improve your ability to write about literature, read the following poem by George M. Horton. Horton was born a slave in North Carolina and went on to become a well-known black poet of the nineteenth century.

The Fearful Traveller in the Haunted Castle

by George Moses Horton

Often do I hear those windows open
And shut with dread surprise,
And spirits murmur as they grope,
But break not on the eyes.

Still fancy spies the winding sheet,
The phantom and the shroud,
And bids the pulse of horror beat
Throughout my ears aloud.

Some unknown finger thumps the door,
From one of faltering voice,
Till some one seems to walk the floor
with an alarming noise.

The drum of horror holds her sound,
Which will not let me sleep,
When ghastly breezes float around,
And hidden goblins creep.

Methinks I hear some constant groan,
The din of all the dead,
While trembling thus I lie alone,
Upon this restless bed.

At length the blaze of morning broke
On my impatient view,
And truth or fancy told the joke,
And bade the night adieu.

'Twas but the noise of prowling rats,
Which ran with all their speed,
Pursued in haste by hungry cats,
Which on the vermin feed.

The cat growl'd as she held her prey,
Which shriek'd with all its might,
And drove the balm of sleep away
Throughout the live-long night.

Those creatures crumbling off the cheese
Which on the table lay;
Some cats, too quick the rogues to seize,
With rumbling lost their prey.

Thus man is often his own elf,
Who makes the night his ghost,
And shrinks with horror from himself,
Which is to fear the most

– Courtesy Academic Affairs Library, University of North Carolina at Chapel Hill

Writing Prompt

In the poem "The Fearful Traveller in the Haunted Castle," the author uses a personal experience to convey a theme or lesson about life.

Write an essay of 400–500 words about the theme or lesson in this poem. Use examples and images from the poem to explain the theme.

2. Locate the following short stories in your literature book, in the library, or on the Internet:

- Richard Connell's "The Most Dangerous Game"
- Bret Harte's "The Outcasts of Poker Flat"
- D.H. Lawrence's "The Rocking Horse Winner"
- O. Henry's "The Gift of the Magi"

Writing Prompt

Read two or three of these stories. Then write an essay of 400–500 words about one of them. Explain why you liked or disliked this story. Support your viewpoint with examples from the story.

Chapter 12
Writing Technical Texts

This chapter covers the following McREL standard and benchmark for Level III:	
Standard 1: Uses the general skills and strategies of the writing process	Benchmark **13**

In the previous chapters of this book, you learned about the different purposes and types of essays. In addition to essays, you will need to know how to write business and technical documents, which also have different purposes and styles. The chart below describes some of the documents you may need to write either at school, at home, or in the workplace.

Document	Purpose(s)
business letter	introduce, describe, request, persuade, thank
resume	provide information, persuade a person to hire you
cover letter	gain an employer's attention
job application	gather more information on applicant, assess applicant's ability to follow directions

This chapter will explain how to write some business and technical documents. However, there are many other types. Consult a specialized business English book for more information.

BUSINESS LETTERS

In writing a **business letter**, you are communicating with representatives of businesses. A business letter must communicate a clear and concise message. The document must also be free from errors. Mistakes in punctuation, grammar, and spelling are not acceptable.

The margins on the right and left of a business letter can vary from one to two inches. The important thing is to make sure they are equal in width. The top and bottom margins should also be equal. The length of the letter will determine the size of the margins. In the block format that we will demonstrate, all lines of text should be flush with the left hand margin.

In order to write business letters correctly, you must understand each part of a business letter. There are seven parts to a business letter: the **return address**, the **date**, the **inside address**, the **salutation**, the **body**, the **closing**, and the **signature**.

Return Address	The first two lines in the letter are the sender's address. The name is not included. The first line is the street address or post office box number, while the second line is the city, state, and zip code.
Date	The date appears right below the return address.
Inside Address	After the date, skip two to four lines. If you know the name of the recipient and his or her title, it goes on the first line. The name of the company is next; this will be the first line if a specific person is not named. The street address or post office box is written on the next line. Then, the city, state, and zip code are written on the last line.
Salutation	After the inside address, skip one line. When the specific person is unknown, *Dear Sir or Madam* is used. Otherwise, the word *Dear* is followed by the person's title (Mr. Ms., Mrs. Miss, Dr., Rev., and so on), and name, such as *Dear Dr. Jones* or *Dear Mrs. Mitchell*. In some cases, you may want to use the name of a department (Human Resources Department), or a job title (Personnel Manager) without *Dear*. Capitalize the first letter of each noun in the salutation; the salutation is followed by a colon.
Body	After the salutation, skip one line. Begin the body paragraph(s) at the left margin. After each paragraph, skip a line, and begin the next paragraph at the left margin.
Closing	After the body, skip one line. Write a closing such as *Sincerely*, *Sincerely yours*, *Very truly yours*, *Yours truly*, or *Regards*. Capitalize the first word of the closing.
Signature	After the closing, leave three blank lines. Then, type the sender's name. The sender signs the letter between the closing and the typed name.

There are books in the library that show you how to format different kinds of letters in more detail. Ask your librarian or media specialist to help you find these resources.

There are also many online resources. Some Web sites that focus on formatting of letters include the following:

www.dailywritingtips.com (click on Business Writing on the left side menu)

www.writing-business-letters.com

www.letterwritingguide.com

Practice 1:   Brief Business Letters

A. Here is one example of a typical brief business letter that follows a block format.   It is a good model of a well-designed, short business letter. However, it contains three mistakes. Read the model letter carefully and answer the questions that follow it.

451 Landing Way

Napa, CA 94558

September 8, 2008

Four Aces Boat Sales

376 Myrtle Lane

Las Vegas, NV 89111

dear Sir or Madam:

I am currently in the market for a jet ski that my family can use on our lake. Please send me a catalog and a price list of your jet ski's.

Sincerely,

Mary Clifton

1. Which part of the letter contains an error in punctuation?
    A. the signature
    B. the body
    C. the date
    D. the return address

2. Which part of the letter contains an error in capitalization?
    A. the body
    B. the closing
    C. the salutation
    D. the typed name

3. Which part of the letter contains a spelling error?
    A. the closing
    B. the typed name
    C. the inside address
    D. the date

B. On your own paper, or on the computer, write a brief business letter based on the following information. Refer to the previous page for the format of the letter.

Mr. Peter Farley works at the Guiness Car Manufacturing Plant #32 at 6781 Clovis Industrial Boulevard, Arlington Heights, IL 60005. He is in the parts department and needs to order exhaust system parts from the Helios Parts Company. Mr. Farley needs to request six mufflers at $300.00 each. The company's address is PO Box 3659, North Highlands, IN 47810.

WRITING THE BODY OF A BUSINESS LETTER

When you are **writing to a company**, you must be sure that you can communicate in a professional manner, not in the informal style with which you would write a friend or relative.

- **Use formal words and expressions**. Make sure that you do not use contractions, slang, or regional dialect in your letter.

- Using the **block format style**, make sure that you do not indent paragraphs. Instead, leave one space between each paragraph.

- The **purpose and audience** determine the length of a business letter.

- A typical business letter, such as a cover letter you would send with a resume or job application, should not exceed **one page** (four paragraphs), whenever possible.

Just as in a composition, every body paragraph in your letter should have a different focus. Remember to take into account the person(s) who will be reading the letter and give only the information which you believe concerns them or the company. Here is a brief suggested guideline for each of the four paragraphs.

Paragraph I	Describe who you are and why you are writing this company or person.
Paragraph II	Clearly introduce your need or concern.
Paragraph III	Offer further information about your need or concern, and give specifics about the response or solution you want. Provide the reader with contact information for reply; include when, where, and how.
Paragraph IV	Thank the reader for his or her time and consideration.

Now, take a look at this sample letter. James Duncan, who loves basketball and cars, has graduated and wants a summer internship with an automotive research company. James needs an answer as soon as possible so he can let his current employer know how long he will be gone.

123 Pine Street
Metropolis, IN 46900

June 2, 2008

Mr. Calvin Perkins, Director of Special Programs
CellTech Automotive, Inc.
PO Box 123
Metropolis, IN 46900-4321

Dear Mr. Perkins:

Since I was a child, I have been fascinated by the inner workings of automobiles as well as their design. As a high school student, I excelled in my automotive classes by making all As and have also been working part-time at Roberto's Automotive Repair. For years, I have thought about new structural designs for prototype cars, and recently I read an article in *Automotive Trends* magazine about CellTech's new prototype project on the solar-cell automobile. I am very interested in the possibility of working with CellTech's engineers in a summer internship.

I heard about this great opportunity through my guidance counselor at the technical college I will be attending in the fall. I was told that your company's internships usually last between six and eight weeks, during which time a mentor will closely supervise me. I am writing in hopes that there is, in fact, an internship opportunity available at CellTech.

I am anxious to find out within the next week whether or not I can work as an intern. My current employer will need to know so a substitute can be trained. I also need to know whether the length of the internship would be six or eight weeks. I can be available for the entire summer if needed. Please call me as soon as possible at my work phone number, (555)123-4567, or you can email me at jduncan@myemail.com.

Thank you for taking the time to consider my request. It would be a great privilege for me to work with your innovative company on such a creative project. If you need any additional information, please contact me at the work number listed above. I am looking forward to hearing from you.

Sincerely,

James Duncan

James Duncan

Practice 2: Writing the Four-Paragraph Business Letter

Choose one of the following scenarios, or create one of your own, and use the information to write a four paragraph business letter. Use the sample letter as a guide.

1. Jean-Luc Vancant, 154 River Drive, Hays, IN 46708, wants to apply for a job as a political researcher for a company called Research Polls, Inc. He found out about the job opening on the company's Web site, www.researchpolls.com. Most recently, he was the campaign manager for the winning mayoral candidate of his city. Also, he has two years of previous experience conducting polls for political parties and enjoys boating and fishing on the weekends. Research Polls, Inc. is located at 987 Technology Drive, Lafayette, IN 47909.

2. Courtney Bridges, 1612 Lake Road, Cedar Hill, TN 37032, is a full-time student at a community college and works part-time at a day care center. The Chalkboard Dreams Foundation distributes scholarships to worthy applicants. Courtney wants the foundation to understand how her lifelong dream of becoming an elementary school teacher makes this scholarship important to her. She also wants to emphasize that this scholarship will make the difference between her going to college full time and her going to work full-time and quitting college until she has money to return. She has already been accepted to transfer to University of Tennessee. The Foundation's address is 452 Flores Avenue, Clarksville, TN 37040.

3. Green Valley Landscaping needs more information on riding lawn mowers they may want to buy. Marcus Weidower is a part owner in the landscaping company and needs Mowing Frenzy, Inc., PO Box 56789, Franklin, AL 36444, to send him information on the cutting area under the mower, the top speed, detailed warranty information, and the best price if his company purchases three of them. He needs this information within three weeks to make his decision and would like the information sent to his office at PO Box 12345, Franklin, AL 36444.

EDITING THE BUSINESS LETTER

Editing is a critical step in writing a business letter. In many situations, your letter will be the first impression you make on the reader. If the reader's impression from your letter is negative, it will likely be your only chance to make an impression. When writing a business letter, your attention to detail is extremely important. If you misspell the recipient's name or get the name of the company wrong, it may create a negative impression on the reader. Especially if your letter is in reference to a job, you want to communicate that you will be a capable and intelligent employee. Your letter will be speaking for you, so make sure it says the right things!

Revise your letter very carefully; avoid mistakes in grammar and spelling. General neatness is also very important. Use the guidelines for revising any type of writing in chapter 5 and the proofreading chapter (chapter 6). Also make sure you have followed the page format for a business letter provided in this chapter.

Practice 3: Editing the Business Letter

Edit your four paragraph business letter from Practice 2. Be sure to check spelling, grammar, formatting and neatness. Review this chapter to help you in checking any parts you are uncertain about. Exchange letters with a classmate and make suggestions about how you can improve your letters.

RESUMES AND JOB APPLICATIONS

To consider someone as a candidate for most types of work, especially for professional positions, employers will expect to see a **resume**. A resume is a summary of your employment experience, education, special skills and qualifications, and sometimes honors and community involvement.

A job applicant typically sends a resume, accompanied by a **cover letter**, to a potential employer. If qualifications meet those required in the job, the employer may invite the applicant to fill out the company's **job application** and/or come in for an interview.

ORGANIZING INFORMATION ON A RESUME

There are different types of resumes. In high school, you may visit your counselor who can direct you to software programs having resume templates. Formats may vary by field of work or the amount of experience a person has. Many example resumes are offered in resume-writing guides in the library and online. Below are descriptions of some common resume types and uses.

Chronological Resume	Highlights progressive job advancement and skill building. It is easy to read and can be quickly scanned for employment history, education, and so on. The chronological resume is the most accepted type among people who make hiring decisions. We will focus on the chronological resume in this section of the chapter.
Career Objective Resume	Begins with a statement, such as "Career Objective: to become a manager in a national retail store." Experience is organized to highlight work performed in a specific industry and the skills and qualifications needed for the target job. For example, in the case above, any retail experience would come first.
Functional Resume	Focuses on key skills, accomplishments, and qualifications at the top of the resume, regardless of when they occurred. The functional resume highlights what you have done rather than where or when you did it.
Combination Resume	Combines the benefits of both the chronological resume and the functional resume by first summarizing the most impressive qualifications, skills, and accomplishments, followed by listing employment history in chronological order.

In preparing your resume, remember that it will be an important document when you look for a job. Its main purpose is to convince prospective employers to consider you for a position and contact you for the next step toward hiring (usually an interview). As with business letters, you want to make sure your language is professional and that there are no errors in your writing.

For the rest of this discussion, we will focus on creating a chronological resume. There are typically five sections: a **header**, a **profile** or an **objective**, work **experience** in chronological order, **education**, and **skills**.

Header	Your **personal information**, including full name, address, telephone number, and e-mail address if you have one (be sure that your e-mail address contains a name you can use professionally—something like ihatework@dot.com will not make a positive impression). The information may be typed to one side, right or left, or it can be centered at the top. Make your name stand out (boldface or a different type style); remember that your resume may be in a pile of many, and you want people to be able to find it.
Profile or Objective	A **profile** is a brief statement about why you would make an ideal employee, such as, "Profile: Dependable and detail oriented worker with a positive attitude." You may list an **objective** for a specific job type, such as "Objective: Responsible position at a veterinary clinic." Note that an objective will limit you, so do not include one if you are looking for any job or are open to working in a variety of fields.
Experience	List work experience (most recent first), including company names, job titles, and brief descriptions of what you did.
Education	The school you attend(ed), grades or class standing, and degree(s) or certificates earned.
Skills	List any work-related skills or special qualifications.
Community Involvement	This is an optional section where you could include special volunteer activities or committee participation.

What *not* to include: Do not write in your resume how much money you would like to earn. Also leave out personal information such as hobbies, family members, or pets. If there is something personal you feel further qualifies you for a job, mention it in your cover letter.

Take a look at the following sample resume, which is one that James Duncan sent with his letter to CellTech Automotive (the sample letter you saw on page 243).

Notice that James has made it easy for a potential employer to contact him by including address, telephone numbers, and e-mail address.

The section headers stand out and sections are easy to scan for dates, company names, job titles, and so on.

Especially important is how James has stressed his positive points in each of the job descriptions. Words like *responsibility*, *dependable*, and *reliably* in reference to his duties reinforce his value as an employee. Also, mentioning that his responsibility at the garage increased to opening the shop one day a week shows he became a highly trusted employee.

Finally, James included relevant special skills.

James Duncan
Pine Street, Metropolis, IN 46900
Home: (555)234-5678, Work: (555)123-4567
jduncan@myemail.com

Objective Obtain progressively more challenging positions in automotive repair and design

Experience 2006–present Roberto's Automotive Repair
Assistant Mechanic

Work on all major components of domestic and foreign engines, including transmission, electrical system, fuel pump, etc.; given responsibility to open the shop on Saturday mornings in April 2006

2001–2005 Bucky's Diner
Bus Boy

Cleaned tables and assisted wait staff as a dependable team player (in nearly a full year of employment, I missed only two days due to illness)

2002–2003 *Metropolis Ledger* paper route

Reliably delivered the daily and Sunday editions to the Maddock Hills neighborhood, rain or shine

Education 2004–2008 Metro North High School
Graduated May 2008, 2.8 GPA
Lettered in basketball; played JV and Varsity

Skills Computer and Internet literate
MS Office, QuickBooks
Fluent in Spanish

When you first start out, your resume will be brief (a page or less) because you may not have a great deal of job experience that you can list. In the beginning, you will list every type of experience that demonstrates your skills and responsibility, whether or not someone actually paid you to do it. Later, some of the earlier examples will be replaced by new jobs you have had. Think about doctors and lawyers and imagine how long their resumes get! They would no longer list the babysitting jobs or summer camp counseling they did in high school…but you might!

CREATING YOUR RESUME

In order for your resume to be complete, you might need to spend some time thinking about what you can include. If you have held several jobs already, you may also need to go through old pay stubs, calendars, or journals to recall when you worked, at what company, and the details of your job duties.

You may feel uncomfortable at first trying to make positive statements about things you have done. But remember that you need to talk about your skills and accomplishments so that the people reading your resume can tell whether or not you may be qualified for the opening they have. Keep in mind also that it helps to get an outside perspective. Work on your resume with a parent, friend, or your guidance counselor at school.

Practice 4: Creating Your Resume

After reviewing the section about resumes, write one for yourself. Be thorough; your ideal job may depend on it. Begin by making lists in the following categories:

- header information
- profile or objective (optional)
- work experience
- education
- skills
- community involvement (optional)

Some categories may have quite a bit of information, while others will contain very little. You may want to eliminate sections that have little or nothing in them and focus on the others. Include only the relevant information, such as things that an employer would value if he or she were considering hiring you.

Now, create an appealing format for your resume and organize your information in it. Then, share it with your teacher and perhaps fellow students for feedback.

WRITING THE COVER LETTER

The **cover letter** was mentioned several times in the last few pages. A cover letter normally accompanies a resume. It is much like any business letter that you read about in the previous part of this chapter. As you know, business letters have a variety of purposes. The purpose of a cover letter is to interest a prospective employer in looking at your resume and inviting you to apply or interview for the position. Your cover letter should answer the needs of the employer and make him or her think, "Wow, this is exactly the person I am looking for!"

Practice 5: Writing the Cover Letter

Using what you learned about writing business letters, compose brief cover letters that will accompany the resume you created in the last exercise. Write one cover letter to request consideration for at least two of the jobs in the following advertisements.

> **SALES** RVs 'R' Us needs Sales Associates – No RV Experience Needed! Your success will be determined by your desire, dedication, effort, talent, and ability to follow directions. Hands-on training. Potentially earn from $30-45K in your first year. 401(k) and profit sharing, health ins., 5-day workweek – flex schedule, friendly & fun, drug-free work environment. Send resume to: RVs 'R' Us, 700 Price Parkway, Jasper, GA 30143

> **CUSTOMER SERVICE** Dr. Fractal & Associates, optometrist inside LensPlus, seeks full-time front office staff. $9.00–$13.00/hour; retail or health care office exp. a plus; will train. You MUST be outgoing, extremely personable, polite, confident, dependable, and efficient. Professional dress and a positive attitude are also required. Send resume to: Dr. Henry Fractal, 2600 Iris Drive, Kansas City, MO 64119

> ### We Hire Administrative Assistants for Small Businesses!
>
> Earn $15,000–$25,000/year based on experience
>
> **Minimum Qualifications:** High School diploma
>
> **Kind of Work:** Variety of clerical duties including filing, sorting mail, typing documents, taking dictation, proofreading, greeting visitors, and taking telephone messages. The minimum typing rate is 40 words per minute with 10 or fewer errors.
>
> **Benefits** include 9 holidays and 1 week of paid vacation to start (2 weeks after one year of employment).
>
> Submit Resume to:
>
> **Small Business Consortium**
>
> PO Box 30303
>
> 1200 Colossal Blvd.
>
> Goshen, IN 46526

FILLING OUT THE JOB APPLICATION

When your cover letter and resume are successful, you will proceed to the next step toward landing the job: the interview and the **job application**. You may wonder why an employer wants you to fill out the application, which often asks for much of the same information that is already on the resume you provided.

There are several reasons why a company may request that a job application be filled out. First, as you learned earlier, there are many types of resumes that applicants can provide, and some may not be in the format that those hiring can quickly scan and compare with others. Second, when you fill out the company's form, it shows how well you follow directions and also how neatly and accurately you provide information. Third, the company may ask questions on its application form that are not covered anywhere on your resume but may be necessary to assess whether you are a qualified candidate.

On the next pages, you will see a sample application form from the Small Business Consortium, the company in the third ad in Practice 5. Review it, and then complete the exercise that follows.

Sample Job Application

Read the typical job application on the next three pages, and complete the exercise that follows.

FOR OFFICE USE ONLY

Certification

Approved ( )
Disapproved ( )
Contingent ( )
Date & Initial

Small Business Consortium

1200 Colossal Blvd.
Goshen, IN 46526
555.678.1234

SBC

APPLICATION FOR EMPLOYMENT

READ CAREFULLY BEFORE FILLING OUT THIS APPLICATION

I understand and agree that any false information provided herein may be cause for denial of employment or dismissal in the event of employment. As an applicant for a position with clients of the Small Business Consortium, I hereby authorize the release of information regarding my education and work history for use to determine my qualification for employment.

Date: _____ Signature: _____

Name: (Last) _____ (First) _____ (MI) ____

Present Address: (no. street) _____

City _____ State _____ Zip Code _____

Telephone No.(Home) _____ (Work) _____ (Other) _____

E-mail _____ Social Security No. _____

POSITION APPLIED FOR:

Job Title: _____ Location: _____

How did you learn of this opening? _____

Do you want to work: ☐ Full-time? ☐ Part-time? ☐ Day? ☐ Evening?

Have you ever worked for the Small Business Consortium before? _____

If yes, When, Where Reason for leaving? _____

Do you have relatives presently working for the Small Business Consortium? ☐ Yes ☐ No

If yes, state name(s) and relationship. _____

Have you ever been convicted of a crime, excluding misdemeanors and summary offenses? ☐ Yes ☐ No

If yes, describe in full.

_____

Are you legally authorized to work in the United States? ☐ Yes ☐ No
(proof of employment eligibility will be required)

Have you ever served in the Armed Forces? ☐ Yes ☐ No

If yes, what branch? _____

Dates of Duty: From _____ (Month Day Year) To _____ (Month Day Year)

Type of discharge _____

EDUCATIONAL BACKGROUND

Type of School	Name and Location	No. of years completed	Graduated	Major / Degree Received
High School			☐ Yes ☐ No	

College			☐ Yes ☐ No	
Post Graduate			☐ Yes ☐ No	
Business or Trade			☐ Yes ☐ No	
Other				

WORK HISTORY

1

Kind of business organization (*manufacturing, accounting, insurance etc.*)

Dates of employment (*month, year*)
From: _____ To: _____

Place of employment (*city, state*)

Avg. hrs per week

Name of employer (*firm, organization, etc.*) and address (*including ZIP*)

Area code and phone No.

Number of employees you supervised

Salary or earnings (*grade & step, if applicable*)
Name and title of immediate supervisor

Starting $ _____ per

Reason for leaving

_____ per

May we contact current employer? ☐ Yes ☐ No

Describe your duties, responsibilities, and accomplishments

2

Kind of business organization

Dates of employment (*month, year*)
From: _____ To: _____

Place of employment (*city, state*)

Avg. hrs per week

Name of employer (*firm, organization, etc.*) and address (*including ZIP*)

Area code and phone No.

Number of employees you supervised

Salary or earnings (*grade & step, if applicable*)
Name and Title of immediate supervisor

Starting $ _____ per

Reason for leaving

Final $ _____

Describe your duties, responsibilities, and accomplishments

3

Kind of business organization

Dates of employment (*month, year*)
From: _____ To: _____

Place of employment (*city, state*)

Avg. hrs per week

Name of employer (*firm, organization, etc.*) and address (*including ZIP*)

Area code and phone No.

Number of employees you supervised

Salary or earnings (grade & step, if applicable)	Name and Title of immediate supervisor
Starting $ _____ per	Reason for leaving
Final $ _____ per	

Describe your duties, responsibilities, and accomplishments

SKILLS AND QUALIFICATIONS

List special qualifications and skills with machines and equipment (office, printing, word processing, public speaking, computer hardware and software, etc.)

Do you have a current valid driver's license? (If Yes, indicate class) ☐ Yes ☐ No

Upon request, candidate must provide documentation of any achievements claimed on the application form to include: certificates, licenses, visas, degrees, registrations, etc.

OFFICE USE ONLY

Tests Administered	Date	Gross Score	Net Score	Errors	Rating

The Small Business Consortium is an equal opportunity employer and does not discriminate on the basis of race, color, national and ethnic origin, sex, marital status, religion, or disability.

Practice 6: Filling Out the Job Application

Assume you have applied for an administrative position, as advertised by the Small Business Consortium. You only know what you read in the ad and you do know where you may be asked to work. The company received your resume and cover letter, decided you are qualified, and invited you to come in to fill out an employment application.

Complete the application by writing directly in this book, or ask your teacher to copy Appendix A: "Sample Job Application" from the answer key. Share your completed copy with your teacher, or role play with another student who can act as the employer reviewing your application.

CHAPTER 12 SUMMARY

A **business letter's** main purposes are to introduce, describe, request, persuade, or thank.

There are seven parts to a business letter: the **return address**, the **date**, the **inside address**, the **salutation**, the **body**, the **closing**, and the **signature**.

A resume provides information to persuade a person to hire you. There are four main types.

- Chronological Resume
- Career Objective Resume
- Functional Resume
- Combination Resume

A profile is a brief statement about why you would make an ideal employee. You may list an **objective** for a specific job type on your resume as well.

Use a **cover letter** to gain an employer's attention.

Employers use a **job application** to gather more information about an applicant and to assess the applicant's ability to follow directions.

CHAPTER 12 REVIEW: WRITING TECHNICAL TEXTS

Use the diagram of the business letter and the information in the paragraph after the diagram to answer questions 1–4.

```
_____  1
_____  2
_____  3

_____  4
_____  5
_____  6

_____  7
_____
_____
_____  8
_____
_____  9
_____  10
_____  11
```

Jimmy Rawler lives at 2396 Bedford Walk in Redwood City, CA 94065. He wrote a letter on April 15, 2009 to Sid's Bait and Tackle Catalog Company, 4569 Colonial Parkway, Smyrna, GA 30087. He is complaining about a set of defective fishing lures.

1. What should go in area 6 of the diagram?

   A. Jimmy Rawler

   B. Redwood City, CA 94065

   C. April 15, 2009

   D. Smyrna, GA 30087

2. In which area should the signature of the writer go?

   A. area 1   B. area 10   C. area 11   D. area 9

3. What should go on line 1 of the business letter?

   A. 2396 Bedford Walk   C. Sid's Bait and Tackle

   B. Jimmy Rawler   D. April 15, 2002

4. On which line should *Dear Sir or Madam*: appear?

   A. line 7   B. line 1   C. line 3   D. line 8

5. Write a business letter using the four-paragraph method to describe the situation listed below.

   > You are someone who has been involved in many outdoor sports such as mountain climbing and camping. You are requesting more information from Pierpoint Technologies on the operation of a sailboat you recently won on a game show. You have no prior experience with sailboats, so you are also requesting any information they may have on instructors in your area. You also would like to know if Pierpoint sells maintenance agreements for sailboats. You have requested that the information be faxed to your home within three days from receiving this letter. You then want to thank Pierpoint Technologies in advance for taking the time to consider your request and provide you with the appropriate information.

6. Gather job applications from a variety of businesses around where you live, and practice filling them out.

Chapter 13
Writing Research Reports

This chapter covers the following McREL standards and benchmarks for Level II:	
Standard 3: Uses grammatical and mechanical conventions in written compositions	Benchmark **11**
Standard 4: Gathers and uses information for research purposes	Benchmarks **2–7**

Research reports and analytical papers require special planning and organization as well as attention to detail in compiling information as you write. The actual writing of a research report will be similar to that used for any type of essay: you will plan, draft, revise, and proofread. However, incorporating research adds several steps.

Once you decide on your research report topic (or are given one by your teacher), you must **find sources**. Sources are informational materials that will support the points you make in your paper. There are **primary sources** (firsthand accounts) and **secondary sources** (written about the accounts). You will need to **interpret and evaluate** sources to determine how well they fit, and then you must **synthesize** all the material you have gathered. Finally, you will add supporting information into your own writing, using appropriate **citations** and **bibliography**.

WRITING THE RESEARCH REPORT

Ideas for a research report can come from many places.
Sometimes you will be assigned a topic, but often you will
need to come up with the subject yourself. When deciding
on a topic, be sure you choose something that interests you
because you will need to become an "expert" on it!

CHOOSING A TOPIC

Nadia had to choose a research paper topic for her English class, and she was not quite sure how to proceed. She did some freewriting; this brought to mind an article in the paper about cases of rabies in a neighboring town. One person had been bitten by a bat. This made her think of how ordinary animals can get a reputation for being bizarre, or more than ordinary. She wondered how the legend started about vampire bats. When her biology class had studied nocturnal animals—including bats—they had focused only on facts. Nadia decided to explore these connections and began by listing what she knows and wants to know.

What I Know	What I Want to Know
Studied nocturnal animals, including bats, in biology	How did bats get their reputation?
Read *Dracula* by Bram Stoker	How did the vampire legend begin?
Saw movies *Interview with the Vampire* and *Twilight*	Is it based on anything real?
Watched *Buffy the Vampire Slayer*	What's the connection between vampire bats and mythical vampires?

In this example, you see some helpful ways to proceed when considering a research topic. As with any composition, you can do **prewriting** (brainstorming, freewriting) to find ideas. Listing what you know and what you want to know can help you plan what research you will need to do.

It is important to remember that research findings will influence what you write about and how you write about it. You may find information contrary to what you thought was true, or you may find so much information about your topic that you will want to narrow it down.

Before Nadia started researching, she noted what she had established so far:

Topic	vampire bats
Issue:	legend, myth, and superstition surrounding the vampire bat
Research Questions:	what are the connections between reality and myth? what's behind the vampire legend?
Thesis	????

ESTABLISHING A THESIS

Notice in the list above that Nadia does not yet have a **thesis** for her paper. Recall from chapter 3, a thesis states the main idea and includes the major lines of argument. Because Nadia has not begun her research, she does not know what she will find. The information she gathers will greatly influence the point she will make in her thesis and what evidence she will obtain to support it.

Practice 1:   Choosing the Research Topic

Practice choosing a topic for a research report you will write. On your own paper, first do a prewriting exercise (brainstorming, freewriting, and so on) to find a topic. Then, list what you know and what you want to know about it. Finally, list the topic, issue, research questions, and a possible thesis if you have one.

FINDING AND EVALUATING RESEARCH SOURCES

Research should not be scary! We all do research. When you compare a college or technical school you may attend, you are conducting research. Using your topic, issue, and research questions, you can list some **keywords** that will guide your research efforts. In Nadia's case, these keywords could include *vampire bat, vampire(s), legend, myth, Dracula,* and *rabies.*

Research sources are available from many places, including libraries, book stores, and Internet sites. In some cases, people also do **field research**, meaning that they make firsthand observations or conduct interviews about their topic. The keywords derived from the topic, issue, and research questions are helpful in locating research sources.

Nadia started her search for sources on the Internet on a computer in the library at school. She went to her favorite **search engine** (a site that enables searches of the World Wide Web for sites containing specific keywords) and entered the keyword *vampire.* The results told her that there were nearly five million hits (possible sites that match the keyword), and the first few did not contain anything she could use. One was about a gothic bookstore, another was a chat site for fans of *Buffy the Vampire Slayer,* and so on. She decided to ask the librarian for help.

The librarian explained that, with so many Web sites on the Internet, a single keyword will often turn up an enormous and jumbled array of possible pages to view. She suggested that Nadia try narrowing her search by entering several of the keywords at once, simply separated by a space. In that way, sites that contained *all* the keywords would come up first.

So, Nadia typed these keywords: *vampire bat legend rabies.* The results were amazing. She found a scientific document about people getting rabies from bat bites, several articles about whether rabies was responsible for the vampire legend, sites about vampire bats, and sites about vampires being associated with animals such as bats and wolves.

Nadia printed several of the pages she found, so she would have the information when she drafted her paper. She also noted the Web site names and addresses on each printout, which she would need for her bibliography (her teacher had warned her that sometimes Web sites may be difficult to find a second time). She also noticed that the full text of one article mentioned was not available on the Web, so she asked the librarian how to find it. She was directed to the **microfiche** (small sheet of microfilm on which several pages can be copied) of periodicals that the library had, and she showed Nadia how to use the microfiche viewer.

When you conduct your research, remember not to give up after the first few searches. As you saw from Nadia's example, you may need to refine your search to get the results you need. In addition, expand your research to include a variety of sources, rather than relying on just one source for all of your information. Below is a list of some research sources to keep in mind.

- Reference books, such as dictionaries, encyclopedias and almanacs
- Periodicals, such as journals and magazines
- Audio and video collections
- Internet sites and online reference sources
- Firsthand research and interviews

Next, Nadia had to **analyze and evaluate** all of her sources: the printouts from the library, the book she had read, the films she had seen, and the lessons she remembered from biology class. She would need to decide which ones to use and how they might influence her thesis. She went back to her list and made some changes, and she came up with a thesis statement.

Topic:	vampire bats vs. vampires of legend—reality and myth
Issue:	the connections between the real-life vampire bat and the vampires of myth and legend may be the disease rabies
Thesis:	One theory is that rabies, a disease sometimes transmitted to humans by animals—including bats—has symptoms similar to becoming a vampire, and that superstitions in less scientific times connected the bat with the made-up monster.

As you can see, Nadia narrowed her topic to focus on rabies as the connection between mythic vampires and vampire bats. Evaluating her sources, Nadia decided to set aside the films and television shows she had seen. While these sources had plenty of lore about mythic vampires, they had nothing to do with real-life bats or with rabies. Her other sources seemed to fit well.

Practice 2: Finding and Evaluating Research Sources

Begin doing research about your topic. On your own paper, write down the sources you find and what information each adds to your topic. Write and test your thesis statement.

VALIDATION: CHECKING SOURCES

Why should you bother with validating sources? After all, if you can find material on a Web site it must be OK, right? No, not always. Many Web sites are created by students and other citizens, who may believe what they have posted is true but are mistaken. Researchers protect their work by screening the material they find for quality and accuracy.

- Find two or more sources that agree with the information that you wish to use.

- Read material carefully, watching for any bias or particularly strong opinion expressed in it.

- Look at the URL for the source of the material. It should name an organization or individual. If the organization is an educational (.edu), government (.gov), or professional (.org) sources, the material is probably valid.

- Look for links within the text of a Web site; these are an indication of a serious, validated work (they're like footnotes in a book). Go to some of the linked sites to check the accuracy of the source as well as to find additional material.

- Look at the homepage of the source for other related works by the author of the site. The more the author has published on a topic, the more trustworthy the material.

- Check the date on the material. Obviously if your topic is on a current event, the more recent the date, the better the information. Recent data and theories are valuable for any topic.

- If you are using informal sources, such as chat rooms, for clustering or sharing ideas, again, the information needs to be confirmed by two or more other sources before it is validated.

The name of the author or organization and the date when the site was updated (modified) can usually be found at the bottom of the main page. Look at this example:

OHIO HISTORY STORE // CALENDAR // PLACES // RESOURCES // ABOUT // SEARCH //
<http://www.ohiohistory.org/about/index.html> Last modified Tuesday, 19-Jun-2007 11:19:22 EST
Ohio Historical Society - 1982 Velma Ave. - Columbus, OH 43211© 1996-2007 All Rights Reserved.

SAFETY

The use of the Internet, without special safe servers, is basically unregulated and unguarded. This situation brings up concerns about credibility, safety, and privacy issues. The following is an informal listing of ways to make your Internet use as safe and as positive as possible.

- Develop a <u>healthy distrust</u> of much of what you read on the Web. Databases are usually OK, but chat rooms and personal Web sites are open to all sorts of deceptions and second-class information, causing frustrating detours for you.

- Be sure to have updated virus software on your personal computer to avoid viruses, spyware, and other online threats.

- Make sure that you understand and follow the expectations that your school, library, or home has about the way the Internet is to be used.

- Understand that some sites have built-in roadblocks; there is no way for you to exit the site. Should you run into this trap, disconnect from the Internet. Then, sign on again. You will also want to alert your teacher or the webmaster to the problem.

- Watch out for anyone online asking you personal questions. This is a flashing red stoplight. Do not respond to those questions and exit that site.

Practice 3: Validating Resources

Using your list of topic, issue, and thesis, find research sources and validate them. Write a short paragraph for each source describing why it is a useful research source.

THESIS

TESTING THE THESIS

When you establish a thesis statement that you believe will work for your research topic, you want to be sure that you can support it and that it clearly states the point you will prove. Asking the questions below can help **test the thesis** and determine whether it meets these criteria.

- Can you state your thesis (your main idea) even more clearly? Could you use more concrete nouns or stronger verbs?

- Will the thesis be of interest to readers? Can you make it more interesting?

- Can you address the thesis thoroughly in your paper's length and in the time to write?

- Do you have evidence from your research sources to support each aspect of your thesis?

SUPPORTING THE THESIS

Once you have determined the thesis of your research paper, you will develop main ideas to **support the thesis**. These will become the **topics for body paragraphs** in your research paper. Each paragraph should in some way support the thesis. Supporting evidence can include:

- facts and statistics
- definitions
- commonly held beliefs

- hypotheses or theories
- scenarios or examples
- quotations from experts

The next step for Nadia was to develop ideas to support the thesis. Nadia created an **outline** to help her with this. The ideas in her outline would become the main points of the body paragraphs in her research report. Take a look at Nadia's research paper outline.

Research Paper Outline

I.   Introduction: Vampire bats and vampires of legend are linked.

    A. Thesis: One reason could be rabies.

       1. People can get rabies from bats, and people can become vampires after bitten by vampire.

       2. People with rabies behave strangely, which is similar for those bitten by vampires.

II.   Legend of vampires

    A. Origins of legend are ancient.

    B. "Modern" folklore—most famous story created by Bram Stoker.

       1. Stoker borrowed from many myths to create Dracula.

       2. By this time (1897), the vampire bat was well known.

    C. What are the vampires' traits?

       1. drink blood

       2. afraid of sunlight, mirrors, water

III. Connection to rabies

    A. Some symptoms mistaken for vampire traits.

       1. snarling, biting, fear of sun/mirrors/water, deathlike sleep

    B. There were misunderstanding of diseases.

       1. rabies outbreaks in Europe

    C. Other diseases were mistaken for vampirism.

IV. Truth about vampire bats

    A. Why are they named after vampires?

    B. The facts—bat's real diet, rabies cases, beneficial qualities

V.   Conclusion: Vampire bat gets its strange reputation from vampire legend, most likely due to past misunderstanding of rabies.

Practice 4: Supporting the Thesis

Using your list of topic, issue, and research questions as well as your thesis and research sources, write an outline for a research report about your topic.

DRAFTING THE RESEARCH REPORT

Drafting a research report is much like drafting any composition, except that it may be longer to accommodate all of your research material. Review chapter 4, Drafting the Essay, for the steps of drafting, which include improving word choice, developing coherence, writing effective introductions and conclusions, using transition words, and using appropriate formatting.

When you write your first draft, you may already know where in your paper you want to use some of the research sources you have gathered. If you do, then make notes in the draft to remind you where you want to insert each point of support, and indicate where each quote, paraphrase, or summary came from. Be careful not to fill your paper predominantly with information from your sources. The research source information is there to support the point that *you* make, in your own words.

One way to make it easier to keep your sources straight is to organize your notes by subjects. For example, Nadia grouped her articles with those about the vampire legend on top, those about rabies next, then those about Bram Stoker, and finally those about vampire bats.

Now, read the first draft of Nadia's research report. You will see some issues with organization, sentence structure, grammar, and mechanics that need to be fixed at the revision stage.

The Mistaken Identity of the Vampire Bat

On one hand, there are countless tales and legends of the mythical creatures called vampires, which go back centuries and are found in many cultures. On the other hand is the vampire bat, a tropical American bat, named after these creatures. What do they have in common? Both the vampires of legend and vampire bats feed on blood, and they both can make their victims very sick, even to the point of death. But that's where the similarity ends. How did the misunderstood little bat become associated with the evil, undead vampires portrayed in literature and film? One theory is that rabies, a disease sometimes transmitted to humans by animals—including bats—has symptoms similar to becoming a vampire, and that superstitions in less scientific times connected the bat with the made-up monster.

The origins of the vampire legend are ancient. Some myths date as far back as the fourth century. The legend arose in many cultures. There is mythology about vampires from all over the world (Wikipedia). What most stories have in common is that vampires were once living people but are now "the walking dead," and they stalk the living for blood. In most myths, vampires are evil, grotesque beings not unlike demons. The myths arose for various reasons, as reactions to political and religious clashes (Wikipedia) and as superstitious explanations for mysterious diseases (Origins of Belief). Among the diseases now known to probably be mistaken for vampirism is rabies, which was sometimes transmitted to humans through scratches or bites from infected animals, including bats.

Before the nineteenth century in Eastern Europe, where our modern idea of vampires originated, vampires were depicted as raving demons who fed insatiably on human blood. Only after Bram Stoker's *Dracula* did the vampire become a being able to move in society with intelligence and restraint. Stoker did something else innovative to create Count Dracula: he borrowed "from several versions of the vampire myth, and adding some details of his own, Stoker formed the standard for the modern vampire" (Modern Vampires). The name came from Vlad Dracul, a reportedly cruel and brutal Romanian prince. However, nothing in the history of this real person suggests anything about vampirism (Modern Vampires). Stoker probably just liked his name, which means dragon or devil, and the mystery surrounding him. He also incorporated the traits of vampires from various myths, setting down the ultimate definition of vampires that exists in the Western world today: Vampires are immortal, strong, and intelligent, they drink blood, and they sleep in their coffins during the day. They have some weaknesses, though: fear of crosses, water, and mirrors (in which they cast no reflection) as well as garlic and wolfsbane. They can be killed by the sun or a stake driven through the heart. Most importantly to this discussion, Stoker forever linked the vampire bat to the vampire legend by referring throughout his book to Dracula taking the form of a bat, and in one passage even naming the species when Quincy Morris says, [insert quote about it being a vampire bat] (*Dracula* 145). In 1897, when *Dracula* was published, species of bats in Mexico and Central and South American had been referred to as vampire bats for about a century because people had seen them drinking the blood of livestock, and sometimes people, but it did not exist in Europe, where the Dracula story takes place. That didn't matter, and the connection stuck.

Additional influences on Stoker's novel were the diseases rampant throughout Europe in the eighteenth and nineteenth centuries. Rabies outbreaks were particularly feared, and it was not until 1885 that Louis Pasteur discovered the vaccine for the disease. Transmitted by rodents and especially by infected dogs, the disease was so dreaded that people bitten by dogs thought to be infected often killed themselves rather than facing a slow horrible death (Baer). Rabies attacks the

Louis Pasteur

central nervous system, causing violence and convulsions, including spasms in which the upper lip jerks back over the teeth, in an animal-like snarl (Loecher). Rabies victims often tried to bite other people. They also became hypersensitive, resulting in an apparent fear of light and other bright things like mirrors and to smells like garlic, and a strong aversion to water. Because the disease affects part of the brain that controls sleep, rabies victims are often awake at night, but can collapse in a death-like sleep during the day. Once symptoms appear, the disease is always deadly. Finally, like vampirism, rabies can be transmitted through a bite. In a recent article, Spanish neurologist Dr. Juan Gomez-Alonzo reported that, after watching a vampire movie for the first time, he found the similarities of vampirism to rabies striking and said, "Much evidence supports that rabies could have played a key role in the generation of the vampire legend" (Loecher).

Symptoms of two other diseases were sometimes taken for vampirism. Porphyria, a rare disease in which the blood does not produce enough pigment (color), can in severe cases cause sensitivity to sunlight, delirium, and sometimes the look of having a reddish mouth and teeth (due to irregular coloring), as though the person had been drinking blood. In addition, catalepsy, a condition in which a person can freeze up and become very stiff, with shallow respiration and heartbeat, made people appear to be dead. When they woke up hours or even days later, it seems they were rising from the dead, especially if they had been mistakenly buried (Origins of Belief)! None of this explains, however, why the vampire bat, an ocean away, became the culprit that to this day inspires fear and superstition.

While it is true that vampire bats, along with most other bat species, have been known to transmit rabies to people (and more often to animals), they do so no more than other wild animals such as raccoons and skunks (Krebs). Vampire bats sleep during the day in caves or other completely dark areas, and at night they come out to feed. They do drink blood, but they can hardly be classified as people-killers. Rarely attacking human beings, vampire bats usually seek out a sleeping cow or goat and make a small bite, then lap up the blood. "This wound is small and the animal often does not even realize it has been bitten" (Carattini). In fact, they only need about two tablespoons of blood a day (Harris). Bats, including the vampire bat, are in fact very beneficial to human beings. For example, they eat insects, they can pollinate plants, and their droppings (guano) is a excellent natural fertilizer (How Bats Work). There is also research being done now to harness the bite of the vampire bat for medicine. Scientists are investigating uses of the powerful anticoagulant (a substance that stops the blood from clotting) secreted by vampire bats when they bite to help stroke patients (BBC). In fact, the only real thing to fear from vampire bats comes full circle to the rabies they may carry.

Named after the notorious, blood-sucking monster of legends, the vampire bat has been misguidedly feared and hated. The misunderstanding of rabies and other diseases led to suspicion of people being possessed, becoming werewolves, or becoming vampires, but these things can be scientifically explained today. In the same way, the mistaken notion that a bat was really a transformed person coming to make someone else a vampire can be set aside so people can see the unfortunately-named vampire bat for what it really is.

Nadia now has a good start. Her draft needs to be revised for coherence, transitions, consistency of tense and voice, redundancy, and sentence structure. She also must incorporate her research sources appropriately, according to the style her teacher assigned and to add her bibliography. We will discuss how to do that in the next section. First, draft your own paper.

Practice 5: Drafting the Research Report

Using Nadia's draft as a guide, draft your own research report. Work from your outline to make sure you do not forget anything, but don't be afraid to leave things out that do not seem to fit or to change things around, just as Nadia did. Get your ideas down on paper, making notes where you may want to use research sources. You will revise later.

INTEGRATING RESEARCH SOURCES

Working from the outline of your research report, you probably did something similar in your draft to what Nadia did, noting the names of articles or books in places where you wanted to use these sources. That's fine for your draft, but in your final version that you will turn in, you want to be sure to list your **in-text citations** correctly, in the style indicated for the assignment.

When you revise your research report to integrate research sources you found, there are guidelines that will help you. First, you need to decide the amount of research data to use, including enough of your source material to show the thorough research you did, but not so much that the supporting material overshadows your own writing. Next, you need to use correct **documentation conventions** for **integrating source material**, including appropriate punctuation and in-text citations. Finally, you need to decide how to fold in source material, through **direct quotation**, **paraphrase**, or **summary**. Whatever format you use, you must always properly cite your sources. Otherwise, you will be **plagiarizing** (taking someone else's words or ideas and passing them off as your own), which is a form of cheating.

The **amount of source material** integrated into your research report will depend on your topic and purpose. In Nadia's sample draft, she achieved an appropriate balance of original text (her own ideas, written in her own words) to research source material (cited work). Any less may show a lack of research support; much more may turn the paper into a compilation of source material with no sense of the author. An exception to this may be introductory and concluding paragraphs, which often include only one citation or none at all, as they either introduce or summarize an entire content of the paper.

In order to list a source correctly, you must know the **documentation style** in which you are expected to format your citations and bibliography. There are several different styles, and each is used in different fields. The most well known styles are the following:

MLA Style	(Modern Language Association) is widely used for literary analysis and for English Language Arts studies. As it is the most common academic style, we will focus on using MLA guidelines in this section to complete the sample research report.
CMS Style	(*The Chicago Manual of Style*), also called simply Chicago Style, is used in the fields of history, philosophy, and fine arts.
APA Style	(American Psychological Association) is used by writers in the field of psychology, as well as in sociology, economics, and education.
CBE Style	(Council of Biology Editors) is used in the sciences.

Documentation styles have differences that sometimes seem small, but they are important for correctly citing and listing research sources. One example of an important difference is that MLA style uses endnotes to include information that is important but does not belong in the text, Chicago style uses footnotes which are summarized in endnotes, and both APA and CBE styles usually use no footnotes or endnotes. To make sure you cite and list your research materials correctly, be sure you know what style you should be using, and use a style manual or guide. Writing guides like *The St. Martin's Handbook* or the *Hodge's Harbrace Handbook* often list how to use several popular styles. Complete guides for each style also are available on the Internet, in bookstores, and at your local library.

MLA STYLE BASICS

Learning all you need to know about a documentation style will require that you carefully review a style guide, like those mentioned above. Here, we will discuss some of the basic guidelines for using the selected documentation style, MLA.

MLA style uses **parenthetical citations**, which means a reference to a work is placed in parentheses after a quote, paraphrase, or summary. A **citation** is a brief reference in a text to another source that acknowledges where a quote or idea came from. Let's look at an example from Nadia's paper. In the paragraph about how Bram Stoker's book linked vampire bats to mythic vampires, she includes the source information that you will see on the next page.

> Most importantly to this discussion, Stoker forever linked the vampire bat to the vampire legend by referring throughout his book to Dracula taking the form of a bat, and in one passage even naming the species when Quincy Morris says, [insert quote about it being a vampire bat] (*Dracula* 145)

When revising, Nadia will replace this note with an actual quote from the book.

Nadia was on the right track, having used parentheses to enclose her citation information. However, when she checked the MLA style guide, she saw that MLA requires citations to be listed as follows.

- For a work by one author, list the author's last name and the page number where the material is taken– no comma between.

  Example: Two examples of the theory are explained (Dankin 185).

Notice the end punctuation goes after the parenthetical citation. When material is summarized from more than one page, give the page range.

  Example: (Dankin 185–187)

- When the author is cited in the text, put only the page number in parentheses.

  Example: Dankin gives us two examples of the theory (185).

- For a work by two authors, list both names and page number.

  Example: (Dankin and Lex 150)

If there are three or more authors, use the name of the first listed and *et al* (abbreviation for the Latin *et alii*, meaning "and others").

  Example: (Dankin, et al. 176)

- An online source is cited much like a book, with author, if given, or organization.

  Example: (Freudenrich, sec. 1)

In addition, Nadia went on to make sure she included the quotation correctly. In the MLA style guide, she read the following about including **quotations**, **paraphrases**, and **summaries** in her research paper.

- Use **direct quotations** when you wish to include exact wording from a research source. Be sure the wording is exactly as it appears in the original text, and enclose it in double quotation marks (single quotation marks can be used for a quote within a quote). Insert the parenthetical citation after the end quotation marks, but before the end punctuation.

Example: In his analysis of the theories, Dankin notes, "Several years of observation preceded the scientists' formulation of their respective theories" (186).

- For a long quotation (in MLA style, longer than four lines), set off the entire quote by introducing it with a phrase and colon, beginning a new paragraph, and indenting the entire quote one inch or ten spaces.

Example: Dankin discusses the work it took to arrive at the theories:

> Those around them soon tired of their incessant work. The experimentation and late-night work sessions continued, until each had formulated a hypothesis about what was occurring. Little did they know their theories, forged under such duress, would survive to the day. (188)

Note that in this case there are no quotations placed around the source material (setting off the quote indicates it is a direct quotation), and the parenthetical citation is placed after the end punctuation.

- Use **paraphrase** when you want to use your own words to tell what an author is saying. This can be a good option if a direct quote would be a bit too long or if the wording of the quote would not fit well with the original text around it (as in the case of verb tenses being inconsistent).

Example: Dankin tells how the theories were forged through long days and nights, with the scientists unaware how long the outcomes would actually survive (185).

- Use a **summary** to include the main idea from a source that does not lend itself to direct quotation or paraphrase, such as summarizing the content of an entire article.

Example: *The New Haven Herald* noted that Dankin's book was the definitive work on the theories (Porter F1+).

Now, Nadia was ready to complete the quotation and citation. She found the complete quotation in the book and made sure to copy it exactly.

> Most importantly to this discussion, Stoker forever linked the vampire bat to the vampire legend by referring throughout his book to Dracula taking the form of a bat, and in one passage even naming the species when Quincy Morris says, "One of those big bats that they call vampires had got at her in the night, and what with his gorge and the vein left open, there wasn't enough blood in her to let her stand up" (Stoker 145).

BIBLIOGRAPHIES

Each citation in the research report must have a matching entry in the **bibliography** or **works cited** page at the end of the paper, in which complete information is provided about how to find the source cited. A citation in the text means nothing without its corresponding reference listing.

Sometimes, you will be asked to include a works cited page or a references page, and other times you will need a bibliography. What's the difference between these lists? A works cited page, also called a **references page**, lists only works cited in the text. A bibliography, also called a **works consulted page**, is a list of all works that were part of the research and are pertinent to the subject, even though some may not be cited in the text. Sometimes, an **annotated bibliography** may be called for, which not only lists the research sources, but includes a brief summary of each source. Make sure that you are clear about the type of research source list you must include with your research report, and look up the proper conventions and formatting to use in the guide for the style you are using.

In MLA style, the sources are normally listed on a works cited page and include only the sources cited in the text. There are detailed directions and examples in the MLA style guide for how to list every type of source, including books, periodicals, electronic sources, and others. The general guidelines that apply for most sources are below.

- First, list the **author**, last name first, followed by a comma and the first name. If there are more authors, the second subsequent names appear with the first name first. Place a period after the name(s). Works are listed alphabetically by author's last name.

    Example: Jones, Barry, Lisa Davis, and Marquis Hammel.

- Next, list the **title**. In MLA style (and most others), the titles of books, periodicals, reference works, albums and CDs, Web sites, and any other "long" works appear in italics or underlined (not both). Titles of short stories, articles, poems, songs, pamphlets, and any other "short" works appear in quotation marks. If you are in doubt about how a specific source should appear in the works cited, consult the MLA style guide. Again, insert a period after the title.

- Then, list the **publication information**. In MLA style, this includes the city of publication followed by a colon, a shortened form of the publisher's name (for example, Albert A. Knopf is entered simply as Knopf), a comma, and the latest copyright date of the edition being used. All of this information can be found on the copyright page in most publications.

    When there is no author, the title appears first and is folded into the alphabetic organization.

Nadia decided to try listing the source she had quoted in her text, the book by Bram Stoker. The author and title she knew, and she found the publication information on the copyright page in her paperback of *Dracula*. It was on the third page of the book. She read that this edition had been published in New York by Jove Publications, Inc., and there was only one copyright year, 1979. Nadia entered the information as follows:

Stoker, Bram. *Dracula*. New York: Jove, 1979.

She checked with her English teacher before listing other sources. Her teacher said it was perfect. He reminded her that if a source listing exceeds one line, the second line onward are all indented half an inch, or five spaces. He also mentioned that style guides might change how entries should be made, so she should check her guide carefully. Nadia said she would remember. Nadia added an online source to her bibliography with an access date and the URL included:

Harris, Tom. "How Bats Work." *How Stuff Works*. 29 Mar. 2008

<http://science.howstuffworks.com/vampire4.htm>.

Practice 6: Citing and Listing Sources

A. Use a separate sheet of paper for responses. Using the general guidelines provided for MLA Style works cited listings, list the following sources as they should appear.

1. *Shakespeare in the Movies*, by Douglas Brode, published in New York, New York. Copyright 2000 by Oxford University Press.

2. *Wisdom from the Ancients*. Authors: Thomas J. Figueira, T. Corey Brennan, and Rachel Hall Sternberg. Cambridge, MA. 2001. Published by Perseus Publishing.

3. Michael Macrone. *It's Greek to Me!* Published and copyrighted in 1994 by HarperCollins Publishers, in New York.

4. http://www.beowulf.edu, "Golden Seal" by Christopher Golden, Beowulf College, 5-7-04.

B. Now, list the research sources for the research paper you have drafted. Use the guidelines in this book as well as a printed or online MLA style guide.

REVISING THE RESEARCH REPORT

A very important aspect of completing your research report is **revision and proofreading**. Review chapter 5 of this book, and follow the steps for revision and proofreading.

The format of your research paper will be determined by the type of paper you are writing, by the style (MLA, APA, etc.) being used, and especially by the instructions that your teacher gives you for how it should look when it is turned in. The sample research report that follows (Nadia's final copy) represents one possible way to format such a paper.

Here is Nadia's final paper. Along the margin are comments about what Nadia changed, and why, when she revised and edited her draft. Compare this version with her earlier draft.

Nadia James
ELA, 2nd Period
Mr. Reynolds

The Mistaken Identity of the Vampire Bat

In her first paragraph, Nadia corrected errors and made slight revisions to improve word choice and flow. She also revised her thesis to better explain the connections she will explore between vampires, rabies, and bats.

On one hand, there are countless tales and legends of the mythical creatures called vampires, which go back centuries and are found in many cultures. On the other hand is the vampire bat, a tropical American bat, named after these creatures. What do they have in common? Both the vampires of legend and vampire bats feed on blood, and they both can make their victims sick and even kill them, though in very different ways. However, that is where the similarity ends. How did the misunderstood little bat become associated with the evil, undead vampires portrayed in literature and film? One theory is that people once confused rabies with vampirism; when bats in the New World were seen drinking blood, with rabies sometimes resulting, people linked the flying mammal with the disease, and thus with mythic vampires.

Here, Nadia combined and revised sentences to vary her sentence structure. She also corrected some redundant language.

As she revised her writing, Nadia also made sure her source material was correctly worded and cited.

The origins of the vampire legend are ancient, with some myths dating back to the fourth century. The legend arose in many cultures, including those of Australia, Malaysia, the Philippines, Mexico, Brazil, China, and Europe (Wikipedia). What most stories have in common is that vampires were once living people but are now "the walking dead," and they stalk the living for blood. In most myths, vampires are evil, grotesque beings not unlike demons. The myths arose for various reasons, as reactions to political and religious clashes (Wikipedia) and as superstitious explanations for mysterious diseases (Harris, "Origins"). Among the diseases that are identified today, but probably assumed to be vampirism in the past, is rabies. Rabies attacks the central nervous system, has horrific symptoms, and is fatal (unless treated immediately with the vaccine now available). It can be transmitted to humans through scratches or bites from infected animals, including bats.

> Nadia decided that the idea of Stoker making Dracula a "civilized" vampire did not make sense here, until she introduced his many innovations. Therefore, information in this paragraph has been moved around.

> To arrive faster at talking about Stoker linking vampire bats to mythic vampires, Nadia removed a few sentences from this paragraph that she will use later. She also improved sentence structure and corrected citations. She added a reference to an endnote about porphyria, which is discussed in the note at the end of her research report.

> In this paragraph, Nadia corrected inconsistencies in verb tense, as well as non-parallel sentence structure. She also chose new words in a few places to make her descriptions more exact.

Despite the long history of vampire legend, our modern Western ideas about mythic vampires comes mainly from one place: Bram Stoker's novel, *Dracula*, written in 1897. Before then, most vampire myths, including those of Eastern Europe, depicted the creatures as raving demons who fed insatiably on human blood (Harris, "Later"). In creating his main character of Count Dracula, Stoker invented a new type of vampire, one that was not a lunatic beast but could move in society and was intelligent. Borrowing "from several versions of the vampire myth, and adding some details of his own, Stoker formed the standard for the modern vampire" (Harris, "Modern"). Count Dracula's name came from a real-life historical figure, Vlad Dracul, a reportedly cruel and brutal Romanian prince. Some people speculate that Vlad Dracul may have had a rare disease called porphyria[1] (another disease sometimes mistaken for vampirism), and perhaps this is what interested Stoker ("Vampire"). But the author probably just liked his name, which means dragon or devil, and the mystery surrounding him. Whatever his many inspirations, Stoker created the definitive vampire, on which all others have been based. Most importantly to this discussion, Stoker forever linked the vampire bat to the vampire legend. Throughout the book, there are references to Dracula taking the form of a bat, and in one passage the species of bat is even named, when Quincy Morris says, "One of these big bats that they call vampires had got at her in the night, and what with his gorge and the vein left open, there wasn't enough blood in her to let her stand up" (Stoker 145). When *Dracula* was published, species of bats in Mexico and Central and South American had been called vampire bats for about a century because people had seen them drinking the blood of livestock—and sometimes people—but this bat did not exist in Europe, where the Dracula story takes place. Regardless, the connection stuck.

Among the many influences on Stoker's novel were the diseases rampant throughout Europe in the eighteenth and nineteenth centuries. Rabies outbreaks were particularly feared, and it was not until 1885 that Louis Pasteur discovered the vaccine for the disease. Transmitted by wild animals and especially by infected dogs, the disease was so dreaded that people bitten by dogs thought to be rabid often killed themselves rather than facing a slow, horrible death (Baer). Rabies attacks the central nervous system, causing violence and convulsions, including spasms "in which the upper lip jerks back over the teeth, in an animal-like snarl" (Loecher). Rabies victims often tried to bite other people; if they succeeded, the disease was passed on. They also had a strong aversion to water and became

The paragraph about other diseases did not fit into the flow, so Nadia decided to use the information in her endnote. Since it includes porphyria, she placed the endnote reference next to that word (see end of report).

Here again Nadia corrected her citation and made some changes to improve wording, sentence structure, and flow.

hypersensitive, resulting in an apparent fear of light and other bright objects like mirrors as well as to smells like garlic. Because the disease affects the part of the brain that controls sleep, rabies victims often wandered at night but collapsed in a deathlike sleep during the day. Once symptoms appear, rabies is always deadly. It is no wonder that people who had no idea what rabies was jumped to conclusions about people with the traits a vampire was supposed to have: strong, violent, asleep during the day and stalking at night, and afraid of crosses, garlic, water, mirrors, and sunlight. In an interview, Spanish neurologist Dr. Juan Gomez-Alonzo reported that, after watching a vampire movie for the first time, he found the similarities of supposed vampirism to rabies striking and said, "Much evidence supports that rabies could have played a key role in the generation of the vampire legend" (Loecher).

This does not explain, however, why the vampire bat, an ocean away, became the culprit that to this day inspires fear and superstition. While it is true that vampire bats, along with most other bat species, have been known to transmit rabies to people (and more often to animals), they do so no more than other wild animals such as raccoons and skunks (Krebs, et al. 1–3). Vampire bats sleep during the day in caves or other completely dark areas, and at night they come out to feed. They do drink blood, but they can hardly be classified as people-killers. Rarely attacking human beings, vampire bats usually seek out a sleeping cow or goat and make a small cut, then lap up the blood. "This wound is small and the animal often does not even realize it has been bitten" (Carattini). In fact, bats only need about two tablespoons of blood a day. Bats, including the vampire bat, are actually very beneficial to human beings. For example, they eat insects, they can pollinate plants, and their droppings (guano) are an excellent natural fertilizer (Harris, "How Bats Work"). There is also research being done now to harness the bite of the vampire bat for medicine. Scientists are investigating uses of the powerful anticoagulant (a substance that stops the blood from clotting) secreted by vampire bats when they bite to help stroke patients ("Secret"). In fact, the only real thing to fear from vampire bats comes full circle to the rabies they may carry.

Named after the notorious, blood-sucking monster of legends, the vampire bat has been misguidedly feared and hated. The misunderstanding of rabies and other diseases led to superstitious beliefs about people being possessed or becoming werewolves or vampires, but the causes behind the strange behaviors can be scientifically explained today. In the same way, the notion that a bat was really a transformed undead human, coming to drain people's blood or make them vampires too, can be set aside today so that people can see the unfortunately named vampire bat for what it really is.

At the end of her paper, Nadia typed her footnote information.

Notes

[1]Like rabies, other diseases were misunderstood at the time. Specifically, symptoms of two other diseases were sometimes taken for vampirism. Porphyria, a rare disease in which the blood does not produce enough pigment (color) can in severe cases cause sensitivity to sunlight, delirium, stomach cramps, and sometimes the look of having a reddish mouth and teeth (due to irregular coloring), as though the person had been drinking blood. In addition, catalepsy, a condition in which a person can become very stiff, with shallow respiration and heartbeat, made people appear to be dead. When they woke up hours or even days later, it seemed they were rising from the dead, especially if they had been mistakenly buried (Harris, "Origins")!

Finally, on a separate page, Nadia typed her works cited list.

Works Cited

Baer, George M. *The Natural History of Rabies, 2nd Edition.* Baca Raton: CRC, 1991

Carattini, Lisa. "The Vampire Bat." *PageWise.* 30 Mar. 2008 <http://va.essortment.com/all/batvampiredesin_rggj.htm>.

Harris, Tom. "How Bats Work." *How Stuff Works.* 29 Mar. 2008 <http://animals.howstuffworks.com/mammals/bat4.htm>.

---. "Later Vampires." *How Stuff Works.* 29 Mar. 2008 <http://science.howstuffworks.com/vampire3.htm>.

---. "Modern Vampires." *How Stuff Works.* 29 Mar. 2008 <http://science.howstuffworks.com/vampire4.htm>.

---. "Origins of Belief." *How Stuff Works.* 29 Mar. 2008 <http://science.howstuffworks.com/vampire5.htm>.

Krebs, John W., MS; Heather R. Noll, MPH; Charles E. Rupprecht, VMD, PhD; James E. Childs, ScD. "Public Veterinary Medicine: Public Health: Rabies surveillance in the United States during 2001." *JAVMA* 221.12 (2002): 1690-1701.

Loecher, Barbara. "Rabies May Have Inspired Vampire Legend." *Reuters,* 1998. 1 Apr. 2008 <http://www.angelfire.com/nj/woundedknee/vampires.htm>

"Secret of the Bat's Bite." *BBC News World Edition.* 30 Mar. 2008 <http://news.bbc.co.uk/2/hi/health/265227.stm>.

Stoker, Bram. *Dracula.* New York: Jove, 1979.

"Vampire." *Wikipedia.* 29 Mar. 2008 <http://en.wikipedia.org/wiki/Vampire>.

Practice 7:   Revising the Research Report

Review the changes that Nadia made and read her final paper and attachments carefully. Then, revise your research report and add notes (if you have any) and a works cited page. Share your paper with your teacher, or trade research reports with another student to exchange feedback.

CHAPTER 13 SUMMARY

Sources are informational materials that will support the points you make in your paper. There are **primary sources** (firsthand accounts) and **secondary sources** (written about the accounts).

A **thesis** states the main idea and includes the major lines of argument.

A **search engine** is a site that enables searches of the World Wide Web for sites containing specific keywords.

The **amount of source material** integrated into your research report will depend on your topic and purpose.

A **citation** is a brief reference in a text to another source that acknowledges where a quote or idea came from.

A **works cited page**, also called a **references page**, lists only works cited in the text.

A **bibliography** is a list of all works that were part of the research and are pertinent to the subject, even though some may not be cited in the text.

An **annotated bibliography** lists the research sources and includes a brief summary of each source.

Plagiarizing is taking someone else's words or ideas and passing them off as your own.

There are four main **documentation styles**:

- MLA Style
- CMS Style
- APA Style
- CBE Style

Once you have written your final draft, be sure to **revise and proofread** your research paper to catch and correct errors.

CHAPTER 13 REVIEW: WRITING RESEARCH REPORTS

Sometimes, you will be able to choose a research topic, and other times you will be assigned what to write. Even when the topic is assigned, you will need to do some prewriting to focus on the subject, narrow down what you will talk about, generate possible keywords to research, and organize your ideas. Using the topics below, fill in the chart for topic 1. Then, on your own paper, create charts for topics 2 and 3.

1. Topic: preserving famous works of art

What I Know	What I Want to Know

2. Topic: life before computers

3. Topic: underground transportation

Review your notes about the topics that you explored above. Now, use the same kind of chart, and make a list of research sources you would most likely use to begin your search for information. How and where might you find them?

4. Topic: preserving famous works of art

Possible Research Sources	How/Where I Would Find Them

5. Topic: life before computers

6. Topic: underground transportation

Consider the three topics you have been working on. Which one is most interesting to you? For which one do you think you could find the best research sources? Now, choose one of the topics, and complete the steps below.

7. Write a clear thesis statement for a research paper about each topic. If you need to, review Establishing a Thesis on page 259. Keep in mind that you may actually need to do part of the research to create an effective thesis statement. Then, test the thesis, following the steps you learned about earlier.

    *   Can you state your thesis (your comment about the topic) even more clearly? Could you use more concrete nouns or stronger verbs?

    *   Will the thesis be of interest to readers? Can you make it more interesting?

    *   Is your thesis one that you can address thoroughly in the length of paper you are writing and in the time you have?

    *   Do you have evidence from your research sources to support each aspect of your thesis?

8. Develop an outline for a research report you would write about each topic, using the thesis which you wrote and tested. Nadia's sample outline on page 263 can serve as a guide.

List the research sources described below in MLA style for a bibliography. Refer back to the section about Citing and Listing Sources, if you wish. It will be even more helpful to consult an MLA style guide.

9. *Decoding Egyptian Hieroglyphs* is a fascinating reference book by Bridget McDermott, with a foreword by Dr. Joann Fletcher. Its latest copyright is 2001, and it was published by Chronicle Books of San Francisco, California

10. There was an article about modern-day blacksmiths in the *Calhoun Herald*, called "A Really Big Shoe." It started on page B1 and continued on B9 of the May 23, 2004, edition. The community reporter, Martha Wenslow, did a great job writing it.

11. A great deal of information about how much stamps are worth can be found in current catalogs, like the *Mystic's 2009 U. S. Stamp Catalog*, volumes 1 and 2. Published each year by the Mystic Stamp Company of Camden, New York, it contains photographs, descriptions, and pricing for thousands of collectible stamps.

12. An interesting history of our nation's flag can be found at a Web site called *Founding Fathers*. There are links to various points in the flag's history right from the home page at http://www.foundingfathers.info/. While the *Founding Fathers* site doesn't list authors, the links that lead to other sites do have articles with authors listed.

Basics Made Easy

Chapter 14
Scoring the Essay

Since you are a student writing the essay, not a trained scorer grading the essay, why should you practice scoring essays? There are two reasons: (1) Scoring will help you improve your writing, and (2) you will learn about holistic scoring, a scoring method commonly used to assess writing proficiency.

An important part of the writing process is reviewing. A good writer steps back from his or her work, takes time away, and returns to the work with a fresh outlook. Then the writer can see more clearly which ideas are unrelated and which need more development. Errors in grammar and punctuation stand out more, and the writer can hear whether the tone is appropriate and consistent throughout the essay.

When teachers and students learn about holistic scoring, they are better able to evaluate writing. To determine a score for an essay, you must distance yourself from the work and use an objective scale to evaluate the work. This process will help you develop better skills in reviewing your own written work, thus making you a better writer.

When you take a writing test required by your state, it will be scored based on a state **rubric**. A rubric is a table of points you can earn and the skills that you must demonstrate in each area of writing. In this chapter, you will use a scoring scale that is similar to many state rubrics.

As you or your teacher score your own paper and the papers of your student peers, you will be using the same **criteria** (standards) as when you are writing an essay. For scoring practice, this chapter is set up so that you may focus on one trait at a time to score. (Example: The first two essays will be scored for their ideas only.) In this process, you will become more familiar with the writing skills that the trained scorers will evaluate. Then, you will be better able to include those skills in your own writing, so you can write a better essay for the written test.

This chapter provides you with a scoring overview, as well as detailed scoring information about four analytical **traits**. The traits provide the guidelines for scoring a writing exam. They include the following areas:

- Ideas
- Organization
- Voice
- Writing Conventions

This chapter also contains some sample essays for you to practice scoring. The best practice, however, is for you, your teacher, and your peers to review your own essays and work together to score them. Then revise your writing as needed to improve your scores.

SCORING OVERVIEW

This chapter will evaluate the four traits using a six-point scale for **holistic grading** of your essays. (Holistic grading means the essay will be scored as a whole and not simply by counting the number of errors.)

RECOMMENDATIONS

To make sure your paper can be graded properly, do the following:

- **Write on the assigned topic.** Make sure you clearly understand the topic, purpose, and audience for your assignment. Keep a clear focus, and do not stray from it.

- **Write in English.** This test is intended to evaluate your skill in writing Standard American English.

- **Write legibly.** You want the graders to be able to read your essay easily. You may have great ideas, but if the graders can't read them, you will not get credit for them.

- **Write a well-developed composition.** Though you may have only a certain amount of time, you must take some time to organize your ideas for each essay.

- **Write in prose.** This isn't a test in poetry. Extended use of poetry or musical lyrics will not be graded.

- **Write respectfully.** Essays that use offensive language or discuss offensive content may not be graded. If you can't express your ideas without vulgarity, then don't express them.

- **Write your pre-writing and your essays either on your own paper, or on paper given to you by your teacher, or in the appropriate, labeled spaces provided in an answer document.** Pre-writing can be a simple cluster diagram or a quick listing of the major points you want to make about the topic. From this you can develop a central idea and tone. Be prepared to change the tone of your writing as you move from one prompt to the next.

- **Write your own essay.** You may not copy a published source or another student's writing.

By following these recommendations, you make sure only that your paper will be graded. For your paper to receive a passing grade or an excellent grade, you must demonstrate skill in the **four traits** (areas of writing skill) outlined in the next section which professional graders generally use to evaluate writing proficiency.

TRAITS

As you read in the introduction to the diagnostic writing exam at the beginning of this book, scorers will assess your essays according to criteria similar to the four traits and their corresponding components.

1. **Ideas:** The writer develops a clear, focused main idea or ideas related to the prompt. In addition, he or she demonstrates completeness in his or her writing through the use of documented support, elaboration, anecdotes, images, or carefully selected details that build understanding or hold a reader's attention. This trait includes the following components:

- Response to assigned task

- Clearly established main idea(s)

- Sufficiently relevant supporting ideas

- Clearly developed supporting ideas appropriate to the audience, purpose, and topic

2. **Organization:** The writer uses his or her organizational method to provide logical links in each detail or new development in the essay, leading the reader to a turning point, key revelation, or well developed conclusion. The writer also provides smooth transitions between details or events in the essay. This trait includes the following components:

- Clearly discernible order of presentation

- Logical transitions

- Natural flow of ideas

- Clear description of topic found in both the introduction and conclusion

3. **Voice:** The writer uses his or her ability to emotionally connect with the audience through using the following components:

- Varied and effective sentence structure

- Tone consistent with topic and purpose

- Sense of audience

4. **Writing Conventions:** The writer forms sentences correctly. This trait includes the following components:

- Appropriate usage (clear pronoun references, subject-verb agreement, etc.)
- Appropriate mechanics (proper spelling, capitalization, punctuation, etc.)
- Appropriate end punctuation
- Complete sentences
- Legibility of text

Based on the six-point scale on the next two pages, there will be a range within each score assigned. For example, one paper may be a "high 3" and another may be a "low 3," but both papers receive the same score. In judging between scores, it may help to think that if the paper is more like a 3 than a 4 and more like a 3 than a 2, then 3 is the appropriate score. Generally speaking, an essay receiving a score of 4 or higher would be passing. A score of 3 or lower would be considered failing.

HOLISTIC GRADING

When you score essays, consider each essay as a whole. For example, an essay may show a good command of mechanics and usage overall, even though there are a few errors here and there. In this case, you can consider the errors as oversights due to the time limits of the test. However, if a paper consistently has repeated errors in it, then the writer has demonstrated a lack of skill in this particular area. Also, don't count errors. A short essay may have few errors, but it may not give enough evidence that the writer has good writing skills. On the other hand, a longer essay may have a number of errors, but overall, the paper also shows that these were exceptions to the generally good performance of the writer.

Scoring an essay is a little like judging an apple pie. As long as care has gone into the making of the whole pie and the slice which you try tastes good, then a few cracks in the crust can be ignored.

Score	Explanation
6	A **six** paper is superior. It does ALL OR MOST of the following: Focuses and develops ideas in a sustained and compelling manner, showing creativity and insight. / Clarifies and defends or persuades with precise and relevant evidence; clearly defines and frames issues. / Effectively organizes ideas in a clear, logical, detailed, and coherent manner using appropriate structures to enhance the central idea or theme. / Demonstrates involvement with the text and speaks purposefully to the audience in an appropriate, individualistic, and engaging manner. / Uses multiple sentence structures and word choices effectively and with a sense of control for stylistic effect. / Commits few, if any, errors in standard English rules for grammar/usage and mechanics.
5	A **five** paper is distinctly above average. It does ALL OR MOST of the following: Focuses and develops ideas in an effective and detailed manner. / Defends and/or persuades with important and relevant evidence; defines and frames issues. / Organizes ideas clearly and coherently using structures appropriate to purposes. / Communicates a sense of loyalty to the topic and to the audience's involvement. / Uses varied sentence structure and word choice effectively. / Commits few errors in standard English grammar/usage and mechanics.
4	A **four** paper is adequate. It exhibits ALL OR MOST of the following: Adequately focuses and develops ideas with detail. / Defends and/or persuades with support and clarity, using relevant evidence. / Organizes ideas in a satisfactory manner with adequate coherence and logic. / Uses a voice that is appropriate to audience and purpose. / Uses a variety of sentence structures and word choice, but occasionally displays some wordiness or ineffective diction; sentences may be predictable. / Commits some errors in standard English grammar, usage and mechanics that do not impede meaning; indicates basic understanding of conventions.
3	A **three** paper is inadequate. It is clearly flawed in SOME OR ALL of the following: Focuses, but may not display mature or well-developed content. / Attempts defense or persuasive stance but position is unclear and/or evidence is brief, tangential, or based solely on personal opinion. / Displays minimal organization; contains irrelevancies, digresses, rambles, or lacks logic. / Lacks sincerity of purpose in the writer's attempt to involve the audience appropriately. / Uses sentence structure and word choice that are somewhat limited, simplistic, mundane, or otherwise inappropriate. / Contains flaws in Standard English rules of grammar/usage and mechanics that don't confuse meaning; indicates some consistent misunderstanding of the conventions.

285

Score	Explanation
2	A **two** paper is very weak, revealing serious, persistent problems in communications. It compounds the weaknesses of the 3 paper in SOME OR ALL of the following: Lacks focus and development; may list items with little or no supporting detail. / Defense or persuasive stance is unclear or absent; evidence is vague or missing. / Contains serious flaws in structure, organization and coherence. / Attempts, but fails to involve the audience appropriately. / Uses sentence structure and word choice that are highly limited, simplistic, or otherwise inappropriate. Displays consistent violations in Standard English rules of grammar/usage and mechanics that impede understanding.
1	A **one** paper is extremely weak. It has few good qualities. It mentions the topic, but generally fails to communicate with the reader. It does SOME OR ALL of the following: Simply repeats the topic or fails to provide adequate development. / Fails to establish a position and/or develop persuasive view; evidence is not apparent. / Shows almost no structure, organization or coherence. / Doesn't address the audience appropriately. / Uses limited and/or immature sentence structure and word choice. / Overwhelms the reader with serious violations in Standard English rules of grammar/usage and mechanics.

IDEAS

Your teacher will assess your essays on how clear, focused, and interesting they are. He or she will also be looking for them to hold the reader's attention. Relevant anecdotes and details should enrich the central themes or story lines. The best ideas are fresh and original. Ideas are the heart of the message, the main thesis, impression, or story line of the piece, together with the documented support, elaboration, anecdotes, images, or carefully selected details that build understanding or hold a reader's attention.

ASSIGNED TASK

Each writing prompt asks you to create a particular type of written work on a given topic. This is your assigned task.

CENTRAL THEME OR STORY LINE

The writing has balance; main ideas stand out. Your paper must be clearly organized around a **thesis** or **central idea**. The central idea is a brief summary of your focus and purpose for the essay. Though the central idea may be implied, stating the idea directly is helpful to the reader. A direct statement of the central idea can also help you maintain your focus while you write. Your response is expected to have ideas that are creative and insightful pertaining to the prompt.

RELEVANT SUPPORTING IDEAS

Supporting, relevant, telling details give the readers important information that they could not personally bring to the text. The writer needs to be writing from experience and showing insight: a good sense of how events unfold, how people respond to life and to each other. The writer should use facts and appeal to emotion to support the central idea. This support may include assumptions, reasoning, emotion, irony, humor, examples, testimony, or data. Make sure that your **supporting ideas** are related to your argument. Because the test does not allow time for research, you will not be graded on whether these ideas are factually correct or incorrect. However, they should make sense and sound reasonable as well as being enlightening and entertaining.

SENSE OF COMPLETENESS

The readers must have a **sense of completeness** about the paper as a whole. You must be sure that there are no gaps in the information you present. In addition, the concluding paragraph must lead the grader to a sense of ending and a summary of the whole essay. This displays the control the writer maintains to the end of the essay.

Practice 1: Scoring Ideas

Read the following essays. Using only the guidelines for *ideas*, assign each essay a score based on a six-point scale (pages 285–286). Then, explain why you gave each essay that score.

Students wrote the following two essays, based on this topic:

> Write a story about an adventure, either in work or elsewhere in life, that you have experienced. The story can be real or imaginary.

1. I was working at a local ski resort over the winter holidays looking for some extra cash. My job was to test the slopes every morning and check for problems such as obstructions in the slope and to make sure all of the lights were working. You see, at this resort, people can ski at night because the trail is lit up like a Christmas tree.

   On the early morning of December 23, I trudged out to take a run down the expert slope. I turned on the outdoor lights and watched as my breath spread out like a thick, smoky fog. I worked up the skis and got ready for a slow, methodic descent. It is my job to pick up any rocks, sticks, or trash left in the pathways. Once that is done, the resort can open the slope. Out of the corner of my eye, I saw a furtive movement to my left.

   I had to investigate, so I yelled, "Hey you, you're not supposed to be on the slopes yet."

   Every so often, some idiot decides to run the slope which is closed, usually getting hurt in the process. When I saw the vague shape move faster away from me, I knew I had to pursue.

   As I raced down the slope on my skis, the shape grew larger and took on more definition. As I moved closer to the person, I became more frightened. The shape looked huge, white, and very furry, and it was no longer moving away.

"Hey, a, a, you need to get off the slope!" I stammered. The creature was hunched over and looked as if it was saying something. It turned and glared at me with these red, piercing eyes. I decided it was best to ski quickly down the mountain—away from the creature.

As I continued skiing, I heard the creature scream, "My mountain!" He heaved a snowball at me the size of a boulder which came down to the right of me.

I notified the authorities from an emergency call box at the bottom of the mountain, but the creature could not be found. In fact, I never saw the creature again. I was just happy I lived to tell the tale.

2. I remember an adventure that started when I wasn't even looking for one. I was walking down the street in my hometown of Las Vegas, Nevada on a Saturday morning. I was headed to the library to check out some materials for a school project on the lost city of Atlantis. I walked past our local pizzerias and couldn't resist. I had to go in and stuff up some food.

I went inside the place and ordered me a calzone and a Pepsi. There were just a couple of people in the place—an old man reading the paper and a mom there with her daughter. My big surprise came when the food was brought to the table by what must have been the most beautiful girl I had ever seen. She looked like some sort of supermodel.

I asked her, "So, I haven't seen you before, are you from around here?"

"Yeah, as a matter of fact, I am," she said "I go to school right here. You know, Las Vegas High School? I'm on the basketball team."

"That's great," I said, kind of nervous, "That's kind of funny, I'm on the swim team. How come I've never seen you?"

With our mutual interest in athletics established, we started going out and now we're going to the prom together.

ORGANIZATION

Organization is the internal structure of the piece. It is both skeleton and glue. Strong organization begins with a purposeful, engaging lead and wraps up with a thought-provoking close. In between, the writer takes care to link each detail or new development to a larger picture, building to a turning point or key revelation and always including strong transitions that form a kind of safety net for readers so that they never feel lost.

Your essay should include a clearly structured introduction, body and conclusion. Within this structure, one idea should flow logically to the next, and each detail should support the main idea of the paragraph and the overall essay. Do not simply state your key ideas but **develop** them with appropriate explanation and detail.

SEQUENCING

Your paper should follow a definite **sequence** or pattern of organization. There are many ways to arrange ideas in an essay. Whatever type of sequence is used, there should be an inviting introduction and a well-thought-out conclusion. Types of sequences are found in chapter 1 of this book, discussing four methods including spatial order, time order, order of importance, and contrasting ideas. You may use any one of these for each essay, but the order you choose should be clear to your readers.

LOGICAL TRANSITIONS AND PROGRESSION OF IDEAS

Your paper should have smooth transitions both between paragraphs and within paragraphs. If the scorer doesn't know how you got from one idea to another, you are missing a transition. You want to lead the reader through the essay with one idea naturally flowing to the next. Your ideas should progress through the paper, moving the reader smoothly through the essay.

Practice 2: Scoring Organization

Read the following two essays. Using only the guidelines for *organization*, assign each essay a score based on a six-point scale (pages 285–286). Then explain why you gave each essay that score.

Students wrote the following two essays based on this writing prompt:

> What characteristics must a student possess to be successful in college?

1. When students decide to go to college, they have many responsibilities to obtain their college degree. After they have been accepted into college, they must remember some points on how to be successful. Students could be successful because they have good attendance, and they have good study habits.

    First of all, students must have a good attendance record. They have to be in their classes each class period, so that they do not miss important information. You must maintain passing grades. These grades have to be at least an A, B, or a C to pass any college class. You must attend learning labs. You have to participate in these labs to help you understand your class better. These labs also help students to comprehend their class information.

    Last of all, students must have good study habits. They have to learn to dedicate themselves to their course of study. They must manage their time. Students have to be involved in their class. They must attend lectures. All of these things help students to complete their course of study. When students have graduated from college, they could give themselves credit for all the hard work. They know how to be successful in college. So what, college was difficult. Students would have learned that college was worthwhile.

2. Today, more than ever, it is important to receive a quality education in order to be successful. In receiving a quality education, a student must possess certain characteristics. The characteristics that students must possess are good study habits, good note taking skills, and good listening skills.

First, students must have good study habits in order to be successful in college. To ensure good study habits a student should make a study schedule in order to allow him or her to have time to study every day. This way students will not have to cram the night before an exam. When a student is studying, he or she should be in a studying frame of mind. The student should think about what he or she is doing, so that they can get the most out of their time. He or she should try to keep focused and have a good attitude. Also, the students should pick a study place like their room, if it is quiet. If the student's room is not quiet, then they should pick a place that is. One that has no distractions. Usually the library and lunch room are not good places to study because there are to many distractions. For example, the students eating lunch and the clouds outside. The students can not keep focused, therefore they do not learn the material as well.

Second, students should have good note taking skills. The students should review there material before they start so that they can get an idea of what they will be taking notes on. Also, students should take notes on what they are studying and what the teacher is going over. When the teacher is lecturing the students should try to abbreviate and not write sentences so that they can get as many notes down as possible. The students can always go back and fill in the sentences later if they like writing in sentences. If the students are still having trouble, then they should ask another student if they could look at their notes.

Finally, the students should have good listening skills. If the students do not have good listening skills, then their note taking skills will probably be poor too. The student should try to be attentive and asservive. Also, the students should try not listen to what their classmates are saying next to them and should not talk in class. The students can not learn if they are talking. Another suggestion to better help the students listening skill is for them to eat a good healthy breakfast. This will give the student energy and help them stay awake. The students can not learn if they are asleep.

In conclusion, one can see that there are many important skills and habits a student needs in being successful in college. The students not only need to be successful, but also do their best. No matter how hard college gets, the student should not give in because the reward of a degree will be wonderful.

VOICE

Voice is the presence of the writer on the page. When the writer's passion for the topic and concern for the audience are strong, the text virtually comes alive with energy, and the readers feel a strong connection to both writing and writer. The language needs to be natural but stirring.

Copyright © American Book Company. DO NOT DUPLICATE. 1-888-264-5877.

VARIED SENTENCE STRUCTURE

A series of similar sentences may be clear and correct but lacking in style. Each sentence in an essay is connected to those around it. By varying the structure of your sentences, you create interest and emphasize certain points. Return to pages 108–109 in chapter 5 for a discussion of sentence variety.

TONE AND LANGUAGE

Tone is the attitude you express toward the topic and the audience. Make sure the tone of your paper is appropriate for your audience and purpose. Different examples of tone include *sarcastic, humorous, candid, ironic, respectful*, etc. Keep your tone consistent so the readers will not be confused about your meaning. To accomplish this, you need to also use appropriate language for your audience. Choose effective words that convey your ideas and feelings through your writing. For example, if you were writing a letter of concern to the principal about a new dress code ruling, you wouldn't write, "Hey, man, like, I think it stinks that we can't use green hair color! It's a free country, you know." A more appropriate written response would be, "Mr. Caliente, I'm really worried that this new dress code ruling will infringe on the rights of students to express themselves. I would urge you to offer this matter up in a school discussion."

SENSE OF AUDIENCE

The writing prompt will indicate that you should address **a particular audience**. It may be other students, parents, a legislator, or some other person(s). Each audience is concerned with certain issues. The support for your position should take that into account. Also, your word choice and tone should be appropriate for the specified audience. For example, if you are writing to the zoning board to approve an under-21 club in your city, you will want to point out how a club would keep teens out of trouble and not focus just on entertainment. You will also want to use a respectful and formal tone.

SENSE OF WRITER

The writer must have a strong presence on the pages of the essay. The two elements—the vivid voice of the writer and addressing a specific audience—allow for a feeling of interaction between the writer and the reader. The writer needs to have a clear sense of purpose when writing, so the reader is clear on the point the writer is making.

Practice 3:   Scoring Voice

Read the following two essays. Using only the guidelines for *voice*, assign each essay a score based on the six-point scale (pages 285–286). Then, explain why you gave each essay that score.

Students wrote the next two essays in response to the following prompt.

> Provide a detailed description of any room in your home or apartment.

1. Walking into my brother's room is such a traumatic experience. First thing you notice is the smell: pungent odors of dirty socks and shirts assault me immediately. Then there's the smell of the hamster cage, which he cleans once every two months. Yuck! If you've never smelled the room before, it will bring you to your knees! By this point, I usually attach a clothespin to my nose and prepare to wade further in.

    There is no clear path in the room: clothes, textbooks, comics, half-finished homework papers and old food bits are strewn all over the floor.

    What is even scarier is the feel of the room. You can't sit down too long in one place before you get the tingly sensation of ants and roaches crawling over your body. Once I felt the creamy feel of an old banana's insides touch my warm fingers when I extended my arm back on his bed. I found it inside his pillowcase.

    If you have allergies, watch out! Light and fluffy dust bunnies fly easily through the room and multiply faster than real bunnies. We're talking sneeze city.

    At night, you can hear the scurrying of small rodents, the chattering teeth of small mice looking for a quick meal, hamsters nestling in their feces-rich cage, and the raspy mating calls of crickets. It's amazing my brother can sleep in this mess!

2. Describing my kitchen is fairly easy to do. Our kitchen has three windows and two doors. One door faces outside to the deck, the other door connects to the living room. The kitchen has pots and pans, forks, spoons, and knives. There are several appliances in the kitchen such a microwave oven, a blender, a stove, and an electric oven. All appliances work fine and are all black. The floor is made of linoleum vinyl squares. There is wallpaper on three of the walls. The fourth wall has the three windows, so we decided to paint it yellow instead. There is a ceiling fan to take away any food odor in the middle of the room. There are a large number of electrical outlets, fifteen, in fact. The kitchen has approximately six cabinets and twelve drawers of various sizes. The wooden cabinets and shelves are stained a reddish color, and the hinges are painted with a gold trim. Several hanging plants are suspended from the ceiling. We have two puppies who stay in the kitchen. The kitchen sink made of stainless steel and also comes with a black sprayer. All in all, the kitchen is very well planned and beautiful.

WRITING CONVENTIONS

Almost anything a copy editor would attend to falls under the heading of **conventions**. This includes punctuation, spelling, grammar and usage, capitalization, and paragraphing: the spit-and-polish phase of preparing a document for publication.

For more practice in these areas of writing, *Basics Made Easy: Grammar & Usage Review* (American Book Company) is very helpful.

- **Usage** refers to how you "use" the English language. The scorers will grade your essay based upon the rules and practices of Standard American English. The graders will be looking for clear and correct pronoun references, correct agreement of subjects and verbs, and the appropriate form of adjectives and adverbs. Slang and jargon are inappropriate for a writing test and will reduce your score unless they are used in a quotation from someone. You are also expected to use English words appropriately, including commonly confused words such as *accept/except*, *to/two/too*, *sit/set*, and *lie/lay*. (See American Book Company's *Basics Made Easy: Grammar & Usage Review* for a more in-depth study of usage.)

- Writers are expected to have a strong grasp of **punctuation**. Noting that this is a testing situation, a few errors will be tolerated as long as the essay can be read smoothly without confusion in the logic because of errors in punctuation.

- **Spelling** needs to be generally correct. As with punctuation, a very few errors will be tolerated due to the timed test situation.

- **Format** refers to the appearance of your paper including standard writing practices of margins, paragraph indentation, spacing between words, and spacing between sentences.

- **Stylistic effects** through manipulating conventions are permitted.

- **Proofreading** is the writer's final review of a piece of writing. In this stage of the writing process, the writer corrects errors in capitalization, punctuation, spelling, and grammar.

Practice 4:   Scoring Writing Conventions

Read the two essays on the following page. Using only the guidelines for *Writing Conventions*, assign each essay a score based on a six-point scale (pages 285-286). Then explain why you gave each paper that score.

In response to the following prompt, two students wrote the essays in practice 4.

Some argue that teens under eighteen are too immature to handle the responsibilities of driving. Many teens, however, have come to depend on cars to get them to and from work and school.

Write a paper expressing your opinion about raising the age requirement for obtaining a driver's license. Support your opinion with clear reasoning that will convince your audience to agree with you.

1. Learning to driver is one of peoples main things to learn now. Driving as good and bad pointes. The good thinges are geting from places'es far off to see folks, to work, or shopping to.

    Some people do not understand that drinking and driving killes other people. Druges also as the same effic on killing people. The law now is .02 is drunk driving. i was told it.

    Learning to drive is every 15 'n ahalf year oldes dream. After some pratace they can go out on dates, be with friendes, or just go riding around town, or back roades.

    Teenagers are 50% of the drunk drivers. The state law needs at least to be 18 year or more before geting permited to get a car.

    The reason why it is important to me now is because, it get me home, to see my folks, help me get my billes paied, and get me to school.

2. There is no reason why a person who is sixteen years old should not be allowed to get a driver's license. There is nothing magic about the number of years in a person's age. The real issue when considering whether a person should drive or not is their level of responsibility.

    Driving a car puts you in a position of great opportunity and risk. Driving too fast, or recklessly, puts not only your life in danger, but endangers the lives of everyone else on the road. A good driver must always be alert to changes in road conditions and the movements of other cars and trucks on the road. Listening to the radio or talking to a another passenger have caused many accidents on the road. But a responsible driver has the wide open road in front of them and endless opportunities.

    For a teenager who has already proven to be a responsible person, the ability to drive provides many benefits. For one, it encourages further development in responsibility. By rewarding a responsible teen with the freedom of driving, society teaches the teen that responsible behavior pays off in the long run. Whereas, if a responsible teen is denied the right to drive, he or she may think, "What's the point of trying to be responsible?" This lesson can carry over into school, work, and personal life. The parents of the teen will also benefit by not having to drive their teen around to work, school, extracurricular activities, and so on.

Some people question whether sixteen-year-olds are old enough to drive. My answer is that some are and some are not. The question is not the numerical age of the person, but how mature they are. If mature and responsible teens are given the opportunity to drive, then everyone benefits. Those who are not responsible should not be allowed to drive. But don't punish everyone just because of a few bad apples.

CHAPTER 14 SUMMARY

Holistic grading means the essay will be scored as a whole and not simply by counting the number of errors.

There are four main analytical traits that provide the guidelines for scoring a writing exam. They include the following areas:

- **Ideas:** The writer develops a clear, focused main idea or ideas related to the prompt.

- **Organization:** The writer uses his or her organizational method to provide logical links in each detail or new development in the essay, leading the reader to a turning point, key revelation, or well developed conclusion.

- **Voice:** The writer uses his or her ability to emotionally connect with the audience through using the following components:

- **Writing Conventions:** The writer forms sentences correctly.

CHAPTER 14 REVIEW: SCORING THE ESSAY

On your own or in a group, read the following essays and assign each one a score based on the six point scale (pages 285–286). On a separate sheet of paper, provide an explanation for your scoring. Then, edit these passages for errors in ideas, organization, voice, and conventions.

Essays 1 and 2 are student responses to this prompt:

> Explain a career you would not want to pursue.

1. This is quite an unusual topic. I've never been asked what I <u>don't</u> want to be. I <u>don't</u> want a job pushing papers. I like to work with my hands, and to be free to move about. I can't be locked into some desk job, scribbling and typing my life away. I don't want any job where I am required to look busy or business-like, or make idle chatter by the water cooler or coffee machine. Barely can I stand the choking stench of an "office" (A.K.A. Claustrophobic Nightmare). A place of physical and mental decay, where drones trade their souls for a pension and a paycheck. Not me, dear

heart, not I. I must be where clouds roam like buffaloes of yore and sunlight, like a tidal wave, drenches and covers all that it can. I do not want a stagnant job in a stagnant city. Driving my stagnant car and living my stagnant life. To that I kindly reply "No, Thank You. I'll just sit over here in the corner and paint something . . ."

2. President of the United States used to be the sole dream of my early childhood. Having been born outside of the United States on a US Naval Base, I was concerned about whether or not I would be permitted to run for the candidacy. After learning that I would be able to run for office, but discovering what politics was all about, my dream was shattered.

Looking back on the idea of being President of the United States now, appears to me to be ridiculous. Without the power Of the Senate behind the President, the office is empty and useless. If the President were to be given more power in the voting process, I would reconsider my opinion. All decisions that come out of Washington D. C. now, are nothing more than a breakdown between the Republicans and the Democrats. Besides, the President will always have to worry about pain and death, not only to himself, but to all of the American people as well.

One quote from William Shakespeare would be a great description of childhood, "Ignorance is bliss". In childhood one does not have to worry about whether or not his dream is plausible or what all that dream would include. Overall, I have decided that the office of President of the United States will be better suited to someone who enjoys the game of politics, and not by myself who would actually like to enjoy life without the pressure of rejection.

Essays 3 and 4 are student responses to the following prompt:

> Explain how individual actions can affect the environment. Use clear examples and convincing arguments to persuade other students.

3. There was once an adult and a child walking along the beach. Every time the boy saw a starfish washed up along the beach, he would pick it up and fling it back into the water. The man turned to him and said, "There must be thousands of starfish washed up on this beach. What difference does it make to throw a few back?" The boy looked at the starfish in his hand, then turned to the man and said, "It makes a difference to this one." In the same way, efforts spent to conserve and restore the environment matter. Anyone can make a difference.

The easiest way anyone can help is through recycling glass, plastic, aluminum, and paper recycling. Recycling just one can conserves enough energy to run a television for two hours. At a nearby high school, one student wanted to share her commitment to the environment. Now, the entire school recycles paper and aluminum. If she had not been devoted to this cause, many trees would have been cut down. One person saved all of them.

296

Some people argue that they do not need to change their lifestyle for a couple of trees. Yet, if they save the trees' lives, they will save their own as well. The entire planet is like a global village. An event happening in one region affects all of the others. When too many trees are cut and not replaced, levels of carbon dioxide increase and global warming occurs.

Another way to make a difference in the environment is through energy conservation. Gas consumption can be reduced through the use of mass transit and carpooling. Simply turning off the lights when you leave the room can also help. When these fossil fuels are used, it can literally take millions of years to replace them.

Protecting the environment does not simply rescue a tiger or save a tree from extinction. Environmental quality affects everyone. If someone does not want to conserve in order to retain their own quality of life, that person should do so for the sake of their children.

4. Everyone can make a difference. I, also, felt the task of making the environment cleaner or safer was daunting and believed there was nothing I could do. However, that was just an excuse, an easy way out. All things start with one person—you. Others usually follow a leader and convince others to go along with the movement, this phenomenon is called peer pressure.

    Most of the time, peer pressure is discussed as a negative term, with destructive effects. Drug abuse, the growing acceptance of pre-marital sex, alcoholism, and even the growth of gangs and teenage suicides. Peer pressure is a forceful tool, we need to grasp it from those using it to undermine society and use it to the advantage of everyone.

    You, as one member of a global village, can accomplish many things using peer pressure. To begin with, you can recycle your own garbage such as old newspapers, aluminum cans, and glass bottles. Next, convince your friends to be part of your effort by telling them of all the advantages, and how they can make a difference.

    There are many problems which come from lack of care for the environment. Someone at a particular point in time must seize the initiative to fix these problems. If you truly believe in the cause, you will do your part. Get started today.

    Sometimes you may get discouraged over the way things are going, or lack of going anywhere. Do not lose heart. Keep in mind, you took the initiative when no one else would. You've planted seeds that change minds in the many people around you. You can't fail. It's not your task to change the whole world. Even small changes in our backyards can go a long way.

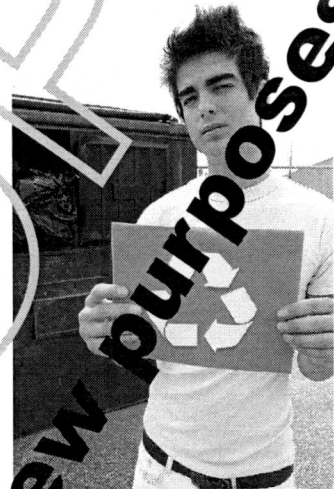

Essays 5 and 6 are student responses to the following narrative prompt:

> Tell a story about the most *challenging* experience you have had.
> Include details such as who you were with and what occurred.

5. I should have known there would be a problem when I saw the oil bubbles rising near the engine of the motor boat. We just thought it would be fun to try out the boat. Freddie the recreational director gave us such a good deal on it. $5.00 per hour plus fuel costs! Me and my best friend, Shelly, each had our older sisters us—just us girls having some summer fun, we thought. We suited up and jumped in the boat. With a little tug, we were off.

    My sister, Mary, screamed as we crashed through the waves others had made. Soon, we were in an alcove on a deserted island in the middle of the river. Freddie told us that this was as far as we could go before needing to turn back because we would have used half our fuel.

    After walking the island a couple times, Shelly's sister, Amy, glanced at the fuel gauge and almost fainted. She screamed, "It's on empty! It's on empty!" While we had looked around the island, an oil slick as big as a mack truck surrounded our boat. "No!" we all screamed. We rushed back in the boat and decided we would paddle back using our hands if we had to. Suddenly, instead of enjoying where we were, we were consumed with the need to get back to our every day lives. We cupped our hands and paddled to get the boat to its correct location. I shuddered as I felt the slimy mouths of fish attacking my fingers as if they were a mound of worms.

    Getting to the island took 1/2 hour, while getting back to the dock took over 6 hours! My arms were killing me, I was sunburned, and my fingers had been nibbled so much they felt like strips of raw hamburger! We marched into Freddie's office and gave him a piece of our mind. He trembled in his old Hawaiian shirt as we told him how his lack of attention to detail caused us unbelievable misery. Hours later, I remembered the saying, "If something's too good to be true, it probably is." I finally understood that.

6. In computer class, they told us we were going to learn something cutting edge, fun, and very effiecient. "Networking for beginners." It was called. I was excited as I imagined the possibilities. 20 computers—all using the same printer and Internet connection. I can't wait to learn how! The teacher started by words I was only beginning to grasp. "cat-5," "Fiber optic," "Wireless," and "Ethernet" immediately come to mind. Along with "scuzzy," "ghosting," "DSL," and "T1." Our teacher, Mrs. Hayworth, told us she needed two volunteers to network the computer lab at school for their final grade. My teammate, Julie, and I agreed to network the 20 computers in the lab. Over one weekend, we used cat-5 cable and routed 20 computers to one server. We had cables going all over the place and kept tripping over the wires! Once we had the cables set, we had to individually program every computer to align itself

with the server! We did not sleep at all that weekend. I was sick from lack of sleep and could not make it to school Monday. This task was definitely the most difficult thing I had ever done. However, the rewards were unmistakable. The network worked beautifully, we both made A's, and the article in the local newspaper landed me a summer job with a network company. It was a challenging experience but definitely worth the rewards.

Essays 7 and 8 are student responses to the following descriptive prompt:

> Describe a place you would like to visit. Include details such as the geography, attractions, and climate of the place you have in mind.

7. My dream location to visit would have to be Hawaii. Every time I see a picture of those islands I feel as if I am looking at a piece of paradise. The land, people, and waves paint a vivid picture of the island, transporting me to a place outside of my everyday life here in Spring Valley.

The land of Hawaii looks like a tropical paradise. Colorful birds stream past orchids in full bloom. The sands of the beach glisten with a glassy reflection in the sunlight. Depending on where you are, the sand can be bone white or as black as the shiniest coal. Palm trees cover the island, and coconuts cascade down streams of pure water.

The people are so warm and inviting, wearing brilliantly colored Hawaiian shirts. The lifestyle of the people is laid-back and easy. The people welcome tourists with flower necklaces and their happy smiles. Every day is a holiday there, and the tourists themselves are ready to let their hair down and enjoy the moment.

The climate of Hawaii is very even throughout the year. While the rest of the United States is in a deep winter freeze, Hawaii is enjoying temperatures in the upper 70s. As a result, the climate keeps the roads salt-free and generally clear of the damage that comes from frequent freezing and thawing. The rains which come over this island are very calm, gently caressing the soil to make it fertile for growing juicy pineapples and sweet sugar cane.

To recap, the land, people, and climate of Hawaii paint a beautiful picture of a paradise on earth. The natural wonders of the Hawaiian landscape sweetly call out to the souls of all those who visit. The people do nothing but complement the landscape. There is a sense of contented harmony that you can find here and nowhere else. The climate adds to the splendor of the island by being mild in both the winter and the summer. Yes, the picture of Hawaii is full of the incredible splendor of the colorful land, the warm people, and the always perfect weather.

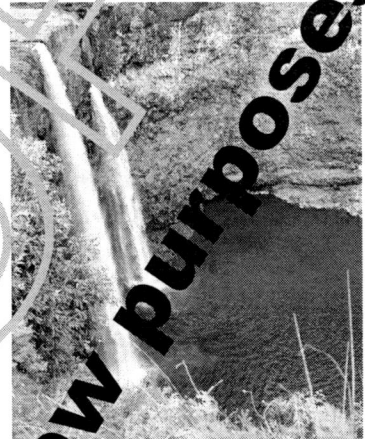

8. For those who are interested, the wintry wonder of a holiday vacation in Colorado can be more than worth the flight there. The beautiful outdoors, the cozy cabins, and the skiing adventures make Colorado an unforgettable experience.

   The outdoors is full of snow, and the snow is white. There are wolves and coyotes outside. You have to wear layers of clothes when you go outside and be sure you remember how to get back to your cabin.

   The cabins are nice. They are usually log cabins, and they are heated with fireplaces. The wood looks plain and the tables are simple. used to, but after that, its a lot of fun. Furniture usually consists of sofas, beds, and rocking chairs.

   Skiing is popular in Colorado, too. People either want to ski or to snow board. You ski by putting your pole in the ground and pushing off on you feet. Your feet have these metal track things on them.

   Overall, Colorado is an unforgettable experience. The cold takes some getting used to, but after that, it a lot of fun.

Essays 9 and 10 are student responses to the following prompt:

> Have you ever read a book that made you look at life a little differently, or made you think about the people around you differently? Think about the last book that made a difference in your views, and describe how the book made this happen for you. Use as many examples and details as you can from the book.

9. Literature can change readers' perspectives on life by drawing them into characters' inner thoughts and the events in their lives. When readers begin to sympathize with a character, they begin to see life through the eyes of that character. One of the books that changed the way I thought about something was *I Know Why the Caged Bird Sings,* Maya Angelou's autobiography about her childhood in the South.

   When Maya's parents divorce, she and her brother are sent to live with their grandmother in rural Stamps, Arkansas. The children observe and are subjected to the cruelties of the racism rampant at that time. Maya and her brother are sent to live with their mother in St. Louis when Maya is eight years old. Life in St. Louis is different but not better for the children. Her mother's boyfriend molests and eventually rapes Maya, inflicting physical and emotional damage on the child. Before the boyfriend can be tried in court, he is sentenced to death by a less merciful and more swift lady justice. The young Maya feels personally responsible for the man's death and decides to stop speaking to everyone, except her brother, Bailey.

The children's mother sends them back to their grandmother in Stamps where Maya is introduced to literature through Mrs. Bertha Flowers. The power of literature breaks through Maya's long-held silence. One evening, after spending several hours reading Mrs. Flowers' books, Maya returns to her grandmother's house full of things to say. In her excitement, she casually turns to Bailey and says, "By the way,. . ." Before she can finish her sentence, she is punished for taking the Lord's name in vain. (The Lord is the Way, thus "by the way" is blasphemy.) Maya returns to her silence.

It is this part of the book that most affected my ways of seeing the importance of literature and words. This incident brought to light both the positive and negative power of words on a child's delicate perception of the world. A victim of abuse and racism, Maya needs escape. Literature provides her with the means to escape her world into another where she may have some control. She can enjoy, through the authors' eyes, parts of the world and experiences she may never see. She can learn things she may never learn in school...

Words are multifaceted. One word can carry several meanings. Idiomatic phrases and slang can often be misconstrued by someone who is not familiar with the current language. A popular example is the phrase "get outa here" to mean that something is unbelievable. Someone who is unfamiliar with the phrase might actually leave the room. Maya's grandmother, who is deeply religious, feels that the "way" is God, and to say "by the way" Maya was saying "by God." To her grandmother, this was blasphemy. To Maya, the phrase was a casual way of saying "Oh, I almost forgot . . ." In this way, a simple phrase may take on two different meanings depending on who hears it.

The power of words is the caged bird's song and has become the theme of Maya Angelou's life story. When Maya stops speaking, it is because she believes that her story in court, her words, brought about a man's death. Her speech is brought back through literature and squelched again by her grandmother's religious fervor. *I Know Why the Caged Bird Sings* became a reminder to me to watch what I say because my words can be more powerful than I intend them to be. It also reminds me to be precise and weigh my words carefully so that what others hear is what I intend to say.

10. *I Know Why the Caged Bird Sings* effected me for three reasons: the book taught me about the South; it gave me a firsthand view of racism; it was a true story.

I grew up in the North, so I didn't know what the South was like for a little girl. I never really saw racism, and this book showed pictures of racism in Maya Angelou's time. It was a true story and described an important part of American History that we are not taught in schools.

What happened to that child growing up was awful. No one should have to go move away from home because they felt unsafe but Maya and her brother had to leave Arkansas because lynchings and other kinds of racism made their home unsafe. I wonder how many other little girls and boys had to leave home because of racism in the South?

I Know Why the Caged Bird Sings taught me about the South, racism, and a part of American History that students should hear more about.

Basics Made Easy

PRACTICE WRITING TEST 1

This practice writing test can help you answer the questions of how well you would do on an actual exam and in what areas you would perform the best. This practice test can also show you where your strengths and weaknesses lie when writing essays.

For assessment purposes, this practice writing test will consist of completing one essay based on one of two writing prompts. Read the instructions carefully.

How to Use Your Time

Allow about one hour for your essay. Follow the steps below.

Planning/Prewriting

During this part of the test, you will read each writing prompt carefully, choose one prompt, make quick brainstorming lists of your ideas, and organize those ideas in a simple clustering diagram or outline. From this, you can develop a central idea and tone. Be prepared to change the tone of your writing as you move from one prompt to the next.

Drafting

Once you have organized your ideas, you will write them in complete sentences developed into well formed paragraphs.

Revising

Now is the time to read over your draft and make improvements. You want to make sure all of your ideas are developed in a logical order and supported by relevant reasons and examples. You also want to eliminate unrelated ideas and unnecessary words. This is a good time to improve your word choices as well. Make sure all of your corrections are neat and legible.

Proofreading

Take advantage of the last few minutes of the testing time to review your essay one more time. This time look for errors in capitalization, punctuation, and grammar. These small corrections can make a big difference.

Review the **Checklist for Your Writing** before turning in your paper.

After you write each essay, you or your teacher should complete the **Writing Evaluation Chart** on page 6. An additional progress chart can be found in Appendix C. It will help you identify your areas of strength and areas for improvement in writing essays. You can also use the **six-point scale** in chapter 14 to help you evaluate your essay.

Test 1: Writing Application

Below are five **writing prompts** that give you instructions about writing an essay. Read each prompt carefully and write an essay based on one of these prompts. Then, use the **Checklist for Your Writing** to help you write an effective and interesting essay.

Use your own paper or an answer document provided by your instructor for your planning, drafting, and final copy. Your instructor will tell you when to begin and when to stop writing. Do your best, and remember, the purpose of this practice is to improve your writing proficiency.

Writing Prompt 1

> Surviving in strange or hostile places is a popular topic on television these days. Many people enjoy the challenge of surviving in these environments.
>
> Imagine that you are stranded on a tropical island for two weeks. Besides three days of food and clothing, you can take only three other personal items.
>
> Write an essay in which you list these items and tell why you would take them. Include details and examples to support your discussion.

Writing Prompt 2

> Across cultures, people often find that meals are events which they can describe with great detail. In your own words, describe as fully as possible the most memorable meal you have ever had.

Writing Prompt 3

> Should the personal life of the President of the United States reflect the high moral standards on which this nation was founded? Or is the personal life of the President of the United States irrelevant to his or her public contribution? Take a position on this issue and argue for your point of view.

Writing Prompt 4

> Choose one of your favorite stories or books. What is the theme? In 350–400 words, explain the theme and justify why you think is the main message. Be sure to tell what you get out of this message personally.

Writing Prompt 5

Do you think our currency needs to be redesigned? Write a letter to the US Treasure Department explaining why or why not. Should we keep the penny and other coins; should we have different denominations or a different look for our paper money? Think about it and perhaps research the currency of other countries, and then compose your letter.

Checklist for Your Writing

The following checklist will help you do your best work. Make sure you

- ☐ Read the description of the task carefully.
- ☐ Use specific details and examples to fully support your ideas.
- ☐ Organize your writing with a strong introduction, body, and conclusion.
- ☐ Choose specific words that are appropriate for your audience and purpose.
- ☐ Vary your sentences to make your writing interesting to read.
- ☐ Check for mistakes in grammar, spelling, punctuation, and sentence formation.

Basics Made Easy

PRACTICE WRITING TEST 2

This practice writing test can help you answer the questions of how well you would do on an actual test and in what areas you would perform the best. This practice test can also show you where your strengths and weaknesses lie when writing essays.

For assessment purposes, this practice writing test will consist of completing one essay based on one of two writing prompts. Read the instructions carefully.

How to Use Your Time

Allow about one hour for your essay. Follow the steps below.

Planning/Prewriting

During this part of the test, you will read each writing prompt carefully, choose one prompt, make quick brainstorming lists of your ideas, and organize those ideas in a simple clustering diagram or outline. From this, you can develop a central idea and tone. Be prepared to change the tone of your writing as you move from one prompt to the next.

Drafting

Once you have organized your ideas, you will write them in complete sentences developed into well-formed paragraphs.

Revising

Now is the time to read over your draft and make improvements. You want to make sure all of your ideas are developed in a logical order and supported by relevant reasons and examples. You also want to eliminate unrelated ideas and unnecessary words. This is a good time to improve your word choice as well. Make sure all of your corrections are neat and legible.

Proofreading

Take advantage of the last few minutes of the testing time to review your essay one more time. This time look for errors in capitalization, punctuation, and grammar. These small corrections can make a big difference.

Review the **Checklist for Your Writing** before turning in your paper.

After you write each essay, you or your teacher should complete the **Writing Evaluation Chart** on page 6. An additional progress chart can be found in Appendix C. It will help you identify your areas of strength and areas for improvement in writing essays. You can also use the **six-point scale** in chapter 14 to help you evaluate your essay.

Test 2: Writing Application

Below are five **writing prompts** that give you instructions about writing an essay. Read each prompt carefully and write an essay based on one of these prompts. Then, use the **Checklist for Your Writing** to help you write effective and interesting essays.

Use your own paper or an answer document provided by your instructor for your planning, drafting, and final copy. Your instructor will tell you when to begin and when to stop writing. Do your best, and remember, the purpose of this practice is to help you improve your writing proficiency.

Writing Prompt 1

Field trips become an important way to experience new ideas, inventions, works of art, and cultures. In a narrative essay, tell about one field trip you were on, what happened, and what you learned.

Writing Prompt 2

An old saying states there is "beauty in simplicity." Discuss important steps you can take to simplify your life.

Writing Prompt 3

We find out about many issues and topics through newspapers, television, and the Internet. What recent issue or event in the news has affected you the most? Give reasons for your opinion.

Writing Prompt 4

Which book, story, or play do you think everyone in your class should read? What does it offer that makes it so special? Describe this literature briefly, and then tell why you think it is a good idea from everyone to read it.

Writing Prompt 5

The mayor is looking for suggestions to get people involved in the community. Consider ways in which people could get involved and make a difference. Write a letter to the mayor explaining your suggestion.

CHECKLIST FOR YOUR WRITING

The following checklist will help you do your best work. Make sure you

☐ Read the description of the task carefully.

☐ Use specific details and examples to fully support your ideas.

☐ Organize your writing with a strong introduction, body, and conclusion.

☐ Choose specific words that are appropriate for your audience and purpose.

☐ Vary your sentences to make your writing interesting to read.

☐ Check for mistakes in grammar, spelling, punctuation, and sentence formation.

PREVIEW COPY

for review purposes only

for review purposes only

for review purposes only

Basics Made Easy

BME
Writing Review

Persuasive Essay Prompts

1. Recently, the newspaper reported that a student shot and injured several students in your school district. The school board is proposing that students in all schools be required to carry clear plastic book bags and purses for easy inspection. In addition, an armed security guard will be hired to carefully check items with a metal detector as students enter and leave the building. This policy has caused mixed reactions in your community. Express your opinion about this proposal in a letter to the editor of the local newspaper.

2. You are entering a contest in which you must write an essay on the following topic. If you were granted one wish to change the world, what would you change and how would you change it? The writer with the best entry will win $10,000. Write a convincing essay for the judges. Include reasons and evidence in your proposal.

3. Persuade your classmates that television's impact on people is mostly positive. Cite examples and reasons for your choice.

4. Persuade your classmates that television's impact on people is mostly negative. Cite examples and reasons for your choice.

5. Are parents or their children more responsible for school success? Explain your viewpoint clearly.

6. Confucius once said: "Choose a job you love, and you will never have to work a day in your life." Agree or disagree with this statement. Provide reasons for your point of view.

7. People sometimes say "Where there's a will, there's a way." What is your opinion about this statement? Explain your response.

8. Some people believe that prayer should be permitted in public schools. Others feel that praying violates the law that separates the church and the state. Write a letter to your state representative explaining whether you agree or disagree with prayer in the public schools. State your position, and support your argument.

9. Agree or disagree with this statement: "Cars are more dangerous than guns." Support your viewpoint with reasons and examples.

10. Shopping on the Internet increases by 300 percent each year. Purchasing products is quick, easy, and usually tax-free. Should Internet shoppers be required to pay federal and state taxes like people who shop at malls and stores? Why? Why not?

11. Skim through the editorial section of your local newspaper. Find a controversial issue in the news and take a position on that issue. Write a letter to the editor explaining your viewpoint.

12. In recent years, pit bulls have injured or killed children and adults in the United States. Should owning a pit bull be illegal? Or should a pit bull be considered a legitimate pet like other dogs? Cite evidence for your point of view.

13. Many professional athletes earn millions of dollars each year while teachers, nurses, firefighters, and law enforcement officers earn much less per year. Is it fair that professional athletes earn such high salaries compared to these public servants? Why? Why not?

14. Some students make fun of other students. They may even pick fights with others, causing injury or disrupting classes. Write your principal a letter in which you propose penalties for students who bully other students.

15. "It's not what you know. It's who you know that counts." Argue for or against this statement. Provide reasons for your point of view.

16. "You will be much happier if you wait for sex until after marriage." Do you think this statement is true? Why? Why not? Support your opinion with specific reasons.

17. After drinking four cans of beer, your best friend wants to drive you and your friends home from a late-night party. Why is this a foolish decision? Develop a convincing argument.

18. As tools for learning, computers are becoming more popular in schools. Do you think computers will replace textbooks as learning tools in your school? Include evidence for your point of view.

19. Some students drop out of school before earning a high school diploma. Should high school dropouts be denied a driver's license unless they graduate from high school or get their GED? Or should all teenagers of legal age be allowed to drive whether they attend school or not? Decide on your viewpoint, and develop a convincing argument.

20. Should separate schools be established for students who frequently disrupt classes? Why? Why not? Provide reasons for your opinion.

21. Citizens and conservationists alike are concerned about the poor air quality in many big cities. Cars, buses, planes, and industry contribute to this pollution. You have been asked to speak at a community forum on this issue. Convince your audience of the best ways to improve air quality in your community. Be specific in developing your argument.

22. Drinking and driving can have dangerous consequences. Should teens who are caught drinking and driving lose their license until they are twenty-one? Or should the courts give them another chance before they lose their license? Include reasons for your opinion.

Expository Prompts

Cause-Effect Essay Prompts

1. You may have lost a family relative at some point in time. Relate the impact this has had on your life or your family's life.

2. Our clothes and hairstyles send a message to others. Why are clothes and hairstyles important in today's society?

3. Deciding on a career is an important step in life's journey. If you could choose any career and money was no object, what career would you choose and why?

4. Your personality often affects others more than you know. Reflect on your own personality. In what ways does it affect those around you?

5. "I'm bored" is a phrase often heard in today's world. What causes boredom? Provide enough details to explain your answer.

6. Perhaps your parents or the parents of someone you know have been involved in a divorce. Discuss the effects of divorce on a family.

7. We all have our favorite person in the news whether it be a world leader, scientist, athlete, singer, movie star, or local celebrity. Choose your favorite person in the news, and tell why you admire this person.

8. Some people in the news can affect us in a negative way. Choose someone in the news that you do not admire, and explain why you dislike this person.

9. Traveling to different places is getting easier all the time. Among ways we can travel are walking, riding a bike, going by car, train, bus, or airplane, etc. What is your favorite way to travel? Why?

10. Many teenagers and adults still smoke even though it is harmful to their health. Write a letter to someone who smokes, and explain the effects it has on his or her health.

11. For some people, television has turned us into a nation of couch potatoes while others believe television improves our lives. Explain the positive or negative effects of television in your life.

12. Teenagers often strive to be different, yet they sometimes dress exactly alike. Explain why this statement is true.

13. Computers influence our lives at home, in school, and in the world. What effects have computers had on your life?

14. Our parents, relatives, or guardians influence our lives in many ways. Choose someone who has influenced your life deeply, and explain why.

15. Name a sport or hobby that you really enjoy. Tell why you enjoy it.

16. Movies are sometimes rated better than they actually are. Name a recent movie you saw that was disappointing. Discuss why it was disappointing.

17. An old Latin proverb states: "Sooner will men hold fire in their mouths than keep a secret." Think of a secret that you or someone else tried to keep. Explain why the secret was so hard to keep.

18. What is your favorite time of the year? Give reasons for your choice.

19. Kingsley once said: " . . . there is nothing more wonderful than a book." Think of a favorite book or story. Why did you enjoy reading this book or story?

20. Sometimes children or teenagers run away from home. What do you think are the main reasons that they run away?

21. Think of a job that you would absolutely refuse to do. Tell why you could never do that job.

22. Have you or someone you know been rejected because of the way you looked or acted? Explain how this rejection affected you or someone else.

23. If you could live in any country in the world, where would it be? Explain why you would want to live there.

24. Setting goals helps us plan ahead. Name one goal you would like to achieve soon. Explain why this goal is important to you.

25. Congress has passed laws to control the pollution of our air, water, and food. Explain the effects of pollution on our environment.

Process Essay Prompts

1. Your teacher has paired you with a new student to help orient the person to your class. Explain to the new student how to survive a typical school day.

2. Some people avoid responsibility by wasting time. Explain how you have wasted a whole day and accomplished nothing.

3. Success in school often leads to a better life. Based on your experience and observations thus far, explain how to be a successful student.

4. A six year old girl has just fallen from a playground swing. She is lying on the sidewalk unconscious, and her leg is bleeding. You are one of the first persons on the scene. What steps would you take to aid in her survival?

5. Life does not have to be boring if we know what to do. Explain how you avoid boredom.

6. When there is money to spend, shopping sprees can be exciting. You have one hour to spend $200 at the mall. What items would you buy, and in what order would you buy them?

7. Weight training is a popular form of exercise today. Teach someone a step by step program that will build muscles and self-confidence too.

8. An old proverb says: "Happiness is a habit to be cultivated." Create a simple recipe for happiness. Explain your recipe step by step.

9. Many people continue debating the issue of crime and violence in our society. Explain the steps you would take to reduce crime and violence.

10. An old saying states: "The only thing worse than hearing the alarm clock in the morning is not hearing it." After you wake up in the morning, explain the routine you follow in preparing for school.

11. The famous scientist, George Washington Carver, once said: "Ninety-nine percent of failures come from people who have the habit of making excuses." Based on what you have seen, people who are failures follow certain patterns. What steps does a person take to become a failure in life?

12. Fishing can be fun and rewarding when we land a big one. Advise someone new to fishing how to catch the fish of a lifetime.

13. You enjoy the company of your best friend except for one thing. This friend is always late. Tactfully tell him how to be on time, all the time.

14. Many people enjoy playing sports. What is your favorite sport? Teach someone to play this sport in a few easy lessons.

15. Your principal has asked you to serve on a committee of students and teachers. Your mission is to tell them how to improve the food in the school cafeteria. Offer your ideas in a short essay.

16. Some people would say more if others talked less. Most people know someone who talks too much. Suggest some specific steps to cure compulsive talking.

17. Everyone has a favorite recipe for a main dish, snack, or a dessert. Using simple steps, teach someone this recipe. Be sure to include all of the ingredients.

18. Staying healthy improves the quality of life. Suggest the best steps to a healthy lifestyle.

19. Some famous words of Victor Borge are: "Laughter is the shortest distance between two people." Residing in a nursing home, an elderly woman with no family nearby refuses to laugh at anything. As a student volunteer there, tell what you would do to make her laugh.

20. Teach someone else how to do something. For example, you might have tried to teach a brother or a sister how to brush their teeth or tie their shoes.

21. Pressure and stress are often part of everyday life. How do you handle stress? Suggest steps you take to reduce stress in your life.

Copyright © American Book Company. DO NOT DUPLICATE. 1-888-264-5877.

22. At times, gaps in communication between parents and teenagers can occur. How can parents communicate better with teenagers? Or tell how teenagers can communicate better with parents? Offer some practical tips for improving the communication process.

Mixed Expository Essay Prompts

1. Compare and contrast two fast food restaurants that you attend on a regular basis.

2. Present your views of your two best friends. How are they alike and yet different?

3. What are the two entertainment places or theme parks that you visit the most? Compare and contrast them.

4. How are you and your Dad similar and different?

5. Compare and contrast two cities or two countries in which you have lived.

6. What high school event or experience has impacted you the most so far in your life? Tell about it.

7. What is the most memorable holiday you have experienced? Was it positive or negative? Tell why it is so memorable for you.

8. By overcoming great obstacles, a young person may acquire greater maturity. What struggles have you experienced lately that have caused you to grow in character? Explain.

9. What lesson(s) did you learn in elementary school that have stayed with you, and benefitted you, through high school?

10. What are the benefits/advantages of your position in your family? (Hint: Are you a first child, last child, only child, or middle child?)

11. We live in a society of rapid and dramatic change. What are the greatest changes you have seen in the city (area) or country where you live?

12. Sometimes people are given a grave diagnosis or have a near death experience that turns their lives upside down. One of the most common responses is "It gave me a new perspective of what is really important in life." What is really important in your life and why?

13. There are people whose abilities and energy take them far past any limitation life tries to place on them. How does this relate to your life? Explain.

14. The Supreme Court has ruled (5/4 vote) that states may give parents money to send their children to religious schools as well as independent non-religious schools and magnet schools. What impact do you think this will have on public education?

15. Harle Wilson Baker once said: "Courage is fear that has said its prayers." What are your sources for courage and hope when you feel discouraged or "down and out"?

16. The Golden Rule states: "Do unto others as you would have others do unto you." Discuss why this statement is true.

17. Listening to good music often lifts our spirits. What kind of music do you enjoy? Explain how it affects you and those around you.

18. In many parts of the world, families are living in poverty. What are the most significant effects of living in poverty?

Descriptive Essay Prompts

1. Have you ever seen a sunset so breathtaking that you just stopped and stared so you could take it all in? Describe that event and its effect on you.

2. If you were going to invent something, what would it be, and what would it look like?

3. What is your strongest character trait, and how does it benefit you in your life?

4. Describe your favorite character from your favorite movie.

5. Special effects in movies have been intensified over the last several years. Describe the best special effects scene you have experienced in a movie.

6. In your travels through various parts of the United States, what scenes or events are the most vivid for you? Describe this scene or event.

7. Theme parks have created more and more daring rides to thrill us. Describe your most intense and thrilling ride that you have ever experienced. Think about which senses were triggered and the sensations you experienced.

8. Describe the car of your dreams. Use specific details.

9. Imagine that you are a reporter hired by a sports magazine to take pictures of a major league game for the upcoming issue. To accompany those photographs, write a descriptive report of what you photographed. Include details about the players and their actions.

10. Describe yourself. What do you think about your height and weight? Because you were created uniquely, what is unusual about you? What color is your hair? What is the color and texture of your skin? Are your eyes close together or far apart? Use as many varied and descriptive adjectives as you can. Consult a thesaurus for added effect.

11. Describe the kindest person you have ever met. What character qualities did this person demonstrate?

12. Suppose you have a creative idea for a disaster movie that you want to sell to a movie studio. Describe the initial catastrophe of the plot and the main character of the story.

13. You are writing a letter to a pen pal, and you want to tell him or her about your bedroom and all the posters and decorations you have. Give your room dimensions as well as a thorough description so the pen pal can visualize it.

14. Government and businesses are trying to improve the quality of people's lives. Have you seen any renovations of historical buildings, parks, warehouses, or apartments lately? Describe the transformation that took place.

15. Jane (or a friend of yours) is a wonderful athlete and is involved in gymnastics. She participates in many competitions. You witnessed her winning performance or the heartbreak of a losing performance. Describe the event and the emotions involved.

16. Ask your parents about some of your ancestors. Listen to their stories carefully. Choose an ancestor that seemed very interesting to you and write a character description about that person.

17. Using a map, select a place such as a city, state, or country. Consult an encyclopedia for additional information about this place. In an essay, give its location and relate descriptively its natural resources.

18. You are planning a trip for your family. You will be gone for one week. You are choosing all the places to visit. Do some research. Create the itinerary you will follow and describe the highlights of the places you will visit. This will be comparable to a travel brochure but in essay form.

19. What is your favorite *Star Trek* or *Lord of the Rings* episode/movie? What visual images stand out the most in your mind when you reflect on one of these movies? Describe the most dramatic scene you remember. Appeal to as many of the senses as possible.

20. Mt. St. Helens is a volcanic peak in the Cascade Mountains of Washington State. It erupted on May 18, 1980. Find a picture of that eruption and one taken afterwards. Describe what you see.

21. Describe a simple childhood experience, perhaps an exploration of yours, and make clear to your audience what you saw and how you felt.

22. Write a description of all that you see and hear on the way to school. If you go the same way every time, use one day to write down what you see, and use another day to take notes on what you hear. Combine your notes for both days into a workable descriptive paper.

23. Usually an eating place has its own special atmosphere. Walking into such a place possibly triggers all five of your senses. It is for sure that your sense of smell and sight will be stimulated first while others will slowly be tickled. Write a description that relates to such an atmosphere and have it appeal to as many senses as possible.

24. Have you ever had an imaginary friend that you created when you were a young child? Think about how you used to talk to that friend, and that friend's response to you at different times. Recall how you pictured that friend. Can you describe that friend for us today? Make it as vivid for us as it was for you when you were young.

25. Have you visited any college campuses in anticipation of where you will go to further your education. What was it like? How did the buildings look to you? What did you think about the students walking around the campus? Were they friendly, or not? What sensations did you feel? Were you excited? Write about that day and all the sensations you experienced.

Story or Narrative Prompts

1. Booker T. Washington rose up from slavery and illiteracy to become the foremost educator and leader of black Americans at the turn of the century. Are you struggling for an education? If so, tell about that struggle. If not, write about your pursuit of an education and the events involved in that pursuit. Include important details.

2. Young people sometimes feel the need to perform daring stunts just to experience the thrill. What is the most daring stunt you have performed? Narrate that event.

3. Have you ever taken a trip with a family pet? Was it an adventure or a disaster? Relate an experience of traveling with/or going on vacation with your pet.

4. Find a favorite picture or photograph. Study it and make a list of important actions and details. Put them in an order that makes sense. Then write a story about the picture or photograph. Attach a copy of the picture or photograph to your story. Add details.

5. Listen to a favorite song or musical composition. Can you picture a story to go with the music? Make notes about your story. Write your story, and give it a title like "The Story in (Name of Song or Musical Composition.)"

6. Think of a recent conversation you had with a friend or family member. Write down what you remember about the conversation. Then write a dialogue between you and the other person. Include details.

7. An autobiography is a story about your life. Make a time line of the key events in your life. Include details about each event. Then write your autobiography from the time you were born to the present. Include significant events only. Use details.

8. What was the most embarrassing moment in your life? Explain what happened.

9. What is the most often told baby story your parents tell about you. Write that story. Develop your story with details.

10. Tell about a situation that occurred when a "good Samaritan" helped you, and no one else would. Develop your story with details.

11. Think about a funny or serious story concerning a pet. Imagine that you are that pet and write the adventure from that point of view.

12. Were you ever the victim of a practical joke? Or have you ever played a practical joke on someone else? Recall what happened, and write a narrative about the experience.

13. Try to recall a situation where a person or group wanted you to do something that you knew was wrong. Tell a story about how you resisted peer pressure.

14. Volunteering to help with the elderly, the handicapped, the sick, or a humane society always expands your horizons. What interesting story can you relate?

15. Who is the most remarkable teacher you have ever had? Recall an experience in which this teacher made an impression on you. Relate the details of the experience.

16. Recall the time you took your driver's test. Recount the emotions, waiting in line, the strain, and the actual test itself. Tell about the experience with details.

17. Tell about the worst weather you have ever experienced. This weather could have been a thunderstorm, tornado, hurricane, tidal wave, avalanche, monsoon, or a snowstorm. Write a narrative about that experience.

18. What is the most amazing sports event you have experienced? Tell about it.

19. Many people experience prejudice or discrimination for various reasons. For example, you may have been treated rudely because of your age, intelligence, race, sex, religion, appearance, opinion, income, athletic ability, etc. Tell about a time when you or someone you know experienced prejudice or discrimination. How did you respond?

20. "Gossip and lying go together." Tell a story of how gossiping about someone caused great harm.

21. Create a story based on your own idea or one of these story starters:

    • While I was walking home one night, I heard heavy footsteps behind me. I was afraid to turn around, but . . .

    • My best friend and I love doing things together. Last week we decided to...

    • The best job I ever had was . . .

22. Mark Twain once said: "I can live for two months on a compliment." Has anyone ever given you a compliment? What were the circumstances that led to the compliment?

Prompts for Writing about Literature

1. You have probably read poems in your English books. Many poems are also now available on the Internet. Review this list of famous poems of the recent past. Choose two or three of them to read and study:

"Psalm 23" by David (<u>The Bible</u>)	"A Dream Deferred" by Langston Hughes
"Messy Room" by Shel Silverstein	"Hope is the Thing" by Emily Dickinson
"I Know Why the Caged Bird Sings" By Maya Angelou	"The Great Way is Not Difficult" by Sengstan
"Metaphors" by Sylvia Plath	"My Nose" by Gabriel Liebermann
"The Road Not Taken" by Robert Frost	"Happiness Epidemic" by David Hernandez

Now write an essay of 350–400 words about one of these poems. Base your essay on **one** of the following prompts.

*   Which poem did you like the best? Provide reasons and examples to support your opinion.

*   Which poem best relates to you and your life? Provide evidence from the poem to support your response.

*   What lesson about life did you learn from the poem? Explain some of the images and figurative language that convey this lesson.

2. Reading and writing essays about short stories is another way of writing about literature. Skim through this list of famous short stories. You can find these stories in a literature book or on the Internet. Read two or three of them, and then choose your favorite one.

"The Metamorphosis" by Franz Kafka	"A Very Old Man With Enormous Wings" by Gabriel Garcia Marquez
"Sweat" by Zora Neale Hurston	"Paul's Case" by Willa Cather
"The Secret Life of Walter Mitty" by James Thurber	"The Pace of Youth" by Stephen Crane

Now write an essay of 350–400 words about one of these short stories. Respond to **one** of the following prompts:

- Which story did you like the best? Provide reasons and examples to support your opinion.
- Which short story best relates to you and your life? Provide evidence from the story to support your response.
- What theme or insight into life does this short story communicate? Discuss how the character (s), plot, and setting help to convey the theme.

Prompts and Activities for Writing for Technical Texts

Business Letters

1. Gather three or four samples of business letters from your school, workplace, or home. Analyze the content and format of these letters. How closely do they follow the business letter guidelines? Are there mistakes in spelling or grammar? Revise these letters as needed. Share your revisions with the class or your teacher.

2. Invite someone to speak to the class about writing business letters. Possible choices could be an advisor from the school guidance office, a business leader in the community, or a business education teacher from your school. Take notes on the presentation and keep any handouts for future reference.

3. Skim through a business writing book or surf the Internet for examples of business letters. What is the purpose for each type of letter? How does this purpose affect the content and format of each letter?

Resumes and Cover Letters

1. Sample resumes are now available on the Internet at such sites as monster.com, hot-jobs.com, or jobstar.org. Download samples of each type of resume: chronological resume, career objective resume, functional resume, and combination resume. Review them, and then write your own resume using the format for each of these types. Choose the one that best suits your job skills and experiences.

2. On these same sites or on others, download sample cover letters. Review them, and write a cover letter that best complements your resume and the job you are seeking.

Job Applications

1. Read several Help Wanted ads in the newspaper or on the Internet. Or make a list of your top four job choices. Then find copies of the Employment Applications for these jobs. Then practice filling out these job applications completely and neatly. Share your work with other students or your teacher for feedback.

2. Employment applications often require detailed information about your education, job skills and experience, driver's license, social security number, next of kin, etc. Recalling this information can be a challenge.

   Pick up a detailed employment application, complete it with all of the relevant information, and keep it in your wallet or purse. As you fill out new job applications, you will be able to use information from your existing application to complete your new employment application.

Prompts and Activities for Writing Research Reports

1. Writing a research report involves planning and organizing your topic, finding, evaluating, and synthesizing sources, writing and revising the draft of your report, and citing your sources in a bibliography. Write a typed research report on one of the following topics. Keep in mind that these topics may need to be narrowed down for a research report:

birds of prey	gun control	animal rights
dinosaurs	terrorism	maturity
sharks	life on other planets	urban crime
endangered animals	comets	urban recovery
dolphins	nanotechnology	drug addiction
kangaroos	robotics	solutions to poverty
earthquakes	black holes	value of volunteers
volcanos	smoking	why read books
hurricanes	stress	modern art
public transportation	carjacking	today's best music
alternative fuels	teenagers today	living a happy life
global warming	new careers	life beyond death

2. Based on your television watching and Internet surfing, identify five of the most frequently mentioned issues in the United States today. Bring these topics to class, and share them with your teacher and fellow students. As a class, then choose the five most frequently mentioned issues from these topics.

   Create a bibliography of six sources you could use for a research report on one of these topics. Make a complete list of these resources as they would appear in an MLA Style bibliography.

Then practice writing a brief summary of each source that could be used for a five page research report. Then develop the research report as a class assignment.

APPENDIX B: WRITING RESOURCES

Web Sites for Writing and Grammar

These Web sites include a variety of information with links to still more sites designed as supplemental aids for students. We visited these sites and devised a rating system for them.

Ratings: Excellent

Good

Fair

Poor

Annenberg / CPB: Learner.org: Theme

A very well presented site. It contains valuable information about the five major topics for reading and writing analysis: theme, plot, point of view, setting, and characters.

Web address: http://www.learner.org/exhibits/literature/read/theme1.html

Rating -

Ask Miss Grammar

For this site, first you must ignore the silly, stereotypical cartoon lady. Then, and only then, does this Web site have a lot going for it. There is an option to look through "archives," where you select an item you wish to learn more about, bring up facts and games, or you could choose the option to e-mail a specific question to the site. The site states that it cannot answer all e-mails, but it tries to answer many of them.

Web address: http://www.protrainco.com/grammar.htm

Rating -

Awesome Library

This comprehensive Web site offers resources and lessons on most school subjects. The section on reading and writing contains numerous links and activities designed to improve the writing of sentences, paragraphs, and essays as well as vocabulary, grammar, and spelling. In addition to English, many explanations and lessons are also available in other languages including Spanish, Portuguese, Chinese, and Arabic.

Web address: http://awesomelibrary.org

Rating -

Classic Reader

Offers almost 3,000 free books, essays, poems, and stories by such authors as Dickens and Twain among many others. Downloads are free but may require registration on the Web site.

Web address: www.classicreader.com

Rating - ✎✎✎✎

English Club ESL Quizzes

There is not so much instruction on this Web site as there is practice. The quizzes are often set up as games so it is a fairly painless practice session. This web site does create a community for English students for all levels of learning.

Web address: www.englishclub.com/esl-quizzes/

Rating - ✎✎✎

English Grammar Quizzes - Easy

This site has a variety of grammar and usage quizzes at several levels for the ESL student. The quizzes provide immediate feedback which could provide a lot of practice for students motivated to learn correct English.

Web address: http://a4esl.org/a/g.html

Rating - ✎✎✎

English Works!

This is the official Web site for Gallaudet University's English Tutoring and Writing Center. It provides plentiful information on the writing process, main types of essays, the research paper, and writing and grammar exercises. This site also contains links to other helpful writing and grammar Web sites.

Web address: http://dept.gallaudet.edu/englishworks

Rating - ✎✎✎✎

Guide to Grammar and Writing

This is an exceptional Web site for English grammar and writing. The site is colorful, interesting, and well organized. There are guidelines for writing elements from simple sentences to full essays. The site has activities, examples, and quizzes. The quizzes, however, lack feedback for the student. There are many links to other English grammar and writing Web locations at this site, including a link for an online grammar textbook. The site includes an option of sending questions and receiving answers about grammar and writing issues.

Web address: http://grammar.ccc.commnet.edu/grammar

Rating - ✎✎✎✎

Paradigm: Online Writing Assistant

This site features long discussions on how to write essays and some tips on revising and editing work. Clearly written and organized, this is a good source for those who want a review of the composition process.

Web address: http://www.powa.org/

   Rating - ✏✏✏

Project Gutenberg

Project Gutenberg is the Internet's oldest producer of FREE electronic books.

This site is a worthy source of classic materials both fiction and nonfiction. It is not the easiest to navigate, however. It takes a little time and patience to find materials. On the site's Welcome page, there is a dialogue box labeled **Quick Search**. This is an index of the complete works that you can find on the site. You may search by author, title, or book. The index is in a "Winzip" file, so there may be certain programs which can deal with the index better than others.

Web address: http://gutenberg.net/index.html

   Rating - ✏✏✏

Wikipedia

This free online encyclopedia provides information on writing as well as a broad range of topics for research reports. Second language learners can access information in their native languages as well.

Web address: www.wikipedia.org

   Rating - ✏✏✏✏

BOOKS AND SOFTWARE FOR WRITING AND GRAMMAR

This section contains a listing of books which provide students with grammar and writing instruction in various formats.

Basics Made Easy: Grammar & Usage Review

This book provides clear explanations and plentiful practice exercises in grammar, punctuation, and usage. Chapter reviews reinforce concepts taught in each lesson. The book is a thorough and excellent support for aspiring writers.

Pintozzi, Frank, and Devin Pintozzi. *Basics Made Easy: Grammar & Usage Review.* Woodstock, GA: American Book Co., 2007.

Web address: www.americanbookcompany.com

Basics Made Easy: Grammar and Usage Software

This interactive software program offers a comprehensive review for grammar, punctuation, and usage. Exercises require students to choose the best answers. The software tracks students' scores and correlates with lessons in the companion text, *Basics Made Easy: Grammar and Usage Review* (American Book Company).

Pintozzi, Frank, and Devin Pintozzi. *Basics Made Easy: Grammar and Usage Software.* Woodstock, GA: American Book Co., 2003.

Web address: www.americanbookcompany.com.

Focus: From Paragraph to Essay

The author, Martha Campbell, presents a practical and easy-to-read text that integrates composition and grammar concepts. She includes plentiful exercises, assorted writing topics, and extensive examples of student writing.

Campbell, Martha E. *Focus: From Paragraph to Essay.* Upper Saddle River, NJ: Prentice Hall, 1996.

Writer's Choice: Grammar and Composition

This hardback text contains lessons in composition, grammar, resources, and literature. The composition activities are particularly helpful for improving writing skills.

Royster, Jacqueline Jones, et al. *Writer's Choice: Grammar and Composition.* New York: McGraw-Hill, 1996.

A Writer's Guide to Transitional Words and Expressions

This book is a helpful companion reference to *A Writer's Guide to Using Eight Methods of Transition* (see below). It contains over 1,000 transitional words and expressions that will make your writing effective, logical, and easier to read.

Pellegrino, Victor C. *A Writer's Guide to Transitional Words and Expressions.* Wailuku, HI: Maui Arthoughts, 1987.

A Writer's Guide to Using Eight Methods of Transition

A brief but excellent guide, this book is an invaluable reference tool that helps writers choose the best transitional words and expressions for a context. The author, Victor C. Pellegrino, provides many examples of how to create effective transitions and connections in sentences and paragraphs.

Pellegrino, Victor C. *A Writer's Guide to Using Eight Methods of Transition.* Wailuku, HI: Maui Arthoughts, 1987.

Writing From A to Z: The Easy-to-Use Reference Handbook

This book is organized alphabetically like a dictionary. Consequently, students can easily find, for example, an explanation of a "paragraph" by looking in the letter "P" section. The book covers a wide range of grammar and usage information.

Ebest, Sally Barr. *Writing From A to Z: The Easy-to-Use Reference Handbook*. Mountain View, CA: Mayfield, 1997.

The Young Person's Guide to Becoming a Writer

Reading this book will be a different experience than reading the others. This particular guide is gently encouraging to those students who want to pursue a career in writing but are not sure how to take the first step. There are sections on writing skills, literary genres, and how to keep a writer's notebook. This is a first look into the world of professional writing, and it is good for everyone to know the ways to enter that world.

Grant, Janet E. *The Young Person's Guide to Becoming a Writer*. Minneapolis: Free Spirit, 1995.

APPENDIX C: STUDENT ESSAYS PROGRESS CHART

Use the writing prompts in Appendix A of *Basics Made Easy Writing Review* for writing practice. Keep all of your essays in one folder. As you practice writing essays, you can use the Writing Progress Chart below to help you assess your progress.

For each essay, work with your teacher or tutor to assign a grade in each category listed. If you have an excellent grasp of the skill, write **E** for **Excellent**. If you use the skill well enough to pass, write **P** for **Passing**. If you need to practice a skill more in order to master it, write **NP** for **Needs Practice**. The number listed next to each skill indicates the chapter which discusses that skill. Your teacher may also use the six-point scale from chapter 14, Scoring the Essay. Review the chapters you need to improve each concept and skill.

There is a copy of the progress chart in the back of the answer key also. Teachers/tutors may copy the chart from the **Answer Key** as needed.

Writing Progress Chart

Writing Skills	Chapter Number	Student Name:					
		Essay 1	Essay 2	Essay 3	Essay 4	Essay 5	Essay 6
Writing Paragraphs	1						
Diction	2						
Planning the Essay	3						
Drafting the Essay	4						
Revising the Essay	5						
Proofreading the Essay	6						
Persuasive Writing	7						
Expository Writing	8						
Descriptive Writing	9						
Narrative Writing	10						
Writing About Literature	11						
Writing Technical Texts	12						
Writing Research Reports	13						
Scoring the Essay	14						